Disaster Pedagogy for Higher Education

Disaster Pedagogy for Higher Education

Research, Criticism, and Reflection

Edited by
Victor Malo-Juvera
Nicholas C. Laudadio

ROWMAN & LITTLEFIELD
Lanham • Boulder • New York • London

Published by Rowman & Littlefield
An imprint of The Rowman & Littlefield Publishing Group, Inc.
4501 Forbes Boulevard, Suite 200, Lanham, Maryland 20706
www.rowman.com

86-90 Paul Street, London EC2A 4NE, United Kingdom

Copyright © 2022 by Victor Malo-Juvera and Nicholas C. Laudadio

All rights reserved. No part of this book may be reproduced in any form or by any electronic or mechanical means, including information storage and retrieval systems, without written permission from the publisher, except by a reviewer who may quote passages in a review.

British Library Cataloguing in Publication Information Available

Library of Congress Cataloging-in-Publication Data

Names: Malo-Juvera, Victor, editor. | Laudadio, Nicholas C., 1973– editor.
Title: Disaster pedagogy for higher education : research, criticism, and reflection / edited by Victor Malo-Juvera, Nicholas C. Laudadio.
Description: Lanham : Rowman & Littlefield, [2022] | Includes bibliographical references and index. | Summary: "Disaster Pedagogy for Higher Education serves as an all-purpose, contextually grounded, and multi-modal introduction to teaching in higher education during times of crisis and disaster"—Provided by publisher.
Identifiers: LCCN 2022001229 (print) | LCCN 2022001230 (ebook) | ISBN 9781475859393 (cloth) | ISBN 9781475859409 (paperback) | ISBN 9781475859416 (epub)
Subjects: LCSH: College teaching—United States—Case studies. | Culturally relevant pedagogy—United States—Case studies. | Universities and colleges—Administration—Case studies. | School crisis management—United States—Case studies. | Emergency management—United States—Case studies. | Disasters—Social aspects—United States—Case studies.
Classification: LCC LB2331 .D535 2022 (print) | LCC LB2331 (ebook) | DDC 378.1/250973—dc23/eng/20220310
LC record available at https://lccn.loc.gov/2022001229
LC ebook record available at https://lccn.loc.gov/2022001230

Victor Malo-Juvera
To Debbie Malo

Nicholas Laudadio
Disasters big and small are more easily navigated when one is supported by a loving community—mine includes Meghan Sweeney and Henry Laudadio, and I wouldn't want to be stuck anywhere with anyone but those two.

Contents

Introduction   1
    Nicholas Laudadio and Victor Malo-Juvera

PART I: RESEARCH AND CRITICISM

1   Give Me Liberty or Give Me a Mask: Pandemic
    Anti-Masking as Anti-Science Discourse   9
    Addie Sayers

2   Education in Times of Crises: The Ontological Imperative
    in Considering the Role of Technology Adoption in
    Remote Educational Settings   25
    Hannah R. Gerber

3   From Meteorological Uncertainty to Missing Muffins:
    How University Emergency Managers Manage
    Uncertainty as a Hurricane Response Strategy   43
    Ian R. Weaver

PART II: EXPLORATIONS AND EXAMINATIONS

4   Nimble Pedagogies for a Liquid Time: Disruption,
    Accommodation, Collaboration, Reinvention, and
    Compromise   73
    Diana Ashe and Colleen A. Reilly

5   Studying Abroad During a Time of Disaster: An Exploration
    of Pitfalls, Pivots, and Possibilities for the Future   93
    Kara Pike Inman, Nicole Desjardins Gowdy, and Jason Kinnear

6	Thinking Through Disasters: Critical Analysis and Research in College Composition Courses *Melissa Sexton*	109
7	How Do You Learn to Teach When You Can't Go to School? Teaching Teachers in the Age of Virtual Living *Alice Hays, Jouselin Martin, Alexandra Chapa-Kunz, and Wade Branch*	127
8	Trauma and Its Lasting Effects After School Shootings: Psychological Considerations for Faculty, Staff, and Students *Anka Roberto*	143

PART III: PERSONAL AND PROFESSIONAL REFLECTIONS

9	Chairing in the Pandemicene: Coronavirus, George Floyd, and the Year of Living Dangerously *Tiffany Gilbert*	157
10	New Literacies, Empathy, and Advocacy: Reconstructing a Pedagogy in Pandemic Times *Suriati Abas*	173
11	In a Crisis, Stories Need to Be Heard: Changing the Digital Landscape to Include Narratives *Kevin D. Cordi*	181
12	Community Is Always the Answer: Columbus State Community College, Compassion, and Care *Barbara Allen*	189
13	Holdfast: An Education in Disaster *Andy Tolhurst*	195
14	A Resident Assistant's Reflections on the Pandemic *Kayli Childs*	203
Index		205
About the Editors and Contributors		207

Introduction
Nicholas Laudadio and Victor Malo-Juvera

Although it emerged in the midst of a global pandemic, this book was initially inspired by a hurricane. No one living and working on the North Carolina coast ignores the inevitability of severe storms, but when Hurricane Florence hit Wilmington, North Carolina, and the surrounding areas in September 2018, it did so with a ferocity not felt in decades. Like much of the surrounding community, the local university—where we are both English professors—was hobbled by the storm: classrooms were destroyed, students and faculty were displaced, and years of research materials and labs were undone in a flash of wind and relentless rain.

When faculty, students, and staff finally made our way back to our classrooms, hastily assembled portable buildings, and halls full of massive dehumidifier ducting, we quickly realized we must adapt to this reality. Like so many institutions and communities across the globe that deal with climate crises, we made it through the year. But as we began to rebuild from Florence, we were impacted by Hurricane Dorian the next year and then, to a lesser extent, by Hurricane Isaias in 2020. As climate scientists and vulnerable communities have known for years, these are no freak occurrences: Storms are getting stronger and more frequent. We knew that fundamental aspects of our pedagogies needed to change to accommodate this shift.

As we found ourselves in another conversation about this run of hurricanes, we would joke that faculty and staff at our institution were now qualified to serve as "disaster pedagogy consultants" because so many of us had found ourselves with classroom and course design skills born of disaster that grew more and more relevant with each passing storm. But once the buildings had been rebuilt and the portable trailers finally moved on, we found that these skills were soon going to work in a larger and longer context. Higher education was soon to experience even greater disruption.

When COVID exploded in the spring semester of 2020, we were knocked back out of the classrooms yet again. The once fluid movement through the semester, from classroom to classroom, assignment to assignment, that we all took for granted, was again disrupted. Students were forced to disengage from their studies and think about evacuation, infection, and the loss of crucial communal connection. We were all—students, staff, and faculty alike—again struggling to rethink our workplace and social lives.

One evening on social media, one of the editors joked that putting together a "disaster pedagogy reader" might not be a bad idea in response to teaching in the early 21st century.

Three weeks later, that joke had become the contract for this book you are now reading. In it, we have tried to capture the roller-coaster ride that is navigating and working in higher education in the midst of major climatological and social upheaval, and we are still riding it as of the writing of this preface as the Delta strain has gripped the United States. The goal here has always been to leave behind a small marker of a time when we began our transition out of the comfortable familiarity of the 20th-century cinder-block classroom with its white boards and damp odors, and into the anthropocene classroom proper. This classroom is more rhizomatic in nature, spreading itself across ZOOM meetings, outdoor classrooms, endless disaster update emails, and long-winded Canvas discussions. But it is one that, as the chapters in this collection demonstrate, is full of promise and the opportunity to fundamentally change some of the more vexing, problematic, and outdated aspects of 20th-century higher education.

The challenges of gathering a collection of chapters on pedagogical issues about teaching during disasters during the COVID pandemic was not lost on us. As we started to spread our call for chapter proposals across professional bulletin boards and social media and through networks of professional colleagues, we were in the summer of 2020, when many of us were still in what we now know was a state of wishful thinking, expecting that maybe the pandemic would be over by fall, or maybe at worst after the winter of 2020/2021. As it became clear that many, if not most, universities would be almost completely online for the fall 2020 semester, many of our potential contributors found that they had to withdraw as the stresses of the pandemic mounted and multiplied. The sense of being overwhelmed was not lost on us either, as events that would be serious life events during any point in time were made that much more difficult to deal with during a pandemic.

In light of these difficulties, we would like to deeply thank all of our contributors who, along with us, completed all of their work, from the proposal stage to final revisions, during the COVID pandemic. We also would like to share our sincerest appreciation for Carlie Wall, our editor at Rowman &

Littlefield, for her assistance and her never-ending patience during our process of putting this collection together.

THE COLLECTION

We are proud to present *Disaster Pedagogy for Higher Education*. We believe we have put together an insightful array of chapters that cover a wide variety of topics such as classroom pedagogy, emergency management, and study abroad, from a variety of contributors including full-time professors, administrators, adjunct faculty, and students. We have organized the collection into three sections: Research and Criticism, which contains three chapters that highlight original research and scholarly critique of topics related to higher education during disaster; Explorations and Examinations, consisting of four chapters that focus on best practices of a specific aspect of higher education during disaster; and Personal and Professional Reflections, made up of six chapters that provide a more personal look into how disasters have impacted faculty, administration, and students in the academy.

The Chapters

Research and Criticism

Our collection begins with Addie Sayers's analysis of anti-maskers' rhetoric in digital and public spaces. In her chapter, "Give Me Liberty or Give Me a Mask: Pandemic Anti-Masking as Anti-Science Discourse," Sayers illustrates how the anti-mask movement realizes anti-science discourses by verbally positioning science as government control, science as oppression, science as conspiracy, and science as subservient to personal belief. Her linguistic discourse analysis reveals how their messages place science as subservient to personal belief, arguing that a social pedagogy of mask wearing reflects larger cultural beliefs that move beyond medicine and virus protection. Finally, she warns that educators should stress pedagogical attention to discourse and rhetoric for understanding public engagement with science, medicine, and health.

Although many educators at all levels were grateful for the technology available during the lockdowns of the COVID pandemic, Hannah R. Gerber's critical chapter, "Education in Times of Crises: The Ontological Imperative in Considering the Role of Technology Adoption in Remote Educational Settings," provides a process for educators to critically interrogate technology. Using the ontological imperative framework as a method for interrogating technological software and platforms, Gerber shows how educators can consider the negative ramifications of the data that are collected that may often violate the privacy of individuals. As disasters continue to impact and often halt face-to-face instruction, Gerber's chapter provides important parameters to help instructors make pedagogical decisions about using different technologies for remote teaching and learning.

Our third chapter in this section, "From Meteorological Uncertainty to Missing Muffins: How University Emergency Managers Manage Uncertainty as a Hurricane Response Strategy," provides a revealing look at how university emergency managers make decisions during times of crisis. Ian R. Weaver's qualitative case study is presented in the narrative of a fictitious (but all too possible) hurricane that devastates a coastal university, which allows readers an intimate look at the processes, dependencies, and compromises emergency managers make before, during, and after a major campus-closing event. Weaver's chapter is a must read not only for those in emergency management, as he provides multiple suggestions for universities to improve responses and communication with stakeholders during times of crisis, but also for anyone who works on or with a university campus who wants to get an eye-opening look at how critical decisions are made.

Explorations and Examinations

Our first chapter in the next section, "Explorations and Examinations," is an in-depth look at the experiences of the directors of a Center for Teaching Excellence and Center for Faculty Leadership at a university. Developed from their years of experience assisting faculty across multiple campus-closing hurricanes and the pandemic, Diana Ashe and Colleen A. Reilly's "Nimble Pedagogies for a Liquid Time: Disruption, Accommodation, Collaboration, Reinvention, and Compromise" provides best practices in assisting college faculty as they navigate through disaster, campus closures, and changes in course delivery modality.

Although disasters impacting higher education are often thought of as geographically located on or around a college campus, study abroad programs can reach anywhere in the world and as such, tragic events that occur thousands of miles away can become of serious concern to universities very close to home. In "Studying Abroad During a Time of Disaster: An Exploration of Pitfalls, Pivots, and Possibilities for the Future," three administrators in charge of study abroad offices at different universities share a wealth of experience about overseas events that have impacted student travel and study. From the night club shootings in Paris, to the Egyptian Arab Spring, and even to volcanic eruptions, Kara Pike Inman, Nicole Desjardins Gowdy, and Jason Kinnear show readers how travelling abroad with students can be far more than a simple trip away from campus.

We move back into the classroom in Melissa Sexton's "Thinking Through Disasters: Critical Analysis and Research in College Composition Courses," which argues that centering disasters as part of curricula can be effective because they involve complex interconnections between natural and cultural factors. Sexton shows that studying disasters can allow students to think critically, approach research from an interdisciplinary perspective, and broaden their conceptions of what constitutes research. By describing her personal experiences of teaching and adapting disaster-themed units during hurricanes and the COVID-19 pandemic, Sexton explores how these units can help students engage with and process disasters, even when they are personally affected by such events.

Teacher education and student teacher internships are the focus of Alice Hays, Jouselin Martin, Alexandra Chapa-Kunz, and Wade Branch's "How Do You Learn to Teach When You Can't Go to School? Teaching Teachers in the Age of Virtual Living." Their chapter details the issues that arose from training student teachers during the first year of the COVID pandemic in virtual settings for face-to-face classrooms. By centering three student-teacher voices during their residency program, this chapter critiques and troubles the way they were evaluated in addition to identifying the potential gaps in their training; moreover, the authors provide suggestions for ways that universities and schools might support early career teachers who completed online virtual teaching internships.

Our final chapter in this section, Anka Roberto's "Trauma and Its Lasting Effects After School Shootings: Psychological Considerations for Faculty, Staff, and Students," shows educators the importance of trauma- and resilience-informed pedagogy. Lessons learned from the aftermath of school shootings and other tragedies are outlined in this chapter to serve as a guide to help academia institute trauma- and resilience-informed practices. Developed and adopted from the Substance Abuse and Mental Health Service Administration trauma-informed care toolkit, faculty, staff, and administrators in higher education will gain the knowledge they need to implement practices that will assist the overall well-being of our student body.

Personal and Professional Reflections

Our final section begins with Tiffany Gilbert's "Chairing in the Pandemicene: Coronavirus, George Floyd, and the Year of Living Dangerously," which reflects on department leadership in a time of crisis and moral drift in America. In this chapter, Gilbert describes how she navigates the intellectual and emotional hazards of "chairing while Black" at the University of North Carolina Wilmington in the vortex of two pandemics—racism and COVID-19.

It further contemplates Wilmington's racially violent history following the murder of George Floyd and the university chancellor's controversial "All Lives Matter" stance in the face of mass mourning and anxiety.

The Global Story Hour, a Facebook page developed by Suriati Abas as part of teaching during COVID in a children's literature course, is the focus of our next chapter, "New Literacies, Empathy, and Advocacy—Reconstructing a Pedagogy in Pandemic Times." Abas's personal reflection on teaching and pivoting to online instruction shows us how she successfully moved a face-to-face literature class dependent on discussion to an online environment with the help of a variety of digital tools.

Similarly, Kevin D. Cordi's "In a Crisis, Stories Need to Be Heard—Changing the Digital Landscape to Include Narratives" details how his shift to online instruction was based in empathy and storytelling—and listening. A master storyteller himself, Cordi shares how he made his students' narratives the center of his pedagogy and how that helped them navigate through their chaotic semester.

How a community college responds on a larger scale to the shifts demanded by the pandemic is described by Barbara Allen in "Community Is Always the Answer: Columbus State Community College, Compassion, and Care." In it, she details how the office of employee engagement often partnered with human resources to create numerous outreach activities for students, staff, and faculty to maintain a sense of community during a time when many were working or attending class remotely.

The ocean waves beckon Andy Tolhurst, the author of "Holdfast: An Education in Disaster," whose chapter takes us through his relationship with the surf and hurricanes. In this chapter, Tolhurst shares his paradoxical relationship between devastating hurricanes and epic waves to surf, chronicling over two decades of hurricanes and sharing how they have changed him as a student, as a surfer, and as a teacher.

A student's experience is the focus of our final chapter, a personal reflection by Kayli Childs, which shows the darker side of how a university responded to the pandemic. Kayli, who was a dormitory resident assistant at the time COVID broke out, shares how the RAs were expected to put themselves at risk of exposure to the virus, or risk losing their jobs. Although short, this is an important chapter to read as it explores the intersections of the academy and student labor, something that is often overlooked when discussing higher education and the pandemic.

Part I

RESEARCH AND CRITICISM

Chapter One

Give Me Liberty or Give Me a Mask

Pandemic Anti-Masking as Anti-Science Discourse

Addie Sayers

As I write this, deaths from COVID-19 in the United States have just surpassed 562,000 (Centers for Disease Control, 2021). Of course, that's if the government isn't lying to us. That's if those people *really* died from COVID. Or maybe, *maybe* those people only died only because of their underlying conditions. And that's if COVID is actually real. Because I don't know anyone *personally* who saw all those people die. And if they *did* die, and COVID *is* real, it's because COVID was planned. The government just wants to push vaccines. They want to cover up 5G network damage. Or, maybe, those people died because masks don't work, because the virus is so small it passes right through the masks. It's my right, regardless, not to wear a mask.

In 1983, Joanna Russ wrote *How to Suppress Women's Writing,* outlining 11 strategies and methods that kept women out of literary canons, ranging from falsely categorizing their work as something other than literature and categorizing them as something other than a writer, to devaluing their content as applicable to women only, to overtly denying that a woman actually wrote the final product. In 2020, several Americans found ways to replicate these denials of agency, but this time, instead of denying the agency of women writers, they denied the agency of science. Similarly to Russ's (1983) argument that women's writing was condemned, denigrated, undermined, and ignored in spite of evidence to the contrary, many Americans also condemned, denigrated, undermined, and ignored the science of COVID-19, in spite of evidence to the contrary. At the center of this denial stood one divisive cultural artifact, weaponized over all others, as a symbol of anti-scientism: the loathed, feared, freedom-stealing face mask.

SCIENCE IS REAL, WHETHER YOU UNDERSTAND IT OR NOT

During the COVID-19 pandemic, the American Centers for Disease Control (CDC) recommended the wearing of face masks to curb disease transmission. As the purpose of masks was to protect oneself and others from the airborne transmission of the virus, several state and local governments issued mask mandates requiring masks in public spaces, including stores, restaurants, schools, and places of business. Despite such recommendations, however, many Americans not only refused to wear masks, but publicly protested the governmental imposition of mask wearing and spread their anti-mask rhetoric throughout digital and other public spaces. Anti-maskers vehemently argued against masks and created several social practices to express their disdain. For example, anti-maskers labeled masks "submission muzzles," created online groups urging mask avoidance, protested mask wearing with public mask burnings, and invented and disseminated the hashtags of #antimask, #nomasksneeded, #maskscauseillness, #IgniteFreedom, and #TheBurnYour MaskChallenge. Anti-maskers used masks to index several political and ideological views.

In this chapter I explore the discourses of anti-mask-wearing during this pandemic. Drawing from a corpus of 100 images of anti-mask protests from a Google image search, I illustrate how the anti-mask movement realizes anti-science discourses by verbally positioning science in four interconnected and often overlapping ways: science as governmental control, science as oppression, science as conspiracy, and science as subservient to personal belief. I demonstrate how masks become synecdoche for ideological stances that use mask wearing to co-opt discourses of freedom, liberty, and protest. I aim to show that a social pedagogy of mask wearing reflects larger cultural beliefs that move beyond medicine and virus protection, as anti-maskers pervert masks to perpetuate their own political agendas that run counter to empirical scientific arguments. Finally, I illustrate the logic of their non-logical arguments.

For my data gathering, I first created a corpus of images by running an image search through Google on December 12, 2020. I entered "anti-mask protests" and "United States" as key search terms in order to limit posts from other countries. I then collected the first 100 non-repeat images for multimodal discourse analysis (Gee, 2018). I chose anti-mask protest images because of the heavy use of protest signs to express protestors' ideas and I sought to interrogate what attendees at protests would read on protest signs as visual, public discourses in the linguistic landscape of protests.

Following the fundamental theoretical assumptions of linguistic discourse analysis, which connects microlinguistic and semiotic features to macrolevel ideologies and belief systems (Jones, Chik, & Hafner, 2015), I first coded the language of the protest images for linguistic meanings, forms, and structures (Gee, 2018). I then grouped these codes into larger themes related to science based on ideologies present in the data (Gee, 2018).

DISCOURSE PATTERN 1—*I WILL NOT COMPLY*

You know, the real problem here is not the disease. The real problem is the government. The government harms us more than any virus does. They just want to control us, and especially those politicians. They just want to manipulate us, take away our rights, and make us submit to their tyranny. This isn't about our health, it's about theirs. They want to keep themselves free while they muzzle us with fascism, communism, and socialism. They stay alive while our freedom dies.

In the first discursive pattern, instead of accepting masks as virus protection devices, anti-maskers argue that masks are tools for governmental control over constituents. That is, to anti-maskers, governments enforce mask wearing as an attempt to assert authority over their citizens. Quotes from protest images illustrate. Some protestors frame this control more generally, arguing to *Stop Government Overreach* of mandated mask-wearing, while others attack mask mandates and mask-wearing more explicitly, charging that *It's not a health crisis it's a control crisis* and that *Safety = Control*.

These assertions of control often coincide with linking government overreach to other forms of authoritarianism as a slippery slope, as in *Welcome to the N.W.O. [New World Order] poverty, famine, death, government overreach, lying media, I do not consent.* Others lexically rename masks various iterations of *muzzles*, with slogans like *No forced muzzles, no mandating muzzles,* and *mandatory mask = mandatory muzzle!!!*, indexing the forcibly silenced, overpowered, and dominated position of a restrained animal. Masks themselves, and COVID-19, by extension, are less dangerous to the citizenry than the government is, as anti-maskers assert that *the Government kills more than COVID*, refer to the mandates of mask wearing as *This is WAR*, and direct the government to *keep your laws off my face*. At a fundamental level, anti-maskers claim government overstep in their appellation of masks as *unconstitutional*.

Other anti-maskers extend governmental authority and align masks with specific political ideologies that they feel seek to rob citizens of freedom, including fascism, liberalism, and socialism. This occurs through adjectival modifiers, changing *submission muzzles* into *fascist muzzles*, and the use of general modifiers such as *liberal, socialist,* and *fascist* as co-occurring descriptions on anti-mask signs. Protest signs that read *COVID19 is a test run at socialism*, *Social distance from socialism*, and *Defy fascist lockdown* exemplify. Anti-maskers also position masks as extensions of liberal governments, and liberal governments' alleged association with other sites of liberal control, like the media. One sign reads *Masks are a symbol of false security we hide behind when we let the media and politicians attack our medical freedom*, while several others urge citizens with *Don't believe the liberal media* when it comes to information regarding COVID-19, masks, and mask mandates. Other examples of anti-mask protest reference conservativism through intertextual and interdiscursive references to political slogans, such as *Make America Free Again* and *Let America Work Again* and their echo of former president Donald Trump's campaign slogan and rallying cry *Make America Great Again*. In these examples, anti-maskers juxtapose the alleged attack and the implied purposeful deception by the media and politicians with citizens who must hide and sacrifice their freedom at the hands of a government that promotes masks as *false security*.

These discursive patterns of masks as governmental control often coincide with a negative evaluation of government officials. Local governors are often targeted for their mask mandates, with slogans such as *We deem our governor unessential*, *Newsom* [governor of California] *We are putting you on notice*, *Stop Gov Cooper* [governor of North Carolina], *Tyrant Communist Cooper destroying NC lives*, *Impeach Whitmer* [governor of Michigan], and *Remove Whitmer's regime*. The latter two examples go so far as to label one governor a Communist and a tyrant, and as to rename the gubernatorial position one of absolute authoritarian authority. The same language also appeared in an attempted plan to kidnap Governor Whitmer. In October 2020 the FBI arrested six White men who began plotting Whitmer's attack in June 2020 because they believed she was *tyrannical* (Kratkov, 2021). Dr. Anthony Fauci, head of the National Institute of Allergy and Infectious Diseases and chief medical advisor to former president Donald Trump, who was in office during the data collection, officially recommended wearing masks as a strategy to combat COVID-19 infection; he is also a frequent target in anti-mask rhetoric through statements like *Fire Fauci*, *Fauci is corrupt*, and *No Fauci, No Gates, No vaccine*. In the latter example, he is joined in parallel syntactic structure with billionaire Bill Gates and the COVID-19 vaccine, in which protestors braid the anti-mask stance of conspiracy theory with the anti-mask stance of government control; anti-maskers position the government, Dr. Fauci, and Bill Gates as coconspirators who not only seek to dominate US citizens, but use COVID-19 as a ploy to insert controlling relics, like microchips, into citizenry via vaccines. Masks are a tool for such domination.

Finally, because anti-maskers frame masks as instruments of governmental power and mask mandates as violations of the Constitution, they interdiscursively link mask protests with other constitutional violations. The most frequently co-opted reference to this end includes the ubiquitous slogan *We will not comply*, which rose historically out of public responses to fears regarding alleged challenges to the Second Amendment. *We will not comply* indexes the anti-government slogans (Neiwert, 2014) of gun control protest movements, as protestors situate themselves as purposeful opponents to, and violators of, unjust laws. When anti-maskers shift usage of this expression to target masks and mask-wearing, they directly imply that they purposefully oppose mask mandates and indirectly associate masks with anti-constitutional removals of medical freedom similar to the claimed anti-constitutional removal of freedom to bear arms. Additionally, anti-maskers also incorporate the words and images of the Gadsden Flag, *Don't Tread on Me* below a coiled rattlesnake, into their protest signs. Historically an American Revolutionary flag, the symbolism of the Gadsden Flag shifted in the early 2000s when the Tea Party, neo-Confederate, and far-right extremists groups incorporated it into their anti-government protests and activist movements (Southern Poverty Law Center, n.d.). It was also used ubiquitously by the attempted government coup on January 6, 2021, when rioters protesting the election stormed the US capital with Gadsden flags in hand (Mascaro, Fox, and Baldor, 2021). Such discourses subtly and indirectly link a pro-gun, militia, oppositional, and anti-government stance with an anti-mask political position; in doing so, they also reinforce the purported fascist, liberal, and social indexicalities of masks themselves. With this rhetorical move, anti-government becomes anti-mask.

DISCOURSE PATTERN 2—*MY BODY, MY CHOICE*

You can't tell me what to do with my body. It's my freedom, it's my body, and it's my choice. I'm not going to live in fear. I can make my own decisions—I have rights, you know. Reproductive freedom? You mean abortion? That's not even the same thing. I'm not hurting anyone if I don't wear a mask.

In the second discourse pattern, anti-maskers use masks to frame science, via mask-wearing, as oppression. Overlapping with science as government control, this rhetoric alleges that wearing masks violates civil and individual liberties and personal freedoms. In other words, mask mandates remove personal rights, and masks represent citizen subjugation at the hands of an unjust government. A common illustrative trend is the use of *tyranny* throughout anti-mask discourse. Examples include several visuals of masks labeled *the new symbol of tyranny*, and anti-mask posters that read *We do not consent to tyranny or forced vaccines*, *Stop government tyranny*, *We the People will not stand for tyranny*, *Freedom & facts not tyranny*, and *This is about tyranny vs. freedom*.

Anti-mask protesters also indict masks as oppressive tools through their juxtaposition of masks versus freedom through distinct rhetorical moves. One theme is freedom versus fear, where anti-maskers metonymize *masks* to represent fear of COVID-19 and *no masks* to represent freedom. In such instances, masks—as symbols and devices of fear—oppress. For example, *I will not wear someone else's fear*, *If you are scared then you wear a mask*, *Your fear doesn't take away my freedom*, *Freedom and masks don't go together*, and *my rights don't end where your fear begins*. Anti-maskers also claim that masks remove freedom more directly, both literally and metaphorically, by silencing citizens. *Don't let the mask silence you* and *Masks only silence you* are common iterations where *masks* are linguistic subjects and agents against *you*, the linguistic passive object of the verbal *silencing*. Finally, anti-maskers frequently collocate masks with freedom in rhetorical contradistinction that implies contrastive difference, as in *Freedom matters, no forced masks*; *No mandated masks or shutdown; Freedom First; Compliance = complacency; Sorry did my civil rights get in the way of your virus*; *My rights* [my rights NOT to wear a mask] *are essential*, and *My constitutional rights are essential*. Some anti-maskers combine this pattern with science as conspiracy, as in *Freedom over fear You R being lied 2*.

Anti-maskers also use mask-wearing to create a false victimization through the appropriation of protest movement discourse. That is, anti-maskers deploy the typical colonizing, racist, and misogynistic patterns of hegemonic discourses (Hill, 2008) to co-opt slogans of both contemporary and historical civil rights protests and to frame themselves as unfairly oppressed and marginalized; they appropriate rhetoric from social movements that many of them, and/or the political stances with which they align, derided, rejected, and/or protested against themselves. The most frequent appropriation exemplifies, with the oft-repeated *My body my choice* and its derivations *My child my choice* and *Choice not mandate* from the reproductive rights movement. Anti-maskers also appropriate discourse from racial justice and anti-police brutality movements, such as Black Lives Matter, with language such as in *'Freedom Matters' No forced mask mandates*; they also align their alleged subjugated subjectivity with that of enslaved Americans with S*laves wore masks*, *A man chooses, a slave obeys*, and *I prefer dangerous freedom over peaceful slavery*. One protestor combines several anti-mask rhetorical positions, uniting White supremacist victimization with government trickery and authoritarian control through *No slave hoax muzzles*. In a gross display of false victimhood, other White anti-maskers inject White supremacy into their protests. In one sickening example, White anti-maskers repeat *I Can't Breathe* on their signs. In doing so, they steal a Black Lives Matter protest slogan coined in honor of Eric Garner, an unarmed Black man, who uttered *I can't breathe* as his final words before dying in a brutal attack by police. In this instance, anti-maskers equate mask-wearing with the severity and injustice of Garner's murder.

DISCOURSE PATTERN 3—*BUT YOUTUBE SAYS IT'S A PLANDEMIC*

You know, I've never had COVID. And I've never seen someone die from COVID. I've heard stories . . . but have you really seen them? Why don't they let us in the hospital when people are dying? And do their "so-called" numbers really represent people who died from COVID, or who died from other conditions that the government labeled as COVID? If you ask me, this is all a government cover-up. A plandemic. It's a way for the government to push their vaccines with their microchips and tracking. It's all lies, and masks are just the first step to make you believe their lies. Masks don't even stop real viruses. Plus, we all know, the liberal media is the real virus. COVID . . . it's a hoax.

In the third discourse pattern, anti-maskers equate science with conspiracy through the discursive positioning of masks in anti-mask rhetoric. On their protest signs, anti-maskers situate mask-wearing and mask mandates within their new lexical blends, as part of the *plandemic* or *scamdemic*, conjoining *plan* and *scam* with *pandemic*, as one sign that reads *Masks Kill! Resist the Muzzle Scamdemic*. The lexicon implies that COVID-19 is not real, and is part of a governmental and social plan, hoax, or scam against US citizenry. Some overtly claim *COVID 19 is a lie* and that the *shutdown is based in lies* or simply state *hoax* and a form of *mind control*. Masks are indicted, as several signs display pictures or drawing of masks with the caption *This is a mind control device*.

In many instances, anti-maskers marry COVID-19 science with other conspiratorial theories, such as those of QAnon. QAnon refers to the idea that there is a secret group of Satan-worshipping, primarily Democrat-leaning pedophiles and that former president Trump is leading the way in fighting this underground group (Spring & Wendling, 2020); QAnon also references the eponymous group of those who believe the theories of QAnon. Other tenets of the meshing of QAnon and COVID-19 science is the unsubstantiated belief that COVID-19 is a planned attempt to cover this child sex-trafficking ring (Spring & Wendling, 2020) and that governments are trying to microchip citizens with forced vaccines to spy, track, and/or poison citizens.

One sign protest reads *Save the Children sent us* and alludes to the QAnon hashtag *#SaveTheChildren* that allegedly targets the pedophiles of this sex-trafficking ring. A different anti-mask protest poster illustrates with *Imprison Gates-Fauci-Newsom for crimes against humanity—Plandemic* indicting Democratic California governor Gavin Newsom, Bill Gates, and Dr. Anthony Fauci, who are frequently targeted as conspirators by QAnon with the planning of COVID-19. In this example, this protestor alleges that Gates, Fauci, and Newsom are collaborative schemers who planned COVID-19 against innocent denizens and echoes the QAnon assumptions that Bill Gates is using vaccines as a means for inserting microchips into human beings. Another poster directly addresses Gates and indirectly invokes QAnon conspiracy with *Bill Gates, you'll have to kill me before you vaccinate me!* Here, masks are a mere cover-up device for the more potent dangers of vaccinations and their consequent microchipping; the plandemic, not COVID-19, is the real danger, so masks are useless, at best, and smokescreens, at worst. Biblical connections to Satan underscore another attack at Fauci, Gates, and seven other named elected officials with *Texas will not take the mark of the Beast, vaccine chip ID2020*. This brings QAnon references full circle in anti-mask discourses, with allusion to the alleged Satanism of the Democrats and doctors in charge of the *plandemic*. Another protest poster links masks with the conspiracy through the intertextual reference of Nazi Germany, adding *This is not Nazi Germany, No testing, no tracing, no tracking, no spying, no snitching, no mask . . . liberty, not tyranny* and positions the QAnon targets as synonymous to Nazis. In such instances, the anti-maskers unite aforementioned themes of government control and various types of oppression with scientific conspiracy linked through masks.

For many anti-maskers, the COVID-19 vaccine is a key component to the conspiracy, so they also position anti-vaccine stances within their anti-mask protest. One sign reads *The cure is deadly* [sic] *than the virus* while others state *No phases, no masks, no vaxxs, Freedom of choice, the vaccine will kill millions more than COVID*, and *No COVID vaccine*. The linguistic presupposition of many signs, like the latter example, is the forcing of vaccines upon American citizens. Just like the joining of QAnon conspiracy theories with anti-COVID viewpoints, anti-maskers have also united with the anti-vaccine movement. One anti-masker illustrates, *I do NOT consent: mandated testing, mandated immunity certificates or microchips, mandated vaccines, tracking*. In several examples this appears framed as concern from parents trying to protect their children from masks, and consequently, from vaccines, with rallying cries such as *Unmask our children* on adults' posters circulating alongside children holding signs that read *I refuse to be your experiment* and *unmask us*. The intermixing of anti-science, anti-vax conspiratorial rhetoric also appropriates and recycles protest language, as previously discussed; in this instance, parental anti-maskers co-opt reproductive rights, as in *my child, my choice*, and Black Lives Matter discourse with *Kids lives matter*. In this rhetoric anti-mask parents appeal to their parental power (Mays 2020) to contend that masks harm children socially and emotionally; because anti-vaxxers object to all vaccines, most medicines, and schools' rights to enforce vaccination policies, they extend their criticism to schools' rights to enforce mask-wearing. Like QAnon anti-maskers, they ground their beliefs around anti-science and anti-government, but with a slightly different focus on schools and medicine over secret government cabals and high-ranking politicians.

Additionally, anti-maskers realize science as conspiracy through their use of unsupported and non-empirically investigated assertions. Some, once again, align *fear* with *masks* to juxtapose it with their cause of *facts*; this time, however, they metonymize *masks* as *fear*, and *no masks* as *truth*, as in the oft repeated *facts over fear*. Anti-maskers claim truth as their own, and those who promote masks as liars who disseminate false information. One target is the media though signs like *the real pandemic is misinformation, Media, do your job! No more lies! No more bias! No more fear!* and *the media is the virus*. Science and scientific inquiry are also suspect, as anti-maskers protest what constitutes proof of COVID-19 and its dangers, claiming that *no scientific proof = no new normal, the models are wrong*, and *conflicting science should not lead no mandates*. Doctors are suspect, as well, as one poster reads *I am being proven right about massive vaccinations . . . the doctors lied*. Some anti-mask protestors overtly deny scientific and medical evidence with their own assertions, alleging that *masks harm health, this mask is as useless as our governor*, and that *face masks lower oxygen to the brain, impede communication, not proven effective, block our humanity* [and] *disempower us!*, while others employ the agency-denying discursive device of labeling something *fake* to discredit it, *social distancing is fake science*. Still others draw upon the rhetorical strategy of unsupported, decontextualized, misinterpreted, and inadequate statistics to downplay the severity of COVID-19, with anti-mask language like *0.00002 does not justify shutdown* and *I'll take the 0.03% chance—open now*.

DISCOURSE PATTERN 4—*MY KOMBUCHA MAKES ME IMMUNE . . .*

See, here's the thing. I've done a lot of research. I mean a lot. Vaccines are the real problem. They make you sick. Not everyone who gets COVID gets really sick. It's not even that big of a deal if you are healthy. I take my vitamins and

I know that my body will protect me. Vitamin D will protect me. My sister's cousin got a vaccine and got autism from it. Yeah, really. So I'm really anti-vax. And like, I just don't want to put those chemicals in my body. I'll be fine. Plus, really, God will protect me in the end. He really will. So I'm not even worried. I mean, I never even get the flu. And you know what, if I did get COVID, I'd want to get it. Because then I'd just build my immune system. I'd be stronger. I have more faith in my God and in my immune system than in a mask.

The final discourse pattern of the anti-mask movement frames science as subservient to personal beliefs. Anti-maskers invoke anecdotal evidence, religious beliefs, and pseudoscience to justify their claims; they also just assert or deny scientific research findings with no evidence. One protestor uses their alleged personal experience to deny COVID-19 science with *Type 1 diabetic survived covid open schools now* while others claim *I'm not sick No mask* and *Unmask us, I'm not sick*. Immunity figures prominently in this rhetorical strategy; one protestor says *Vaccination is genocide, God gave us an immune system for a reason* while others reject masks because their God will protect them. God and religion are enough evidence for many anti-maskers to invalidate COVID-19 dangers; *God is the only essential*, one sign reads. If not God, then individuals' immune systems are all that is required to fight COVID-19, and masks inhibit this process, as the protestors who urge that *masks reduce immunity* and *Build up my immune system not vax schedule*. No evidence, scientific data, or medical support is required to back some anti-masking claims, as protestors renounce masks because *oxygen is essential, masks are unhealthy, masks cause bacterial infections*, and *masks can't stop a virus*. In such instances, anti-maskers flat out deny science as belief and not fact, with masks as the culprits to block oxygen, allow for viruses, cause infection, and inhibit health.

Whereas each of the four discourse patterns—science as control, science as oppression, science as conspiracy, and science as subservient to personal belief—frequently intersect, interact, and mutually reinforce one another, this discourse pattern diverges slightly. That is, while most anti-mask rhetoric indexes and/or indirectly references other social movements, including Trumpism, conservatism, anti-government movements, militia movements, QAnon, and anti-vaccine movements, the framing of science as subservient to personal belief is the one pattern that aligns more with traditionally left-leaning and liberal tendencies. This rhetoric often includes the modifier *natural*, as in *immune systems work, naturally* or *Social distancing is unnatural, hug your loved ones* and draws from a very different semiotic spectrum than fear, control, and manipulation. These strategies appeal to natural health discourses and non-chemical bases for immunity, and echo a stance of hands-off, liberal healing over other assumptive beliefs.

THE TYRANNY OF FACE MASKS AND THE LOGIC OF ANTI-LOGIC

Four discursive patterns—science as control, science as oppression, science as conspiracy, and science as subservient to personal belief—interact to mutually reinforce one another in the rhetoric of anti-masking. These patterns lessen, remove, or denigrate linguistic agency of masks, COVID-19, and science simultaneously. First, anti-maskers use the method of "Bad Faith" (Russ, 1983), a means of denying science through the creation of a social platform that ignores or devalues masks and science. By uniting masks and science as fear together against facts, truth, the Constitution, and freedom; by revealing science's connections to tyrannical governors, mind control initiatives, tyranny, and oppression; by linking science to the enemies Bill Gates, Dr. Fauci, and a Satan-worshipping secret political society; and by situating science against God, nature, and their personal beliefs, anti-maskers make science critique more accessible and more available to numerous, already science intolerant, individuals. Anti-maskers also employ Russ's (1983) concept of "Pollution of Agency," whereby they deny the veracity of science by claiming that science isn't really science at all. Masks and COVID-19 are elements of scams, lies, control, and instruments for forced vaccinations, microchipping, or general harm to the body.

In these processes, masks gain new associative meanings, known as indexicalities, as they are positioned via synecdoche and metonymy as, and thus stand in for, COVID-19 and science, or falsehood and fear; through anti-maskers' use, masks come to represent, indirectly, all sorts of cultural ideas that extend far beyond the traditional connotational and denotational meanings of masks alone. In other words, as masks move through the digital and analog discourses of anti-mask protests, they gain new associative meanings and carry with them multiple layers of semiotic baggage, including intertextual, interdiscursive, and allusionary references to ideologies, cultural beliefs, and cultural events.

These processes of indexicalization, or the acquisition of associative meanings, arise through several discursive means and occur at multiple levels of language—the word, phrase structure, sentence structure, and larger discourse levels, as well in the pragmatic, metaphorical, sociolinguistic, and rhetorical domains of language use. That is, like taking cookie dough from its bowl and rolling it across nuts, sprinkles, and powdered sugar to gain new layers of substance and flavor, so do words across contexts. As one word is mobilized and reentextualized across different instances of use, its nuance of meaning increases; this happens in the use of masks in the language and posters of anti-mask rhetoric.

The challenge of indexicality as a cultural practice is that it works "behind the scenes" in meaning. Indexicality invokes meaning indirectly, via association, implication, and presupposition, in that which is not *directly said*, but what is implied. Indexicality lives and breathes through shared cultural understanding as it points forward and backward to assumed contexts (Blommaert, 2007) and brings those contexts to bear on present interpretations. Indexicality underscores stereotypes, implicit biases, and microaggressions, and is a mechanism for perpetuating colonialism, racism, (hetero)sexism, ableism, transphobia, xenophobia, and other forms of discrimination and marginalization. With respect to anti-mask rhetoric, indexicality functions as a means of anti-scientism, in which objective facts are subject to uninformed question and invalidation by personal, unjustified, and unsubstantiated opinion.

The problem with the indexicality, generally, and in the anti-science of mask rhetoric, specifically, is twofold. First, because indexicality resides in indirect and associative meanings, it is more difficult to recognize and target as a direct and overt form of science denial; the critics who protested, after all, were targeting *masks*. They are attacking *masks*, however, in the same discursive way that asking an Asian-American person *Where are you from, really*? is simply curiosity, or telling an African-American person that they are *so articulate* or a disabled person that they *don't look disabled* are really compliments. They are not. Folk theories of language incline people to believe that some words, like epithets and slurs, cause harm, and that linguistic harm is explicit and intended, while critical theories of language assert that all language can perform social action, and that meaning is about effect and not intent (Hill, 2008). Connecting this to anti-mask rhetoric, I argue that the harm—and the strength of its cultural impact—lies in the negative anti-science and anti-fact effects of this rhetoric, and not in the literal meaning of critiques of masks themselves. In other words, in order to challenge the anti-science orientation of anti-mask rhetoric, one must first wade through the unwritten/unspoken, underlying assumptions created iteratively through lexical items, phrase structure and syntax, rhetorical patterns, metaphor, intertextuality and interdiscursivity, and other discursive devices outside of direct anti-mask and anti-science positions. The damage to science and fact, however, has already been done.

Second, when indexical links are already established, as the anti-science stances of science as government control, oppression, conspiracy, and subservient to belief are in this data, it becomes easier to disseminate other types of anti-objective fact rhetoric. The implied discursive associations already exist to erode the cultural validity of one set of objective facts (science); those who wish to deny other objective facts (mathematical results of an election) already have a set of indexical assumptions to deploy. The anti-government *Stop the*

Steal attempted coup on January 6, 2021, after data collection, exemplifies this. The same indexicalities that weaved through the anti-science, anti-mask protest data gained a new host to which to link in insurrection rhetoric—to the results of an election. The indexes that allowed for subservience of fact to belief and for people to question science without evidence were mobilized as tools to justify storming the capital; this time, protestors used the very same indirect and concomitant meanings to question electoral vote math. Once again, the rhetoric of the attempted insurrection referenced the *tyranny* of the government, its *lies* as it *stole* an election in attempt to *control* its citizens. The Gadsden flag and the invocations of *liberty*, the fight against governmental *silencing* and *fraud*, even references to Governor Whitmer and appellations of *COVID 19 vaccination = death* adorned the siege. The indexes gained new hosts—from masks to a coup—to exponentially strengthen the anti-fact trend. This same cycle continues with anti-vaccine rhetoric, as well, and particularly as President Biden has increased mask mandates and vaccine dissemination. Like masks and elections, the facts and science of vaccines serves to *control, harm, microchip,* or *fail to stop transmission*. Masks didn't work, vaccines don't work, science doesn't work, and facts don't matter.

In word choice, phrase structure, sentence structure, literary and rhetorical devices, allusions, interdiscursive and intertextual links, and references to macro-level ideologies and discursive denials of agency, anti-maskers contribute novel meanings to masks (and to vaccines, and to voting results, and to . . .) that move way beyond face coverings for medical protection. Each iteration of masks in protest language and discourse adds to the indexicality of masks, or the associated, linked, and highly cultural indirect meanings. Ultimately, I draw attention to the concept of indexicality, because it is the layer of nuanced meaning where many shared, accompanying meanings and ideas arise; these meanings are like the unspoken "baggage" attached to discussions of masks. Because these meanings are indirect, they are often felt and echoed in anti-mask rhetoric, but are not often obvious or seen, which makes them less visible and obvious key players in discussions of health rhetoric. Indexicality is critical for discussions of anti-mask rhetoric, because it is indexicality that positions masks in ways that become more difficult for those who support masks to challenge. Indexicality increases the hegemonic power of anti-mask and anti-science positions within cultural rhetoric; critiques, after all, aren't attacking science, they're attacking control, oppression, lies, fascism, and tyranny.

In conclusion, it becomes difficult to critique and discuss the science of COVID-19, particularly in classrooms and in public discourse settings, without fielding it through assumed attacks to individuals' personal ideologies. Just like masks, science and science education themselves become politicized through the process of indexicality. This means that discussions of efficacy of actual masks, and actual science, are often left untouchable, as one must muddle through layers and layers of meaning, discourse, and rhetoric to get to the actual facts of mask wearing. It's not masks, but vaccines . . . it's not masks, but socialism . . . it's not masks, but microchips, it's not masks, it's God . . . and so on, and on, and on. In this chapter, I aimed to use language to show that a social pedagogy of mask-wearing reflects larger cultural beliefs that move beyond medicine and virus protection, into science and fact. Ultimately, I argue for the importance of pedagogical attention to discourse and rhetoric—and indexicality—for understanding public engagement with science, medicine, and health. When it comes to the science of masks and COVID-19, language matters.

REFERENCES

Blommaert, J. (2007). Sociolinguistics and discourse analysis: Orders of indexicality and polycentricity. *Journal of Multicultural Discourses, (2)*2, 115–30.

Gee, J. P. (2018). *Introducing discourse analysis: From grammar to society.* New York: Routledge.

Hill, J. H. (2008). *The everyday language of White Racism.* Malden, MA: Wiley-Blackwell Publishing.

Jones, R. H., Chik, A., & Hafner, C. A. (2015). Introduction: Discourse analysis and digital practices. In R. H. Jones, A. Chik, & C. A. Hafner (eds.), *Discourse and digital practice: Doing discourse analysis in the digital age* (pp. 1–17). New York: Routledge.

Kratkov, M. (2021, January 27). *Suspect pleads guilty in plot to kidnap Michigan Governor, turns government witness.* NPR News. https://www.npr.org/2021/01/27/961215604/suspect-pleads-guilty-in-plot-to-kidnap-michigan-governor-turns-government-witne.

Mascaro, L., Fox, B., & Baldor, C. (2021, April 10). *"Clear the Capitol," Pence pleaded, timeline of riot shows.* APNews. https://apnews.com/article/capitol-siege-army-racial-injustice-riots-only-on-ap-480e95d9d075a0a946e837c3156cdcb9.

Mays, M. (2020, July 2). *From anti-vax to anti-mask: School districts brace for parent resistance.* Politico. https://www.politico.com/states/california/story/2020/07/02/from-anti-vax-to-anti-mask-school-districts-brace-for-parent-resistance-1295968.

Neiwert, D. (2014, December 10). *"Antigovernment" figures to lead "We will not comply" rally in Washington state over gun rights.* SPLC: Southern Poverty Law Center. https://www.splcenter.org/hatewatch/2014/12/10/antigovernment-figures-lead-%E2%80%98we-will-not-comply%E2%80%99-rally-washington-state-over-gun-rights.

Russ, J. (1983). *How to suppress women's writing.* Austin: University of Texas Press.

Southern Poverty Law Center. (n.d.) *Fighting Hate Extremist Files: Neo-Confederate.* Retrieved December 14, 2020. https://www.splcenter.org/fighting-hate/extremist-files/ideology/neo-confederate.

Spring, M., & Wendling, M. (2020, September 2). *How Covid-19 myths are merging with the QAnon conspiracy theory.* BBC News. https://www.bbc.com/news/blogs-trending-53997203.

Chapter Two

Education in Times of Crises

The Ontological Imperative in Considering the Role of Technology Adoption in Remote Educational Settings

Hannah R. Gerber

OVERVIEW

Technology, and the digital spaces made accessible by technology, can seem like a scary place to the uninitiated. There is a constantly evolving landscape of new apps, new platforms, new hardware, new systems. This rapid-fire succession of *new this* and *new that*, creates a system of potential educational economic instability—what I refer to as "keeping up with the Joneses" in educational spaces. Each new system, tool, service, app, platform, hardware, or software often shines and sparkles and promises freedom and salvation for instructors who are often educationally economically depleted—depleted of time, money, and resources and forced to find solutions for teaching and learning that will reach the broadest number of students as possible. However, the rapid-fire succession of *new this* and *new that* that Big Tech continuously pushes out, needs to be reprimanded by the end user: the instructor. Instructors can slow down their dance with technology and digital spaces and extricate themselves from the mosh-pit of shiny new apps and engage in a waltz with wonderment in a deep dive into technology and digital spaces for teaching and learning. This dive need not be something to fear, through using the ontological imperative framework (Lynch & Gerber, 2018), instructors are provided with scaffolding and guidance for interrogating technology and digital spaces to ensure that they are providing their students with the best digital tools, systems, and services.

As evidenced by the COVID-19 pandemic of 2020, our educational system is vulnerable. Whether we look to primary and secondary education, or higher education, we have a system wherein countless individuals are faced with technological insecurity which can lead to educational instability. In this case, insecurity has less to do with how people *feel* about technology, than it relates to how people have the *ability*—or inability—to access and acquire educational opportunity via technology. Similar to food insecurity that plagues nations all across the globe, technological insecurity is brought forth when the educational system requires that a need be met (i.e., learning online) while limiting access to this system by providing unequal access to software, hardware, platforms, and systems. Often, the assumption is that if educational opportunities are provided via technology, then students, professors, and parties invested in education will be able to access said educational opportunities. This could not be further from the truth. Educational opportunities via online spaces, from the outset, are not created equal, nor are they equally accessible by all, nor do many individuals have the knowledge or understanding of the very divisions—versus opportunities—these technologies are capable of creating.

Throughout the years, words of caution have been offered on the dangers of relying upon media and technology too much for key decision-making processes (McLuhan, 1962; Powe, 1987). One would be remiss to ignore these cautions. But one must ask, what is *too much* when we consider media and technology in the educational arena? How does the influx of media and technology impact the ability to read, write, and make sense of the world? How does the influx of media and technology impact the ability to engage in learning to understand the world?

When one considers the central place of technology and educational opportunity that occurs in online spaces, one must first consider the *digital turn* that has brought society to the era of online communications and subsequently how the digital turn impacts learning, literacy, and meaning making within contemporary society. The digital turn harkens memories of how theories have shifted, morphed, changed, and turned across the years. A *turn* recognizes that one must look backward and first examine history in order to understand the contemporary era and future eras to come. From the social turn in the late 1970s and the early 1980s, later expanded by literacy and media scholars such as Brian Street (1984) and Gunter Kress (2003), who suggested that social actions and social worlds of individuals are at the center of meaning making, to the spatial turn in the late 1980s, led by humanities scholars such as Edward Soja (1989) and Homi K. Bhaba (1994), who suggested that one must examine the spatial and temporal connections that exist in how people engage in meaning-making activities, to the digital turn of the current era (see also, Leander & Bolt, 2012; Lynch, 2015; DeCesari & Rowsell, 2020; Williamson, 2016), which explores how haptics, mobility, and the algorithm power online spaces, it is imperative to explore how individuals come to make meaning of the world.

In 1962, Marshall McLuhan, the esteemed media theorist, posited the concept of a hypothetical post-literate society in his seminal work, *The Gutenberg Galaxy*. A post-literate society is one in which multimedia technology has advanced to such a point that traditional reading and writing are no longer the primary forms of communication. In fact, in some of the hypothetical— or maybe even the not so hypothetical—post-literate societies, reading and writing are shunned and considered enemies of the State. One needs only to think of Ray Bradbury's (1953) *Fahrenheit 451* for an example of this type of society, where books are banned, and, in fact, burned. Some scholars argue that society is currently in a post-literate era, and hedge that technology and education have not kept pace in a manner that has coalesced for true education of all citizens. For example, author Bruce Powe (1987) remarking on post-literacy in his book, *The Solitary Outlaw*, wrote:

> Literacy is the ability to read and interpret the written word. What is post-literacy? It is the condition of semi-literacy, where most people can read and write to some extent, but where the literate sensibility no longer occupies a central position in culture, society, and politics. Post-literacy occurs when the ability to comprehend the written word decays. If post-literacy is now, then what happens to the reader, the writer, and the book in a post-literary environment? What happens to thinking, resistance, and dissent when the ground becomes wordless? (np)

In the age of emojis, Instagram posts, social media, fake news, and cat videos, some might argue that we are now in an era of post-literacy. But is society really in an era of post-literacy? Or rather, is society at a crossroads for understanding that teaching, and subsequently learning, just might look very different, particularly when delivered remotely to individuals with diverse hardware, software, and connectivity situations? Furthermore, what does it mean that these very technologies that are being used to deliver content are often for-profit, driven by a mega-corporate mission of *one-size fits all* globalization versus autonomy and sovereignty of the community? These same corporations collect copious amounts of user-generated data, which in turn they use to profit from via advertising revenue, creating profiles and personas of individuals based on aggregate data that might or might not indicate a true picture of the individual or the community from where an individual hails. This aggregated data and building of digital profiles of people, in turn, shapes technology use and development globally, forcing, for instance, individuals from a small rural village in sub-Saharan Africa into the user habits of an individual from Manhattan.

For example, major social media companies such as Facebook and Twitter collect user data that includes, but is not limited to, clickstreams, geolocation, and browsing habits. These companies not only track users when an individual is online using Facebook or Twitter, but also when the individual is off of Facebook and using different media; these companies collect these data and use these data to target advertising, to customize user experience, and to generate larger global profiles and portraits of society. A well-meaning instructor who creates a class study group using Facebook in order to keep students engaged when out of the classroom, is therefore providing Facebook with potentially sensitive user data that Facebook can then later profit from and shape and create global use patterns based on the data aggregate, which might or might not fit the needs of the user in disparate locations such as with the aforementioned example of a user from rural sub-Saharan Africa. As well-meaning as this Facebook study group creation might have been for the instructor—because it is well-meaning to ensure that all students have access to the class material via a platform that has lower data usage requirements than a streaming service like YouTube—the instructor has perhaps unwittingly handed over their student to be exploited by the marketing machine of Facebook. However, it is not just Facebook that collects copious amounts of user data; almost every online system that exists, social media or educational, captures, stores, and often monetizes these data. It is imperative that instructors begin to think through ways to mitigate this collection of data and to make informed decisions about when, where, and how to use digital technologies and online spaces to ensure that students are receiving continual education during remote learning scenarios. Enter, the ontological imperative.

THE ONTOLOGICAL IMPERATIVE FRAMEWORK

The ontological imperative framework (Lynch & Gerber, 2018) was originally created to encourage researchers to critically evaluate the digital tools, systems, and services that are part of their research studies. Because digital technology, and the very data traces that digital technology leaves, are temporal, transitory, porous, and constantly in flux (Gerber, Abrams, Curwood, & Magnifico, 2017), researchers and scholars must engage in a critique of the digital tools, systems, and services that are a part of their studies to ensure that their research is transparent and replicable (Lynch & Gerber, 2018). Although, to-date, this framework has been applied to mixed methods research (Gerber, Lynch, & Onwuegbuzie, forthcoming; Lynch & Gerber, in press), multimethod research (Gerber & Lynch, in press), and qualitative research (Gerber, in press), this framework can also be applied to the critical evaluation of technologies used within pedagogical and teaching situations in remote learning scenarios. The five-question framework of the ontological imperative engages in a philosophical deconstruction of the very nature of what it means *to be* digital. Because of this philosophical deconstruction of the nature of ontology within the digital realm, Lynch and Gerber (2018) stress that epistemological claims are strengthened in a researcher's study. This same analogy applies to the concept that ontologically deconstructing one's digital teaching and pedagogical materials will lead to strengthening of student learning and epistemological understandings of course material.

Technical Demonstration of the Ontological Imperative Framework

The five questions that undergird the ontological imperative framework allow an instructor applying the ontological imperative to work through a critique of the digital tools, systems, and services that are woven into their teaching. The five guiding questions of the framework are as follows:

1. What digital tools, systems, and services are at play in my teaching? Who created them and why?
2. What data do these digital tools, systems, and services render?
3. What hidden limitations might there be to the data rendered via these digital tools, systems, and services?
4. What are the epistemological implications of this ontological analysis?
5. What are the axiological implications of this ontological analysis?

What digital tools, systems, and services are at play in my study? Who created them and why?

This question is concerned with understanding the purpose and design of the digital technologies that will be used for teaching and learning. It encourages instructors to dig into the technologies that they will be using and to interrogate the biases within each tool, system, or service that they will be bringing into their teaching and remote learning scenarios.

What data do these digital tools, systems, and services render?

The point of this question is for instructors to understand the very data that are being collected on their students so that they can make informed decisions about when and how to use the tools, systems, and services in their teaching and remote learning scenarios. It should be noted that although technology companies will make evident some of the data that are being collected by their system, there are other data being collected that companies do not make publicly known, therefore instructors should exercise caution and not operate off of the assumption that the data they can publicly see are the only data being collected.

What hidden limitations might there be to the data rendered via these digital tools, systems, and services?

This question allows instructors to challenge the norms and biases of the tools, systems, and services that they are using within their instruction and teaching. By examining the tool, system, or service, and incorporating the knowledge gleaned in the aforementioned question of the type of data collected, instructors can make educated analyses or suppositions on what other data the tool, system, or service might be collecting both historically and in the future. This can help shape their potential design of instructional units when using the digital tool, system, or service.

What are the epistemological implications of this ontological analysis?

This question primarily is concerned with how the system operates as outlined in the previous three questions and what operational aspects—from companies' data collection processes to user interfaces—could potentially impact the way that a student might engage with the pedagogical content designed by the instructor. Epistemology is concerned with how people come to know what they know; essentially, epistemology is the study of knowledge development. This question on epistemological implications forces instructors to contend with the fact that student learning that occurs, or does not occur, is in fact shaped by the tool, system, or service being used for instruction. Any epistemological claims and learning objectives must therefore then be grounded back into understanding the tool, system, or service used for instructional purposes.

What are the axiological implications of this ontological analysis?

This question asks instructors to challenge their value judgments and the ethics of using the selected tool, system, or service within their teaching and instructional units based on the information gleaned from the four previous questions. In this case, with axiology, the primary concern is with ethics. How ethical is it to use tools, systems, and services if discovered that specific user data is being monetized and could potentially be used to track and trace a student later in life? In what ways should this discovery influence how an instructor chooses to use a digital tool, system, and service?

Empirical Demonstration of Ontological Imperative in Pedagogical Scenarios and Educational Opportunities That Include Online Spaces

This next section provides a walk-through applying the ontological imperative to a digital technology that could potentially be used by instructors to deliver remote instruction and to foster collaboration among and between students. Given the unique situations that have emerged during the COVID-19 pandemic, instructors have scoured the Internet for various tools, systems, and services that can be used to deliver remote instruction to their students. Because of circumstances that some students face with connectivity, hardware, and software constraints, many instructors look for multi-use tools, systems, and services that are free to use and offer multiple facets for instructional opportunities, and that can be easily used in low-bandwidth situations. For the purpose of this ontological imperative analysis, I am going to focus on the digital messaging service Discord, which meets the aforementioned criteria. I will walk through each question of the ontological imperative framework, engaging in a critical analysis of the Discord platform in order to better understand the ontological, epistemological, and axiological implications for using Discord pedagogically during remote teaching and learning scenarios.

Question 1: What digital tools, systems, and services are at play in my teaching? Who created them and why?

Discord is digital software with over 250 million users, as of this writing, that provides users with a messaging service, content distribution platform, and community creation capabilities. Discord is mainly used by gamers, predominantly those in the Esports market of gaming. Developed in 2015 as an offshoot of an existing game communication platform known as Hammer & Chisel developed by gamer Jason Citron, Discord provides gamers a backchannel platform to use during game play. Users create their own servers (similar to a private room) and engage in voice over Internet protocol (VoIP) for communications, which includes chat, video, and voice calls, as well as sharing of multimodal resources, memes, and music.

Discord allows for multiplatform interoperability and is available on Windows, macOS, Andriod, iOS, Linux, as well as available in web browsers. This provides individuals using various operating systems and platforms the ability to engage in using the Discord platform. Of interesting note, during the beginning of the COVID-19 pandemic, in March 2020, Discord changed this company motto from "Chat for Gamers" to "Chat for Communities and Friends." Later, in June 2020, the company moved marketing even more into the mainstream to capitalize on the concept and idea that groups and individuals were looking for platforms for managing communities, and they changed their motto to "Your Place to Talk and Hang Out" and revised their marketing materials to show these changes. These shifts and changes to Discord's slogans and marketing materials, therefore opens up the idea that Discord is a platform that has a wide range of uses and capabilities for multiple end users, even educational communities, and is not just for the gaming community.

Question 2: What data do these digital tools, systems, and services render?

Understanding the forms of data collected by any digital tool, system, and service requires both front-end surfacing and backend metadata mining (Gerber & Lynch, 2017). Front-end surfacing requires an examination of the user interface to understand what aspects of data appear to be collected. Backend metadata mining includes an examination of the developer documentation to understand what metadata are actually being collected via the application programming interface (API) and/or software development kits (SDKs).

In conducting initial front-end surfacing, the opening landing page user interface of Discord shows a system that allows for a user to join multiple channels, rooms, and communities. See Figure 2.1 for an example of the user interface of the landing page. By doing a deeper dive and going into a community (versus the open landing page), the user interface shows the various rooms that have been set up for engaging in different aspects deemed important to the community, as well as rooms for private chat and public chat, including who is online from that community, where the community bots are operating—such as selecting background music channels or answering surface questions from community members—and other facets deemed important by that community, such as livestreaming content and material, or providing instructions for accessing private rooms for future group chats. See Figure 2.2 for an example of the user interface of a community. From this front-end surfacing analysis, it appears that data that could be collected would be various chats amongst user—both public and private—user identification names, and community information, such as individuals who make up a community user base, and potentially collecting information on links between users.

The next level of analysis requires delving into the backend of the system, which requires going into the developer documentation. Almost every digital tool, system, or service has what is known as developer documentation. Developer documentation, sometimes known as developer portal, is where software engineers and third-party developers go to find the specific details needed to create a new digital application or software that will interface with the current software (e.g., another app or software to interface with Discord).

Education in Times of Crises 33

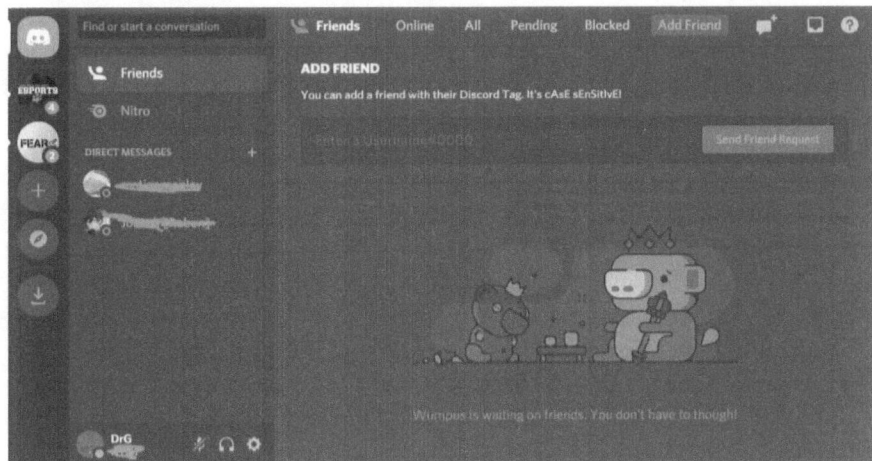

Note: This figure provides a screenshot of the user interface of the Discord desktop app. To the left you can see the various communities that the user is part of, as well as various icons for joining new communities, downloading and uploading material, and engaging in direct messaging services with individuals in the user's friends list. Within each community, there are rooms, channels, and chats for both public and private communication.

Figure 2.1. User Interface of Discord Desktop App. *Screenshot by Hannah Gerber.*

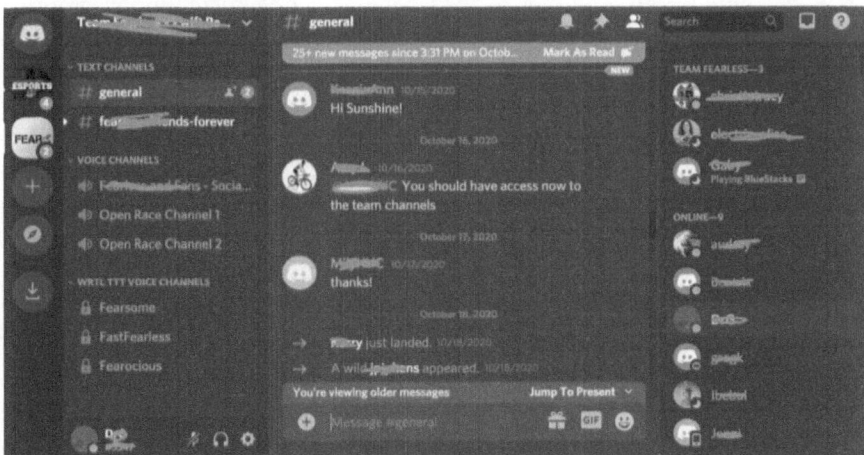

Note: This figure provides an example of a screenshot of the user interface of a community server. In the screenshot you can see which community members are online, the various rooms in which you can engage in voice chat, text chat, as well as engage in private communications.

Figure 2.2. User Interface of a Community Channel/Server. *Screenshot by Hannah Gerber.*

An example of this can be seen in Facebook. Facebook is a social media service that allows other developers to interface with the Facebook system via the API. In the most simplistic terms, this requires that Facebook makes data available to developers so that their product will link and interface seamlessly with Facebook, such as adding third-party apps, like Farmville, to interface with a user's Facebook profile. This new app often requests access to data such as the user's friends list, or other data needed to allow the app to operate within Facebook's interface. A simple understanding of language within programming and using API keys can allow an individual to understand the developer portal/documentation. A Google search, or search within a digital system, for "developer documentation" or "API documentation" will often take the individual straight to the developer documents. A basic understanding of the language used in software app development will help one grasp the way that data are flowing among and between applications and software. For example, "Get," "Pull," and "Grab" are terms used for calling or pulling data from the backend of the system to be used by the third-party application whereas "Post" or "Send" indicate data that the third-party app developer wants sent to the main software.

In order to understand the various types of metadata being collected on Discord, beyond what can be seen at the surface from the front-end surfacing activity, I visited Discord's "Developer Portal." Although one does not need to be a computer programmer to visit developer documentation, a working knowledge of the tool, system, or surface is valuable before delving into the documentation. By working knowledge, I mean a familiarity in how to use the tool, system, and service. This working knowledge will aid in understanding the developer documentation and the types of data being collected. For example, upon accessing the Discord developer documentation, I discovered data that were being collected dealing specifically with user activities, networks, and relationships. All of these data can, at any time, be shared with a third-party app developer. In fact, at the time of this writing, I noticed over 75 discrete metadata points that could be used in the development of third-party applications for interfacing with Discord. See Figure 2.3 for an example of some of these specific metadata. Note, just because the developer documentation makes evident that over 75 metadata points are being collected, it does not mean that these are the *only* metadata points being collected by Discord. Because user data is a revenue stream for almost any application, companies will often shift and change what data that they make available to third-party developers, and they do not always make all of their data available at once nor do they let the public know all of the data points that they are collecting on the user. However, it is worth noting that looking at the data that are made available via the developer documentation, one can get a comprehensive idea of

Activity Struct		
NAME	TYPE	DESCRIPTION
ApplicationId	Int64	your application id - this is a read-only field
Name	string	name of the application - this is a read-only field
State	string	the player's current party status
Details	string	what the player is currently doing
Timestamps	ActivityTimestamps	helps create elapsed/remaining timestamps on a player's profile
Assets	ActivityAssets	assets to display on the player's profile
Party	ActivityParty	information about the player's party
Secrets	ActivitySecrets	secret passwords for joining and spectating the player's game
Instance	bool	whether this activity is an instanced context, like a match

Note: This figure showcases a screen capture that lists select metadata points being collected by the Discord API that can be used by third-party developers. The screen capture shows the name of the metadata, the way that the metadata will be returned in a file (e.g. JSON), as well as an abbreviated description of the metadata. The description is often the most useful category to examine in analyzing the metadata being collected on users.

Figure 2.3. Example of Available User Data for Third-party Development via Discord API. *Screenshot by Hannah Gerber.*

how much, and what aspects of a user profile and/or communications, activities, and relationships are being captured and traced. This type of backend system analysis is important for an instructor to conduct prior to using digital tools, systems, and services because it provides insights into the potential ways that a company might later monetize user information or exploit a user. Instructors should take the insights gleaned from both front-end surfacing and backend analysis into consideration as they engage in selecting digital tools, systems, and services for pedagogical purposes.

Question 3: What hidden limitations might there be to the data rendered via these digital tools, systems, and services?

Even though a thorough analysis via front-end surfacing and backend mining was conducted, this analysis only provided a partial understanding of Discord. As mentioned prior, companies do not make all data available, nor do they show developers and/or users all data that are being collected on users. This is important to consider when making decisions on technology to use within remote teaching scenarios because over time companies change how their product operates, both via the user interface and via the data collected. Because digital spaces and the data produced by digital spaces are often transitory and temporal, it is important to have a historical understanding of the tool, system, or service that an instructor plans to use for teaching. This historical understanding is important because it allows an instructor to acknowledge shifts and changes in the tool, system, or service and how those changes might impact and limit how a specific technology is used from how it was used in the past.

In the case of Discord, the platform has been in existence under the name Discord for approximately five years, so any historical analysis will be limited. To conduct a historical analysis of a tool, system, or service in order to better understand the changes that a digital product has undergone, one needs to use an archival service to conduct an analysis. My go-to choice when I am historically examining a digital tool, system, or service is to use the Internet Wayback Machine. The Internet Wayback Machine is a web crawling platform created in 2001 that has archived almost 500 billion webpages as of this writing. By using the Internet Wayback Machine, an individual can examine webpages as they existed historically, at a given moment in time, whether or not the webpage still exists in contemporary time.

In order to do a single snapshot of one of the original archives and caches of Discord, I launched the Internet Wayback Machine and input the original URL used by Discord. Although the current URL for Discord is www.discord.com, the company launched their product in 2015 under the URL www.discordapp.com. Therefore, in order to historically examine Discord, I needed to use the URL from 2015. Using the Wayback Machine, I was able to access archived Discord pages dating back to March 6, 2015 (see Figure 2.4). Using a random sampling, I reviewed select archived pages from the first two years of Discord's existence. In a deep dive of the archived pages, Discord's advertisements as to their superiority over their competitors—TeamSpeak, Skype, and Ventrillo—were on full display. I was able to delve into some of the developer documentation as well in order to see what features and aspects were supported by earlier versions of Discord, including different entry points in API data and browser support. These two key points are important to note in both epistemological and axiological considerations, which will be discussed in the following sections.

Question 4: What are the epistemological implications of this ontological analysis?

Doing a thorough investigation into the tool, system, or service via the initial three questions of ontological imperative framework, allows an instructor an analysis of the epistemological functions of the selected technology. This may provide a better understanding of what forms of knowledge might emerge

Education in Times of Crises　　　37

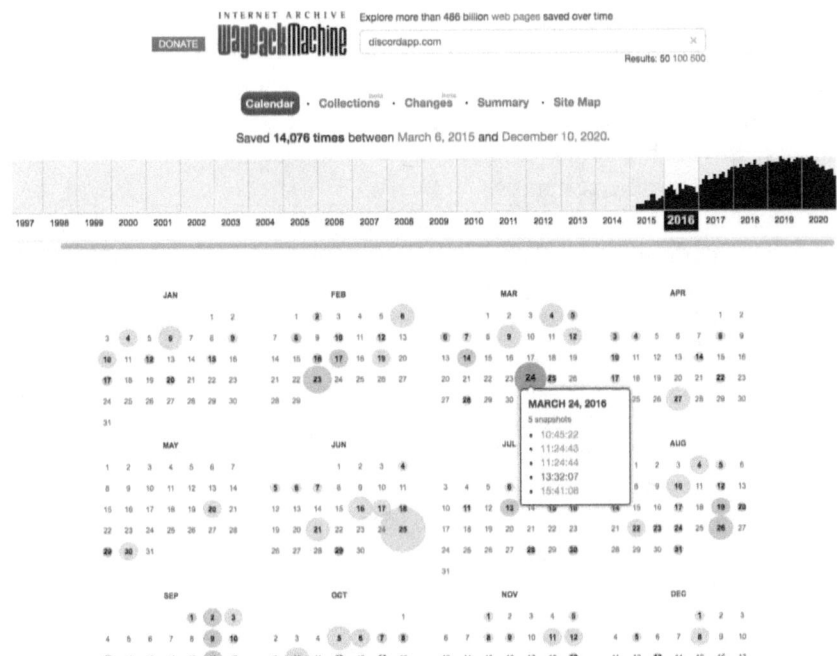

Note: This figure shows a screenshot of the Internet Wayback Machine archive for Discord from 2016. The graph at the top shows how often the web crawler archived pages from Discord. The colored circles by size represent how often on a given day, and/or in a given period, the web crawler archived the pages located on the Discord website. For example, the screen shot shows that on March 24th, 2016, the Internet Wayback Machine web crawler created 5 snapshots, or 5 archival pages, of the Discord website. Time stamps for each capture are shown so that an individual can select what archive to visit.

Figure 2.4.　　Screenshot of Internet Wayback Machine. *Screenshot by Hannah Gerber.*

when students use the technology, and it shapes a better understanding of how the instructor might use the technology pedagogically.

In the case of my analysis of Discord, when examined through the first three questions of the ontological imperative framework, I developed a better understanding for how and why I might use Discord in remote teaching and learning scenarios. Understanding how the original company started—as a competitor to other communication platforms used by gamers—and its subsequent shift into different markets and demographics, provided me the perspective that the company is in continual flux to meet expanding user bases and appears to be open and responsive to community needs. In remote learning scenarios, when students all have differing connectivity, platform, and user needs, it is important that a tool, system, or service meet as wide a range of needs as possible. In my analysis, it was evident that Discord was multiplatform (available on most operating systems from Linux to iOS), accessible via web browser, or downloadable via an app. It was apparent that parts and portions of Discord could be accessed in scenarios that could involve low-tech and low-connectivity issues, making it ideal for bringing it into remote learning scenarios.

A further analysis into what data are being collected by Discord—as determined by my front-end surfacing of the user interface and my backend mining analysis by digging into the Developer Portal—provided me with knowledge that the platform could be used for allowing a deeper community to be built via the sharing of resources, including images, files, and chat, both text and voice. Additionally, I determined from the data structure analysis that community could be built via allowing individual channels to be developed by students, autonomously, therefore allowing students the freedom to lead their own study groups and communities within the class server. Furthermore, in digging into the data structures, it is apparent that networks and relationships can be formed between members of a Discord server, as well as with members outside of the server, allowing information to flow between networks and servers. What this means for pedagogical purposes is that an instructor could create a server for a class and start multiple channels related to course topics with that server, students could start their own subchannels within the server, and students and instructors could connect with others outside of that server in order to share information and/or engage with different unrelated communities. In some ways, this could deepen a student's experience, but in other ways, it could distract and detract from the student's experience. The biggest reminder and takeaway from the ending of the analysis into the epistemological considerations is that Discord was created for entertainment and community, not for educational and pedagogical purposes; however, that does not mean that it cannot serve the purposes of being used pedagogically for remote learning scenarios. The aforementioned aspects from the analysis are all considerations an instructor must make when thinking about the epistemological considerations of using a digital tool, system, or service in remote learning scenarios.

Question 5: What are the axiological implications of this ontological analysis?

As previously discussed, axiology is the branch of philosophy dealing with values and value systems; however, for the purposes of the ontological imperative analysis, in this case, axiology deals primarily with ethics. Understanding the ethical implications of using a particular tool, system, or service for pedagogical purposes during remote learning scenarios is integral to ensuring education that is equitable and inclusive. As mentioned earlier in the chapter, many of the digital tools, systems, and services used in education were created by for-profit companies that have their own specific agendas to meet. This is neither good nor bad; however, it is important to examine when determining what technology to bring into remote learning scenarios (or any classroom or learning scenario).

By understanding why Discord was created and for whom, by examining the data structures via front-end surfacing and backend mining, and by engaging in a historical analysis, I was able to make careful considerations that I would have to use to ensure my students were aware that specific information that they share on Discord could potentially be accessed by a third-party app developer or software engineer. I determined that these data could include personal site usage information, user network information, and potential conversations within the server between members. Furthermore, based on my analysis, I would need to make an acknowledgment to my students that data structures, system missions and purposes, and site regulations change over time and that what they think might be private, could, through changes in Terms of Service and company structure, become public. A prime example of this was raised by Gerber et al. (2017), when they discussed changes made to a popular fanfiction site, Figment.com. At the outset, Figment.com was an independent fanfiction site where users were able to engage in the processes of fanfiction writing, critique, review, and sharing. However, the site was acquired by Random House who then publicly indexed all reviews. This meant what was once private information on the site was now available publicly. This shift from public to private can happen with almost any digital tool, system, and service not protected under FERPA, therefore, it is imperative to consider what harm could be done if student information—such as posts or videos—were later made public. Axiological considerations are core to the ontological imperative when considering digital tools, systems, and services for use in remote learning situations and scenarios.

CONCLUSION

I began this chapter considering what defines and constitutes teaching, learning, meaning making, and literacy in a digital era (e.g., the digital turn) and I challenged the contemporary view of literacy, and took a somewhat negative stance by examining what some scholars posit as an era of post-literacy. However, we are not post-literate. And if digital media trends continue to show us the way that individuals communicate and congregate in and among online spaces, we will develop a new understanding of *a meta-literate society*, one wherein media and technology dance hand in hand with words and books, which, in turn, dance hand in hand with emojis and hashtags. Together they inform, and are informed by, each other and enhance their power. Despite the negativity that many people think exists on the social web, the fake news, politically biased Twitter bots, the trolling, the flaming, the bullying, the social web, Facebook groups, Pinterest, and Instagram-driven professional learning communities, the Internet remains an overwhelmingly productive place where, in fact, remote learning scenarios hold much promise for reaching today's learners.

For example, we can look to hashtags and emojis to understand these phenomena. In 2018, #love was the most used hashtag on Instagram while the LOL emoji is the most used emoji on the Internet and has been a top emoji on Twitter for years (Abidin & Gn, 2018). In overly simplistic terms, although the Internet might be rife with fake news, negativity, brinkmanship, bullying, and passive-aggressive posturing, research suggests that overwhelmingly the most popular emotions displayed on social media are those of love and laughter. Let us not forget this; instead, we should strive to overcome the negativity that seems to exist today. Let us work together to create technology-rich educational environments for all users, for all learners, and for all people. Let us do this together for the next generation of people who will soon be online. Let us work together to cocreate a technology-rich environment where learners bring together beautiful words and mix them with media so that they can engage in a *slow dance*, a waltz, with media, technology, and learning. However, let us not move too quickly. For moving quickly and breaking things, the popular tech industry theme also breaks people. By engaging in the ontological imperative analysis of the various digital tools, systems, and services that are to be used in remote learning scenarios, and taking a slow dance to understand the technology we use, we can create learning that is equitable and inclusive for all, a system that does not break people, but rather builds them up.

REFERENCES

Abidin, C., & Gn, J. (2018). Between art and application: Special issue on emoji epistemology. *First Monday, 23*(9), np.

Bhabha, H. K. (1994). *The location of culture.* New York: Routledge.

Bradbury, R. (1953). *Fahrenheit 451.* New York: Ballentine Books.

DeCesari, D. M., & Rowsell, J. (2020). Teaching beyond a print mindset: Applying multimodal pedagogies within literacy teacher education. In T. L. Gallagher & K. Ciampa (Eds.), *Teaching Literacy in the Twenty-first Century Classroom* (pp. 103–18). Springer Publications.

Gerber, H. R. (in press). Web-based qualitative research. In R. Tierney, F. Rizvi, K. Erican, & G. Smith (Eds.), *The International Encyclopedia of Education, 4th Edition*. London, UK: Elsevier.

Gerber, H. R., Abrams, S. S., Curwood, J. C., & Magnifico, A. M. (2017). *Conducting qualitative research of learning in online spaces*. Thousand Oaks, CA: SAGE Publishers.

Gerber, H., & Lynch, T.L. (2017) Into the meta: Research methods for moving beyond social media surfacing. *TechTrends*, 61(3), pp. 263–272.

Gerber, H. R., & Lynch, T. L. (in press). Mixed methods integration and the ontological imperative in understanding social media analytics. In A. J. Onwuegbuzie & J. Hitchcock (Eds.), *Routledge Handbook for Advancing Integration in Mixed Methods Research*. New York: Routledge.

Gerber, H. R., Lynch, T. L., & Onwuegbuzie, A. J. (forthcoming). *Making big data small: Integrated digital approaches for social science researchers*. Thousand Oaks, CA: SAGE Publishers.

Kress, G. (2003). *Literacy in the new media age*. New York: Routledge.

Leander, K., & Bolt, G. (2013). Rereading a "pedagogy of multiliteracies": Bodies, text, and emergence. *Journal of Literacy Research, 45*(1), 22–46.

Lynch, T. L. (2015). *The hidden role of software in educational research: From policy to practice*. New York: Routledge.

Lynch, T. L., & Gerber, H. R. (in press). Social media analytics as mixed methods analysis. In A. J. Onwuegbuzie & B. Johnson (Eds.), *The Routledge Reviewer's Guide to Mixed Methods Analysis*. New York: Routledge.

Lynch, T. L., & Gerber, H. R. (2018). The ontological imperative when researching the digital age. *International Journal of Multiple Research Approaches, 10*, 112–23.

McLuhan, M. (1962). *The gutenberg galaxy*. Toronto, ON: The University of Toronto Press.

Powe, B. W. (1987). *The solitary outlaw*. Toronto, ON: Lester & Orpen Denny Publishers.

Soja, E. (1989). *Postmodern geographies: The reassertion of space in critical social theory*. London, UK: Verso Press.

Street, B. (1984). *Literacy in theory and practice*. Cambridge, UK: Cambridge University Press.

Williamson, B. (2016). *Big data in education: The future of learning, policy, and practice*. Thousand Oaks, CA: Sage Publications.

Chapter Three

From Meteorological Uncertainty to Missing Muffins

How University Emergency Managers Manage Uncertainty as a Hurricane Response Strategy

Ian R. Weaver

This chapter reports the results of a qualitative study of university emergency managers (EMs) and their responses to crises and disasters. It reports the participants' experiences of a hurricane response from interview data, and it considers how emergency managers might manage uncertainties as opportunities for improving crisis communication. To preserve anonymity, I present the study in narrative form, telling the story of a fictional hurricane named Kyle, which combines the events of three separate hurricanes the participants experienced.

INTRODUCTION

A disaster can bring education to a halt. A hurricane can pause a semester for weeks, suspending any educational activity until infrastructure is repaired. A pandemic like COVID-19 can press into everyday teaching activities (I teach in my living room now to the acoustics of my two toddlers and one baby), causing disaster conditions to linger over long periods of time. Whether education is interrupted and resumed abruptly or interrupted for a year-and-counting, disasters are disruptive and how universities respond to these disruptions impacts thousands of individuals.

Disasters and crises are characterized by the uncertainty that follows disruption (Ulmer, Sellnow, & Seeger, 2017). For universities, emergency managers are key individuals who help campus prepare for and recover from disasters. "Emergency Manager" is usually a specific job title that one or two people hold on campus, but the concept of senior administrative leadership managing an emergency caused by crisis or disaster can describe a large group of people. For this study, I use the term Emergency Managers (EMs) to refer to those administrators and staff who respond to hurricanes. Emergency managers serve as a "critical link" during a crisis, mediating between the threat and the community (Morrow & Lazo, 2014, p. 1) and are the pivot point for risk assessment and communication for universities during disasters. By acquiring, interpreting, and verifying information, they make time-sensitive decisions to help protect and inform the campus community (Baumgart, Bass, Phillips, & Kloesel, 2008). Not only do they protect and inform, but their interpretations of risk and its many probabilities impact the educational experience of the entire campus community.

A Rhetorical Framework for Uncertainty

Scholarship in atmospheric science and risk communication affirms the benefit of learning how individuals interpret uncertainty in weather-related disasters (e.g., Morss, Lazo, & Demuth, 2010), and how people interpret forecast uncertainty influences their decisions (e.g., Demuth, Morss, Morrow, & Lazo, 2012). Many researchers have studied EMs' critical role, looking at how they make use of and interpret forecasts (e.g., Wernstedt, Roberts, Arvai, & Redmond, 2019); others have observed how EMs make decisions (e.g., Baumgart et al., 2008). Some scholars have looked specifically at university EMs, considering how the diversity of such communities influences response (e.g., Simms, Kusenbach, & Tobin, 2013), including how specific populations respond to different types of communication (e.g., Abukhalaf & von Meding, 2020; Rainear & Lin, 2021). Only a few studies have considered administrators' roles as EMs on a university campus during a disaster (e.g., Moerschell & Novak, 2020). There is a dearth of research that focuses specifically on how managing uncertainty can be a particular response strategy for EMs on a university campus.

Managing uncertainty as a response strategy is important to this study because how EMs interpret technical and social uncertainties impacts university students, faculty, and staff in a crisis. Rather than uncertainty being a concern of knowledge only—or a lack of knowledge—technical communication scholars also consider uncertainty to be a site for deliberation and dialectic over the best course of action. Particularly helpful is framing uncertainty as an opportunity for stakeholders to work out what is most possible and most valuable and as a group decides on a course of action (e.g., Grabill & Simmons, 1998). Walsh and Walker (2016) proposed categorizing different types of uncertainty—technical uncertainty, personal uncertainty, and public uncertainty—to show how arguments shift between groups of stakeholders.

Differentiating between these types of uncertainty is a fairly new approach to assessing emergency management (e.g., Lambrecht, Hatchett, Walsh, Collins, & Tolby, 2019). The differences are important because uncertainties invite the need to consider how knowledge is made, who makes the knowledge, and who receives what type of information. These spheres, developed by Goodnight (1982) and adapted to uncertainty and risk by Walsh and Walker (2016), help identify the types of arguments or deliberation present in risk communication. When dealing with technical uncertainties, arguments that favor explaining statistical probability are persuasive. When dealing with personal uncertainty, arguments that cite personal safety and commitment (and others) can be persuasive, and arguments that deal with public uncertainty can be persuasive when citing concerns of justice or reputation. These three types or spheres are not necessarily excluded from one another. Instead, Walsh and Walker (2016) posit these spheres overlap in what they call "hybrid forums." Rather than seeing uncertainty simply as a lack of knowledge, hybrid forums can encourage framing uncertainty as "creative rhetorical topoi (strategic stances or launching points) for inventing new discourses and new communities around shared risks" (p. 72). Thus, this model can offer emergency managers an analytical framework for considering how they build resilient and informed campus communities.

Purpose of the Study

The purpose of this study is to give insight into one university's response to hurricane events. This chapter seeks to explicate the processes, dependencies, and compromises EMs make due to the uncertainty of hurricane events. Understanding how administrators manage uncertainty and respond to events might help educators understand administrative decision making and may also shed light on where decision-making processes of university EMs might become more collaborative, even participatory, among all campus community stakeholders (e.g., students, parents, faculty, staff, etc.). In addition, the basic strategies university administrators use to respond to hurricane events can give insight to educators on developing their own response, helping educators be more purposeful and informed. In doing so, this chapter aims to foster understanding and appreciation between those who manage hurricane response on university campuses and those who do not. This chapter reports the participants' experiences from three hurricanes from four interviews and one focus group.

Participants

The participants in this study included three females and four males who were members of a university administration that directs emergency preparation and response during disasters and crises. At this specific university, emergency management was separated into three leadership teams defined in Figure 3.1.

Emergency Teams	Responsibility
Decision Team	Made major decisions, e.g., whether and when to close and reopen the university
Management Team	Served as liaison between the Decision and Operations Teams; monitored hurricane threats and filtered technical knowledge from the National Hurricane Center to the Decision Team; coordinated preparation, response, and recover activities; implemented emergency plan protocols
Operations Team	Enacted decisions made by the Decision Team; led individual university departments' (e.g., facilities, police department, housing, etc.) preparation, response, and recovery activities

Figure 3.1. Emergency Management Leadership Teams. *Created by Ian R. Weaver.*

The three teams interacted with one another in that the Management Team assessed all technical uncertainties and advised the Decision Team accordingly. I interviewed individuals from all three teams: decision, management, and operations.

METHODS

Research Questions

This study sought to understand how emergency managers responded to specific hurricane events. The following research questions guided the study:

- What uncertainties do university emergency managers experience while managing hurricane response?
    - Who articulates these uncertainties?
- What type of information do university emergency managers navigate (i.e., weather) to address uncertainty?
- What decisions do university emergency managers have to make and how does uncertainty play a role in these decisions?

Methodological Framework

My approach was based in case study methodology (Yin, 2014), which seeks to understand a specific situation in context. Such an approach values analyzing "social action from the actor's standpoint—a concept often referred to by using the German word *verstehen* ('to understand')" (Tracy, 2013, p. 41). The large sums of often inaccurate and complex information emergency managers juggle during a crisis makes decision making and communication difficult (e.g., Ulmer et al., 2017). Verstehen, then, helped me seek "empathetic understanding" and gain insight into the complexity of crisis decision making.

In addition, because this collection seeks to find ways educators can prepare and respond to disasters, I sought to gain a holistic perspective of what contributes to hurricane response on a university campus. This hermeneutic approach helped me examine the interview and document data by "imagining the experience, motivations, and context" of the participants and iteratively analyzing the texts (Tracy, 2013, p. 42). This followed the advice for qualitative researchers to respond to the needs of the research, following the data and adjusting the study as it emerges in context (e.g., Miles, Huberman, & Saldaña, 2014). As a case study, then, my research evolved, including more variables than I could account for, while at the same time providing opportunity for me to listen and adjust my research.

Data Collection—Interviews

I conducted four semistructured interviews and one focus group with administrators who manage crises on one university campus. Using Zoom video, I interviewed a total of seven administrators, four individually and three as a small focus group. The interviews ranged from 45 to 90 minutes. I chose to interview three participants in a focus group because they shared similar roles and tasks during hurricane events. My sampling choices followed snowball and critical incident sampling rationales (Tracy, 2013). Critical sampling made the chosen university a purposeful choice because of the number of hurricanes it has experienced in the last twenty years. Snowball sampling helped me find participants in each of the three administrative teams: decision, management, and action.

Interview questions were developed based on emergency management and communicating uncertainty literature (e.g., Morss et al., 2010) as well as Spinuzzi's (2013) advice for studying institutions in context. The interviews began with warm-up questions inquiring about the participants' histories with hurricanes and as university emergency managers. I then asked participants to give a sort of "tour" (Tracy 2013, p. 147) of what it is like to manage a university through a hurricane, which gave a sense of timeline and themes that participants valued or felt were important. Specifically, the tour question asked, "Can you give me the big picture? What is the life cycle of the whole process like during a hurricane?"

Follow-up questions included asking compare and contrast, typology, elicitation, in vivo language, and member reflection questions (Tracy, 2013), which inquired about their experiences from specific hurricanes, using weather forecasts, interpreting uncertainty, making decisions, and communicating. The interviews ended with catchall and identity-enhancing questions that invited participants to offer their advice for emergency managers.

Data Analysis

Using the Zoom transcription of the interviews, I edited the transcripts for errors and reformatted them to indicate conversation. Following Miles et al. (2014), I wrote postinterview memos and annotated interview notes. After each interview, I recorded initial impressions and details. Before I compiled the data, I revisited these notes and added to them. To analyze the interview transcripts, I used MAXQDA qualitative analysis software, using two rounds of coding and then some after coding during the writing phase (Tracy, 2013). The first round included descriptive, holistic, initial, simultaneous, and versus coding (Saldaña, 2013). Holistic and initial coding follow a more grounded theory approach that allowed me to label chunks of data while remaining open to multiple interpretations. Holistic coding was also directed by my research questions. I used versus coding to help me explain the moments when participants talked about the dichotomies of disaster: expected vs. unexpected, normalcy vs. disruption, prepared vs. unprepared, vulnerable vs. secure.

The second round of coding was iterative in revisiting data and creating data displays. I used focused, axial, and theoretical (also known as selective or conceptual) coding. Focused coding and theoretical coding helped me identify larger categories and themes with the codes, which led to specific data displays such as Figure 3.2 (Saldaña, 2013). Data displays (Miles et al., 2014) were then used to compare coding schemes with theoretical constructs about uncertainty from professional and technical communication studies (Walsh & Walker, 2016; Lambrecht et al., 2019). Coding and creating data displays were documented in memos that were then compared to create categories for discussing results and findings.

RESULTS

In this section I introduce categories and themes found in the data and give examples to illustrate. The coding process explained above resulted in the following list of codes, categories, and themes (Figure 3.2).

First Round Codes	Second Round Codes			Categories		Themes
People	Students		Administrative Response Teams	Decision Team		
	Admin			Management Team		
	Faculty/Staff			Operations Team		
	Contractors					
Stability/Disruption	Technology					
Look/see				Assess	Before/After	
Infrastructure						
protocol						
Decision	Discussion			Deliberate	Before/After	Disruption and Stability
	Questions					
Uncertainty	Spheres	Technical	Managing Uncertainty	Decide	Before/After	
		Personal				
		Public				Spheres and Parallels
Interpret	Sources					
	Characterizing storm			Communicate	Before/After	
Before						
During						
After						

Figure 3.2. Codes, Categories, and Themes. *Created by Ian R. Weaver.*

The Emergency Managers

The emergency managers interviewed were members of three separate emergency teams. This section provides a short characterization of each team and manager as the specific role managers played in hurricane response contributed to the unique perspective the results report below. The following pseudonyms (e.g., "EM1," "EM2," etc.) are listed in order of appearance in the story below.

- EM1: In charge of assessing meteorological uncertainty and defining level of threat; detailed worker who excels at analysis and thrives on piecing together complex strings of data.
- EM2: Supervises the management team, a master puzzler with vision of how the little pieces fit together to form a big picture, including managing institutional safety and reputation.

- EM3: In charge of specific management team tasks and a master planner who can understand the best strategies for how various university entities can and should coordinate during a hurricane.
- EM4: Works with the housing group on the operations team and as such takes a student-advocacy approach to their work.
- EM5: A decision maker through-and-through, not afraid to ask questions or express opinion to ensure movement takes place yet does not agree with top-down management practices like Incident Command structure.
- EM6: Works on the decision team but is primarily a communication strategist, seeing both the big picture and understanding the rhetorical needs of an individual university.
- EM7: A member of law enforcement, bringing a perspective of the unique needs of security during hurricane events as well as offering an empathetic perspective on the experiences of students, faculty, and staff during hurricane events.

Figure 3.3 lists what teams the emergency managers were a part of, providing a summary of the types of comments and details each shared.

Emergency Teams	Emergency Managers	Interview Themes
Decision Team	EM5 and EM6	The difficulty of making decisions, exacerbated by concerns of personal safety and academic and management uncertainties; the people and personalities and how these influenced major decisions; managing institutional reputation.
Management Team	EM1, EM2, and EM3	The technical uncertainties: tools and strategies for collecting, assessing, and discussing uncertainty information; the planning aspects of preparing for and responding to hurricanes, the management techniques and team-driven perspective such as FEMA's Incident Command structures.
Operations Team	EM4 and EM7	The specific challenges of assessing damage after storms, dealing with the public; the protocols of preparation work and how simple decisions were as a result; the required people and labor needed to prepare for and recover from the hurricane.

Figure 3.3. Emergency Management Teams and Interview Themes. *Created by Ian R. Weaver.*

Hurricane Kyle

Three Weeks Before Impact—The Ingredients Mix

Hurricane Kyle begins as a tropical wave off the coast of Africa. This low-pressure strip of air drifting westward appears insignificant, and this pre-Kyle storm is merely one of many tropical waves that will dutifully march west across the Atlantic this fall. Though seemingly innocuous at this point, pre-Kyle's latent destructive potential lies in its path, where the perfect ingredients for hurricanes mix in the froth of such thunderstorms. Emergency

Manager 1 (EM1) has already tagged pre-Kyle as a potential threat. "Pretty much from June 1st to November 30th, EM1 is giving me a daily update on any storm off the coast of Africa," EM2 explains. EM1, EM2, and EM3 manage emergency response on campus, coordinating preparations amongst a team of 25 to 30 university emergency managers. EM1 heads the university's hurricane assessment for the six-month-long season. If the National Hurricane Center has identified a tropical disturbance in the Atlantic, EM1 is monitoring it, sending EM2 and EM3 daily reports.

2.5 Weeks Before Impact—The Storm Forms

Over the next 72 hours, the National Hurricane Center labels pre-Kyle with a yellow and then red "X," marking it for possible hurricane formation. As pre-Kyle glides toward the Caribbean, the Atlantic's warm water and moist air get caught in the tropical wave's low-pressure vacuum. The earth's rotation clicks the storms into motion, and the temperate storms fracture, billowing into a massive, convective cyclone. Air rises, cools, and plunges over and over in a continuous pattern. Like a piston, this convective action converts warm water into fuel, and Kyle emerges, cycles through Tropical Storm conditions, and morphs into behemoth status: the official forecast labels Kyle a Major Hurricane.

10 Days Before Impact—Do We Close Campus? If So, When?

"The university's first call is whether or not we're going to evacuate campus," EM4 stated. This decision directs all hurricane response. As a member of the university housing team, EM4 helps coordinate the student exodus once the decision has been made to close campus. "If you think about what needs to happen . . ., we have to have students pack up all of their valuables, identify a place to go, which for most of our students is home, and then have time to get there without" experiencing any severe weather. Therefore, explained EM4, "I probably become more concerned about [hurricanes] earlier than anybody . . . at the university." To prepare for this upheaval of confused and concerned students and parents, the housing team needs two things: official word from the administration that campus is closing and assurance that the threat is real, and really worth evacuating. They need to know: Will the hurricane hit them? How big will it be? What damage can they expect?

Eight Days Before Impact—Kyle Is Coming

"Once it becomes a Category 1, we are going to have a closing point; we are going to have a stopping-classes point," EM1 dictated. Although Kyle's track has not pinpointed campus yet, the National Hurricane Center's (NHC) Cone of Uncertainty points directly at the coast. Though the widest tip of the cone expresses the greatest uncertainty, its visual contrast as the largest element in the graphic presents an ominous weight: Kyle is coming. "As soon as the university and our area gets put within the cone of uncertainty, parents start wondering if we know that the hurricane is actually out there," EM1 mutters, "kind of like we are oblivious to hurricanes and they just appear and we don't pay any attention to anything else that's going on."

Seven Days Before Impact — Should We Be Talking About This?

It takes a fair amount of assessment to decide whether and when to close a university. EM4 has been watching Kyle closely for a week now, but preparatory work for university housing and other units does not "get granular until EM1 starts sending us models of what could be heading our way." The university relies on EM1 to assess Kyle's probable threat, a task which suits him well. EM1 is a detailed worker, not afraid to jump into analysis. He thrives on piecing together the details of hurricane models, current weather data, and NHC forecasts. "We use . . . two different platforms" for assessment, he explained. One is the NHC forecast and the other is a "separate emergency management-specific . . . decision-maker forum called 'Hurrevac,'" which is a web-based program with limited access. With an internet browser, EM1 can use Hurrevac's primary map display to click through a number of overlays that show a broader range of uncertainty than what the public sees in NHC forecasts.

In tandem with Hurrevac, EM1 spent the past few days on phone calls and in webinars with the local National Weather Service (NWS). EM1's conversations with meteorologists are crucial for helping make sense of the probabilities, and the meteorologists are growing more confident that the storm will impact the local town. At home, EM4 is watching The Weather Channel animate the Cone of Uncertainty; it inches closer. EM4 texts their supervisor: "should we be talking about this?" The first decision team meeting is held that evening.

Six Days Before Impact — Too Much Uncertainty

"A lot of it depends on what kind of agreement the models have," EM1 said, explaining why official discussions had not started until last night. "The GFS and European [models] track our way," he clarified. The decision team's discussion last night was somewhat contentious. "We have an explanation we have to make when we are dealing with the decision makers about the uncertainty," EM1 continued. The administrators, "the Board of Governors, the support trustees, they're all seeing this," he pointed to the NHC's Cone of Uncertainty; "they aren't seeing the uncertainty on the other side."

The takeaway from the decision team's first discussion was that too much uncertainty remains to decide whether to close campus or not, a decision made after some disagreement. The unintended certainty expressed in the NHC's Cone of Uncertainty graphics led a couple of EMs to advocate for immediate action to begin evacuating campus. Being six days from the coast, however, Kyle's position is too far from landfall to make such a decision. This was a point of tension in the meeting. It all depends "on the subtropical ridge [and whether it is] weakening," EM1 elaborated: because if it does, Kyle will "turn slowly more this way." EM1 referred to the rotating parcels of invisible air at varying latitudes in the atmosphere, which acted as steering mechanisms for Hurricane Kyle. Using Hurrevac, "we are able to actually create the movement of the storm," he explained. "We use [this] to provide kind of a context for administrative staff," EM1 explained. The university "has got to plan for this range of possibility: if this [ridge] completely disintegrates, it's going to hit right on top of us at a category four or five, even though the public-facing" forecasts do not verify this.

Making such distinctions concerning uncertainty is central to decision making, contended EM1. EM2 and EM3 supported making this distinction because it was all about the planning: "If we think it's going to come in as a category four, our protocols are we don't have very many people, if any, on campus. Whereas if it comes in as a two, then we're more geared up, more [people are] available." EM2 and EM3 are the university's master puzzlers and coordinate the entire team of 20 to 25 emergency managers. As Kyle churns, a decision needs to be made, and EM1 felt the pressure: "Eighty-four hours out from the start of tropical storm force winds, there has to be a decision made: What is it going to be like? Will it be a category four or five when it hits?" he said to himself. EM3 clarified: "There are benchmarks, 24 hours out, 48 hours out, 72 hours out of things that are happening, processes that have to take place on campus."

Six Days Before Impact — Who Is In Charge?

Meteorological uncertainty was not the only element delaying the decision: "The big question to me was who's in charge?" EM5 said. There are about seven decision-team emergency managers, and EM5 is one of them. EM5 is not afraid to ask questions, seek clarification, and state her opinion. In retrospect, EM5 explained "here we had [a university president] who had not lived in a coastal community before, had never dealt with a major hurricane like this." Comparing the university's hurricane response to the US response to the COVID pandemic, EM5 said, "On the one hand, we didn't have a national plan" yet we had a university president who "likes to be Trump and to be in charge, but on the other hand, [they] didn't take a hold of it well." The university's emergency plan dictates who makes the final decision in a crisis, but for some reason this predecided protocol was unclear for the decision team. "It was confusing in the beginning about who is going to be in charge, and that put us behind a bit," explained EM5.

Five Days Before Impact — Students Are Held Hostage by Us

"When do we need to tell [students] to go home?" asked EM6, one of the decision team's communication EMs. "We want to make sure we provide them with an adequate window to exit," she clarified. Student safety was a recurring theme. EM1 added, "Most students can't leave unless we tell them it's okay and we shut down." If "students don't have enough time to get home, they're kind of held hostage by us. Because if they leave and we haven't closed, then they could possibly be penalized" because of grading and attendance policies. EM7, a member of the law enforcement team, explained that the university wants "students to have . . . I think it's six to eight hours of driving before Tropical Storm force winds arrive." As a coastal university, giving students this amount of time to travel means considering the possible weather hazards they could experience and even how "the tourist [and local population] traffic impact the capacity on [the interstate]; can we put our students into it?" EM7 explained.

Five Days From Impact — The Decision

The Cone of Uncertainty has enveloped the university in its five-day forecast. The university community has grown antsy, and parents are voicing concern. Tensions are high because the last 48 hours of discussion have been hijacked by constantly changing forecasts. "That was one of the reasons we met so constantly those first few days for updates, sometimes [twice a day], in the morning and late in the day," explained EM5. Displaying Hurrevac on the monitor, EM1 again takes the decision team through their latest discussions with the local NWS. On the screen he shows the NHC's forecast trend of Kyle over the last 48 hours. Each forecast published in this period (a total of eight) appears on the map as a separate-colored line in Hurrevac, which displays the forecasts erring to the east, meaning there is still a good amount of uncertainty in Kyle's current projection.

EM5 spoke up, "So are we any closer? Should we tell the students to pack up? What should we do? And how about the [students] who can't go anywhere, what do we do with them?" No one directly mentions it, but each person at the table knows their reputation is at stake if they decide to evacuate too early, but the safety of the university community takes precedence. Pointing out that there is only five days until impact, a veteran EM on the decision team argued, "It's always better to communicate early, better to get [students] off before we're in the middle of this." With this advice and the added pressure of being within the Cone of Uncertainty, the decision team makes the final decision, and the first email is sent announcing a voluntary evacuation to begin immediately, to be followed the next day by a mandatory evacuation.

Hurricane Kyle is now a major hurricane with no obstacles standing in its path.

Four Days Before Impact — How Do We Prepare Campus?

Like a trip wire, the voluntary evacuation announcement springs hurricane preparation protocols into action. Once the decision was made to evacuate/close the university, a cascade of predetermined decisions followed. The first goal was "to get everybody out of the buildings," explained EM4, then "to secure campus." University police help check buildings to ensure people leave, and university housing begins answering a flood of phone calls and emails from concerned parents. Meanwhile, the university president notifies the board of governors of the evacuation order as university workers begin prepping resources. The IT department starts backing up servers, and faculty and students lift their hands from their keyboards, mid-sentence, to enact their portion of response: "According to the university's evacuation policies," the email reads, "classes are officially canceled and grading and attendance policies are suspended." EM1 clarified, a voluntary evacuation "puts faculty in a position to make their own decisions about class."

At midday, university communications send the mandatory evacuation email, and though protocols guide most of the preparation decisions and tasks, some decisions are still unclear. "The next confusing thing to me," explained EM5, "was who's going to go where and why? And oh my . . ., such confusion over that. Like personally [do] my [spouse] and I leave town? We thought we probably should. And then trying to decide where to go . . . and where was [the university president] going?" EM5 clarified, "The leadership group has to stay together to some degree, now together on the phone is fine," but the group has to be able to discuss and make decisions. EM4 added, "I remember [my supervisor] and I talking. [They were] like, I think we should stay. And I was like, ma'am, this is a major hurricane; I'm not staying.... I don't think I want to be trapped here."

72 Hours Before Impact—Campus Entrances Are Barricaded

The campus is close to empty; all students and most faculty have left. While campus workers secure loose objects, the university police designate one open entrance to campus and barricade the others. The remainder of campus finishes preparations: staff park university cars in garages, researchers secure their data, and academic leadership backs up employment documents. Food services begins an inventory and makes a meal plan for after the storm.

48 Hours Before Impact—Emergency Operations Center Is Up and Running

University workers board windows, check waste and water capacity, and position extra fuel. Food services empties freezers and donates perishable food to local charities. Most equipment is powered down. EM1 and a handful of department supervisors transition to the Emergency Operation Center, a secure location on campus reinforced to withstand severe weather, including major hurricanes. Emergency management protocols start a reporting train, each campus unit begins check-in protocols with EM1 and the EOC to ensure communications work and Incident Command structures function properly. EM2 and EM3 coordinate with EM1, acting as liaisons to the decision team, who is now spread throughout the surrounding area.

24 Hours Before Impact—A Calm Silence

EM4, housed in the Emergency Operations Center, inspects their hurricane box, ensuring flashlights work and double-checking they have hard copies of all housing floorplans. IT officially shuts down the network, removing internet access and all network functionality such as printing. The university police have set up round-the-clock campus monitoring. "Our law enforcement function doesn't stop," EM7 explained, "but . . . it shifts a little bit as we're dealing with a whole lot fewer people." By this point "it transitions very quickly to security and you might almost in fundamental ways refer to it as a night watchman service." A calm silence settles over the campus. Other than high humidity, small gusts of wind, and an overcast sky, there is no evidence yet of Kyle.

Landfall—We Cannot Yet Assess Campus

Kyle is in full force. Though it weakened in category before it hit, the winds are strong enough to knock down trees and rip back some metal stripping. The EOC has already had preliminary reports of water damage in one building. The university police have reported downed power lines from fallen tree limbs. From an off-campus location, EM6 and her communications team sends an email to the university community: "We hope you have fared well during [hurricane Kyle] so far. As [the storm continues to] impact the area, we cannot yet effectively or comprehensively assess the impact on our campus. As a result, we are unable to determine at this point when we will reopen."

24 Hours Into Impact—When Do We Reopen?

"And then it happened so quickly. The community wants to resume normal life," EM7 stated matter of factly. "There was a lot of pressure from our audiences: students, parents, prospective students, faculty, staff, community partners, leadership, the board," EM6 agreed, describing the deluge of questions from stakeholders, even in the first 24 hours since landfall. People kept asking, "What is the status? How fast can we get cleaned up?" And they did not stop. Kyle has stalled since making landfall. The winds still pound the university, the water accumulates, entryways flood. The conditions are too dangerous to begin a full-scale damage assessment. EM6's team sends another email: "The university remains closed until further notice. . . . It is still too early to confirm a date for reopening, as we won't be able to complete our damage assessment for another few days."

48 Hours After Impact—No One Knew How Bad It Was Going to Be

"No one thought the storm [was] going to be as bad as it was," EM5 reflected on the entire after-storm recovery. There was flooding in some buildings and others had been shredded by debris; windows were broken, roofs torn. But the real damage came from slow recovery. The decision team and EMs 1, 2, and 3 were "all trying to have conference calls after in the aftermath to check on things," EM6 remembered. From the EOC, EM7 spoke with one of the decision team members, reassuring them that "I've seen all this before; unless there's something going on in the buildings, we'll be open in a week" they assured confidently. EM7 confessed exasperation, "I had no idea what was going on in the buildings, the amount of moisture and growth that was already beginning because the systems were turned off." Everyone was stunned at the extent of damage.

EM6's team sends another campus-wide email: "Thank you for your patience as a very small but dedicated team of employees continues to assess campus damage. The university will be closed through [Friday]. This does not mean we will reopen on [Monday]. It simply means we can confirm at this point that we will not reopen this week."

72 Hours After Impact—Check the Window, Touch the Floor, Touch the Wall: Is There Water?

Assessment progressed at tortoise speed, so it took days to discover the extent of damage. The moment Kyle's winds subsided, the EOC staff and police began "with the damage assessment, a windshield assessment, where we just drive around campus [to determine] the general condition of campus, [noting] areas that might need attention, might be dangerous for people to enter," EM3 explained. Then they moved assessment inside the buildings. "We start with some key areas. We're looking at our research areas . . ., doing a screening of hazardous materials" EM3 continued. Assessing the inside of buildings took time. "[We had] to go door-to-door with floor plans, mark them up, check the window, touch the floor, touch the wall. Is there water on the floor or near the window?" EM4 detailed. It took more than a cursory glance to label a building "all clear." What made it worse, "there was a staffing challenge on campus, period," EM6 said. "Having enough people to handle anything was a challenge because there was so much damage in the area."

Five Days After Impact—People Came Back Helter-Skelter

"The decision on when to reopen is a big one," EM1 said. EM2 added, "I mean, all the variables that you were dealing with before, you're dealing with every bit of that and many variables and more afterwards, [including] you're trying to get people back on campus." Campus was difficult to access because, as happens in most major hurricane scenarios, Kyle damaged the town and surrounding areas to the point that accessing campus was nearly impossible at first. "People came [back] sort of helter-skelter," EM5 stated. "And again we were like, all right, what's the next step?" By "people" EM5 meant emergency managers, contractors, and other staff. It was not until days 4 and 5 that the first couple of decision team members finally arrived back to campus. Again, EM5 expressed the confusion over the university's planning, "One of the pieces that . . . I didn't think we had taken the time to look [at was the] emergency plan; no one really guided that I didn't think." This was in contrast to the experience EMs 1, 2, and 3 expressed, but it could not have helped that everything was in disarray for the extended period after Kyle.

Seven Days After Impact—Who Stole My Muffin?

By this point, EM6 explained, the decision team started "making decisions based on: what is a known factor? And, what can be shared, what cannot be shared?" EM6 remembered that the decision team said a couple of times, "'We are going to open.' [Then], 'Oh, we can't open. We found this other thing that has prevented us from opening.'" The slow assessment is to blame, but the university community is on edge. People want to know what happened to campus. Is it destroyed? Do they have an office? Will their classes resume? What happened to their stuff? Do they have a job to return to? "By 'not shared' I mean sometimes you don't want to share things that are 'maybes' because if they don't pan out people start moving in that direction," EM6 clarified.

One result of waiting so long, remembered EM7, was "a lot of people's thresholds had fallen. We [had] reports of theft filed, one report was for a washcloth that went missing. And someone else, I think a muffin, there may even have been fruit. And so, you know, you try to put it in context."

Though the emails from EM6's team have expressed the uncertainty in assessing campus, no images have been shared. The campus community is in the dark. By day seven, the university community only has a vague description of campus, this time from the university president: "As we continue to move through the aftermath, I want to take a moment to thank all of you for your patience as we continue to assess damage to our campus and develop a plan for our reopening. While we don't yet have a date confirmed, we expect to have one for you by the end of the week."

Eight Days After Impact—News Is 24/7, But We Can't Work 24/7

The university communication team posts the first set of official campus pictures on social media. Before today, "unauthorized photos of damage to campus" had been floating around various social media pages. These were photos "that no one had vetted, no one had discussed. [So] there were people who were looking at the pictures and theorizing what caused the damage, but of course those theories were not accurate because [these people] were not on campus to gather the actual information," EM6 complained. Providing accurate information to the university community was of utmost importance to EM6. Even if it meant slowing the pace of communicating campus details concerning damage and recovery immediately following the hurricane (and in this case up to 8 days later), EM6 contended accurate information is worth it. A "challenge that we face is news is a 24/7, 365 [day] world, and getting information and finding out about it is not [like that after a hurricane]. It can't move fast; it has to be done more thoroughly to be accurate. Our team can't work 24/7, 365," EM6 said. As the communication team considers what photos to share, they asked, "Are they showing anything that would compromise security? Are they showing anything that would compromise health and life safety? [Maybe] accidentally, but are they? Those are not going to be shared."

Nine Days After Impact—People Want to Be Involved

"We're . . . just trying to keep people off campus," EM7 said with exhaustion. Access to information was important for the broader university community, but so was access to campus. People were ready to come back, "they want to come and walk and ride, and it's just not safe on campus. And we're trying to [tell them] in a very polite way: 'Hey, the campus is closed. The entrances are blocked.'" It is not just about access but also being part of the decision making. People wanted to be involved. You could see this in the emergency managers and their staff. You could see this in people trying to get on campus. EM7 explained, "What I found out is, particularly supervisors wanted to be at the table and participate in the conversation." They did not want to "just be told, 'nothing has changed.'"

2.5 Weeks After Impact—The Decision

"Honestly," EM4 said with appreciation, ending the semester "was never entertained . . ., was never a consideration that I recall in any conversation." EM5, on the other hand, admitted that she kept looking at the situation, "thinking, oh my, how are we going to keep this" semester? Nevertheless, EM5 tipped her hat to the university president's persistence in ensuring they saved the semester. "As a leader, [the president] showed [up with their] fanny pack and boots on and hat, [climbing] on top of buildings, looking at rooms." EM4 added, "I think you could probably imagine the university's leadership was very keen on our reopening." Some of the last conversations before the final decision to reopen considered the details about how academics would be affected, and eventually the decision team decided, "We couldn't just make all these decisions on our own, nor did we want to," EM5 emphasized. In the end, a number of university administrators and faculty collaborated, meeting "day after day for, gosh, four or five days after we returned in person, [sitting] around the big table asking, 'How many hours have we lost? What will the state allow us to skip? [What about] our accrediting agency?'" The conversations led to some arguments, but eventually they developed a plan: "I felt good about it being a collaborative plan that both faculty and administrators had bought into," EM5 highlighted.

The decision was made. The university would reopen over the weekend, and invite everyone to return Tuesday, almost three full weeks after Kyle made landfall.

DISCUSSION

Using semistructured interviews, this study sought to explicate the process of how one university managed uncertainty during specific hurricane events. At first appearance, the EMs followed a hierarchical decision-making process in which predefined protocols for gathering and evaluating trustworthy information guided their crisis response. However, a spheres model of uncertainty (Walsh & Walker, 2016) revealed how managing uncertainty was more about EMs coordinating deliberative and dialectic moments rather than outputting a simplified institutional response. The spheres model of uncertainty categorizes uncertainty into three types—technical, personal, and public uncertainty—which help explain how uncertainties interact and "circulate through situations, genres, and forums" (p. 72). To coordinate deliberative moments, EMs engaged in a series of activities that helped them balance multiple uncertainties at once, and the spheres model highlights four types of activities EMs engaged in to manage uncertainty: assessment, discussion, decision making, and communication. These activities culminated in a response strategy that participants did not explicitly identify. The EMs response strategy is best explained by the unique characteristics of each activity: (1) assessing—wading through uncertainty, (2) discussing—weighing probability and defining risk, (3) deciding—anticipating points of disruption and stability, and (4) communicating—authorizing official narratives.

Assessing—Wading Through Possibilities

Identifying assessment as an important emergency management activity aligns with other researchers' findings (e.g., Baumgart et al., 2008); more specifically, however, this study supports Demuth et al.'s (2012) observation that EMs need and seek uncertainty information. To be clear, though EMs seek to reduce uncertainty to make decisions, they also purposefully gather uncertainty to account for all possible scenarios. Without seeking uncertainty information and wading through possibilities, EMs would make ill-informed decisions. An important finding, then, is although uncertainty is often framed as an impediment to EMs' purpose (e.g., Ulmer et al., 2017), this study suggests that uncertainty is an unavoidable and instructive component for effective decision making.

This finding highlighted two important characteristics of assessment activities: One, assessment required access, and two, access called attention to a power disparity between EMs and the university community. Before the storm, access to Hurrevac allowed EMs to analyze meteorological possibilities and therefore justify why EMs waited to evacuate campus as long as they did; in addition, after-storm access to campus enabled EMs to walk through, touch, and see hurricane damage, giving them insight for delaying a return to campus. The university community, however, did not have such access and therefore had little to no understanding of why and when these decisions were made, revealing the disparity between those who did and those who did not create the technical narrative of the hurricane event. Before Hurricane Kyle made landfall, meteorologists had the capability to provide access for EMs to assess uncertainty, and the power to offer access shifted to the EMs after the storm. Having a tool to assess technical uncertainty helped EMs consider all possibilities; likewise, the campus community may benefit from assessing technical uncertainty alongside EMs, and the community is dependent on the EMs for such access.

Emergency Managers should consider the forms of access they provide the campus community. With or without access to the technical uncertainties EMs have, the campus community will assess the hurricane event on their own terms (e.g., Grabill & Simmons, 1998). Though EMs limited the university community's access to both campus and information for purposes of safety and accuracy, lack of access may have included missed opportunities for the campus community to gather reliable uncertainty information and understand EMs' complex decision making during a hurricane event. As the NWS provides a tool for access to reliable data and assessment strategies, EMs might consider developing a similar tool for their constituents. To be clear, "wading through possibility" was not an unguided plunge into complete and total uncertainty for EMs, as Hurrevac provided boundaries and internal structure to help EMs suspend decisions and consider all possibilities. Using dark sites (e.g., Moerschell & Novak, 2020), internally created template webpages that remain unpublished until needed, is a good first strategy, but the site should be simple to manage and provide interactive elements for the university community. A new class of note taking apps, such as Notion, may offer an alternative. Notion allows users to manage information in chunks and databases, making the material modular and thus flexible. The university community may appreciate using a Notion database (which is like an interactive table), and EMs could manage information in synced chunks in multiple locations, easily updated from a single page. This might simplify and encourage the management of fast-changing information.

Discussing—Weighing Probability and Defining Risk

Not surprisingly, discussing uncertainties with colleagues was a crucial activity for EMs as they prepared to make decisions. Two characteristics of this activity shed light on the EMs' strategy. First, EMs needed to weigh the possibilities they waded through in their assessment activities, and the relationships EMs fostered to do so contributed to their ability to manage uncertainty, which echoes the findings of other emergency management scholarship (e.g., Demuth et al., 2012). Before a storm made landfall, for example, EMs benefited from bouncing ideas back-and-forth with meteorologists as they sought to validate their own assumptions, question evidence, and eliminate unlikely possibilities. The way meteorologists talked about uncertainties through tone of voice or habitual cues helped EMs weigh what was most probable, a finding similar to Ernst, Ladue, and Gerard (2018).

Defining risk was the second characteristic of discussion activities, which highlighted how discussions became hybrid forums in which multiple types of uncertainty influenced decisions. Walsh and Walker (2016) warned not to "[conflate] technical uncertainty, which expresses the probability of outcomes, with risk, which assigns values to those outcomes" (p. 71). Doing so eclipses the act of assigning value. When the EMs decided when to close campus, for example, discussions centered on the probability of the track and intensity of Hurricane Kyle until an EM from housing argued that the students' safety was paramount. Thus, discussions became sites for the values of personal and even public uncertainties to influence decision making.

EMs should maintain and build relationships that foster helpful discussion, and they should consider ways to extend such opportunities to the campus community before and after a hurricane event. Of course, doing so could be problematic during a storm as direct back-and-forth may deter from making decisions quickly and keeping people safe. In addition, the EMs had a limited number of staff to complete their tasks let alone field such discussions. EMs could therefore consider using a Virtual Operations Support Team (VOST) made up of university volunteers from faculty and staff. VOSTs are groups of volunteers who mediate information between EMs and the public (Roth & Prior, 2019). Traditionally, VOSTs collect data from social media to inform EM decision making. For universities, however, trained volunteer faculty and staff could accept the risks to mediate assessment and discussion activities between EMs and the university community. VOST members could access campus after the storm alongside EMs and record footage and document conversations of EMs. They might use TikTok or Marco Polo to post continuous updates in which EMs on camera discuss assessment details and list what possibilities they are considering.

Deciding—Anticipating Points of Disruption and Stability

The emergency managers' decision-making activities were defined by two moments: when campus closed and when it reopened. These two points in time marked points of disruption (halting education to evacuate and close campus) and stability (initiating plans to return to and reopen campus and resume education). EMs therefore structured all preparation and response decisions around these two points, making the process and details that went into these decisions articulate and well-thought-out. EMs made these decisions collaboratively, distributing the decision making throughout assessment and discussion activities. Nevertheless, community members were puzzled as to why decisions to close campus felt delayed, and they wondered about the condition of campus for an entire week before they had concrete details. In other words, despite EMs anticipating points of disruption, the community still reported feeling in the dark.

The problem, however, was that the university community was not included in the assessment and discussion activities before and after the storm. Weighing probabilities and defining risk with the meteorologists helped EMs anticipate the most likely hazards and in turn determine what at the university would be most susceptible to Hurricane Kyle. These discussions enabled EMs to then decide which part of the university's emergency operations plan to initiate, which directed how they prioritized risks. The university community, however, had little information to evaluate what recovery options were possible, let alone plan for what recovery actions and outcomes were most likely. Without discussing uncertainty with EMs, the university community's decisions were constricted to a small amount of information and, perhaps above all, speculation. The spheres model highlights that being involved in decision making implies being included in assessment and discussion activities, not necessarily at the table when decisions are made, but part of the making-sense-of-things. Decisions, then, were distributed throughout assessment and discussion activities because of the range of information and time needed to define risk and draw conclusions.

Community members should recognize that emergency management decisions are more complex than they appear to those outside the decision-making process. EMs should recognize, too, however, that the campus community's tendency to simplify the decision-making process is partly due to the process being hidden. Though the intent behind obscuring the decision making may be to avoid making promises that cannot be kept, lack of information tends to leave campus communities to fill in the gaps on their own. Therefore, rather than keeping decisions black-boxed as a strategy to anticipate disruption, EMs might consider ways in which the decision-making process could be extended and distributed to the campus community. To do so, EMs should make the university's emergency operations plan public. If such plans contain sensitive information, a condensed and usable version should be distributed. The university community would benefit in particular from a before-storm timeline that showed when EMs anticipate making major decisions; in addition, a post-storm timeline might unify recovery efforts with some of the campus community's expectations, especially if the timeline explained the dependencies influencing the decisions.

Communicating—Authorizing the Official Narrative

Unsurprisingly, EMs sought to control the Hurricane Kyle narrative as it related to the university. Their approach sometimes followed technocratic strategies for communicating crisis, favoring a conduit model of communication where knowledge is generated by the sender (EMs) and transmitted to the receiver. This strategy is practical when it comes to crises, which is important during hurricane events when EMs do not have time to implement more participatory approaches. A pitfall of the conduit model, however, is it posits the official narrative as the only narrative, making little room for other interpretations. We know, however, in a crisis, individuals, whether experts or nonexperts, assess risk and interpret hazards with or without an official narrative (e.g., Grabill & Simmons, 1998). In other words, "alternative" narratives generated by the university community will always exist alongside the university's; therefore, facilitating assessment and discussion activities with the community may help EMs account for and even adapt to these narratives.

Indeed, for the EMs, other interpretations bubbled up after Hurricane Kyle: faculty reported a case of stolen wine from their office after hurricane recovery, and a student reported the theft of a muffin and other seemingly trivial items. Although not considered a traditional "uncertainty," reporting a missing muffin might represent an individual's effort to make sense of the "aftermath" of Hurricane Kyle. While the EMs sought to assess the physical damage to property, this individual sought to understand where their possessions had gone. Returning from a hurricane evacuation can be overwhelming and being victimized by the theft of personal possessions can compound distress. Although we can rightly say that a missing muffin is of little consequence compared to, for example, restoring power to the university, the juxtaposition explains why crisis communication strategies that focus on power outages alone may seem unsatisfactory and incomplete. Therefore, EMs should see their communication as an argument for how to interpret the uncertainty of a hurricane event. Official narratives do not supplant or displace unsanctioned (by the institution) narratives. EMs should learn what concerns the university community has and find ways to speak to their concerns, such as perhaps explaining what the university is doing to ensure personal possessions stay safe while contractors enter dorm rooms to complete repairs. Reports of missing muffins and wine are opportunities to wade through and discuss uncertainty, not impediments to entrenching an official narrative.

A limited view of communication, then, may obscure strategies that could help in hurricane events. Importantly, the EMs' communications aligned with the advice of well-established crisis communication practices, such as communicating directly after an event, staying in contact with all stakeholders, and stating what is known and what is not known (e.g., Ulmer et al., 2017). However, EMs should recognize that while their messaging transmits consequential emergency information, their control of the technical narrative affords them the opportunity to build effective relationships. Before the storm, meteorologists encouraged an important relationship for EMs to enable them to assess and discuss uncertainty. As the technical experts, the meteorologists generated forecasts but also supplied the EMs with a tool—Hurrevac—for wading through possibility. In addition, meteorologists made themselves available for discussing and weighing probability. After the storm, the author of the technical narrative shifted, moving from meteorologists to EMs. If establishing and maintaining effective relationships is important to their discussion activities, EMs need to acknowledge this shift in who creates the technical narrative. Effective messaging is important, but EMs should recognize that their messaging does more than transmit the technical narrative and build credibility; it also defines their relationship with the university community.

EMs should view their entire response (assessing, discussing, deciding) as a communication strategy, and communication plans should account for this. Emergency operations plans detail the role administrators play in managing emergencies, such as spelling out Incident Command protocols that assign tasks and decisions to each EM. Similarly, EMs might add what role the university community plays during a hurricane (in consultation with the community). Such additions could include specific assessment and decisions activities and resources, which could include links, descriptions, and protocols such as how often EMs intend to post a TikTok during a specified time period. The EMs should also consider reassessing which social media platforms the university uses to account for multiple demographics (i.e., using more than just Facebook) and the ever-shifting landscape of social media. Lastly, the university community should adapt a culture of emergency management and collaborate with EMs to cocreate tools that support pedagogy and research. With disasters becoming more frequent, EM websites, resources, tools, and strategies should become part of how faculty and students view education.

Future Research

This study was limited in that it reports interview data from one university and only seven EMs. Future research should consider ways in which the four activities (assessing, discussing, deciding, and communicating) these EMs addressed might apply in other hurricane situations. Another limitation is that although hurricane events are relatively stable disasters usually predicted days in advance, many crises arise with no warning. In addition, hurricanes have a clear conclusion and require a straightforward recovery process, even if it is disrupted by uncertainty. Thus, future research might investigate how these uncertainty management activities hold up in more complex crises and disasters, such as how universities are handling the COVID-19 pandemic. Lastly, applying the recommendations in this report will take time to learn how to do so in the real-time chaotic moments of a hurricane event. Research is therefore needed to consider how such recommendations may apply in a real-world scenario. Such studies could observe the EM process during live events, using ethnographic techniques to identify where these recommendations could apply. In addition, participatory design and UX studies might consider how EMs and university communities can cocreate EM tools that meet safety protocols as well as faculty and student needs.

CONCLUSIONS

Ultimately, this chapter echoes Walsh and Walker (2016) and argues that uncertainty is opportunity for dialogue, not a deficiency in knowledge; therefore, strategies that help us discuss or dialogue in productive ways can help us manage uncertainties as opportunities—instead of impediments—for improving crisis communication during hurricane events. Productive ways may include accounting for the fast-pace movement of crisis information in the moment; moreover, considering the increase in emergencies and crises across the nation's universities, finding productive ways to manage disaster uncertainty in educational environments has become even more crucial.

As we consider how the university is impacted by disasters and crises, we need to consider the role university emergency management plays in providing a safe place for education. Although hurricanes continue to threaten coastal universities, the worldwide COVID-19 pandemic poses a challenging scenario for emergency management supporting quality education. Hurricanes can be political, revealing power and privilege regarding economic pressures and racial disparities within a community (Fleetwood, 2006). But in terms of institutional response to a hazard, the COVID-19 pandemic has brought a new level of politics that is worth comparing.

Consider the difference in the nature of the threats between hurricanes and the COVID pandemic. COVID is not a visible mass on weather radar nor a crushing cyclone of wind and rain; the disease itself is invisible to naked eyes, evident to the general population only through one's own symptoms or through others who are symptomatic. Consider the different influences individual decisions have in hurricane events vs. the pandemic. Preparing for a hurricane event, one may choose to stay or leave town, and this decision will impact one's own safety and perhaps the decisions of family and friends. Deciding how to act in regard to COVID, however, becomes consequential for classrooms, universities, and communities. Consider the institutional responses, what information do EMs seek to make hurricane response decisions? How do they assess this information? If we base hurricane response on scientific knowledge and practices, why would it be any different for a pandemic? As universities prepared for the fall 2021 semester, why was there still such confusion over the effectiveness of wearing masks to prevent the spread of COVID? Why were vaccines not mandated at every university? A spheres model reminds us that communication about subjects like COVID-19 is an argument for how to interpret uncertainty, and official narratives (perhaps in this case, the scientific narrative) do not easily displace political narratives.

Comparing a university's institutional response to a hurricane event vs. COVID may provide clarity for EMs and those of us trying to salvage semesters. Humans have always lived and died with weather; we are practiced, both individually and institutionally, at responding to atmospheric risks, even if there is much room for improvement. We are less practiced, however, at responding to pandemics, including both the medical and political risks involved. The discussion points in this study ask university EMs to consider how they make knowledge by interacting with meteorologists and then to consider how the EMs, in like manner, interact with their publics, the university community, to make knowledge. EMs should do the same for COVID. Recognizing that personal uncertainties, public uncertainties, and technical uncertainties weigh on individual and university decisions, a spheres model of uncertainty may help us find opportunities for discussing the uncertainties that still exist in science while also finding more resolute movement in providing safe education.

REFERENCES

Abukhalaf, A. H. I., & von Meding, J. (2020). Communication challenges in campus emergency planning: The case of Hurricane Dorian in Florida. *Natural Hazards, 104*(2): 1535–65.

Baumgart, L. A., Bass, E. J., Philips, B., & Kloesel, K. (2008). Emergency management decision making during severe weather. *Weather and Forecasting, 23*(6): 1268–79.

Demuth, J. L., Morss, R. E., Morrow, B. H., & Lazo, J. K. (2012). Creation and communication of hurricane risk information. *Bulletin of the American Meteorological Society, 93*(8): 1133–45.

Ernst, S., Ladue, D., & Gerard, A. (2018). Understanding Emergency Manager forecast use in severe weather events. *Journal of Operational Meteorology, 6*(9): 95–105.

Fleetwood, N. R. (2006). Failing narratives, initiating technologies: Hurricane Katrina and the production of a weather media event. *American Quarterly, 58*(3): 767–89.

Goodnight, G. T. (1982). The personal, technical, and public spheres of argument: A speculative inquiry into the art of public deliberation. *Journal of the American Forensic Association, 18*: 214–27.

Grabill, J. T., & Simmons, W. M. (1998). Toward a critical rhetoric of risk communication: Producing citizens and the role of technical communicators. *Technical Communication Quarterly, 7*(4): 415–41.

Lambrecht, K. M., Hatchett, B. J., Walsh, L. C., Collins, M., & Tolby, Z. (2019). Improving visual communication of weather forecasts with rhetoric. *Bulletin of the American Meteorological Society, 100*(4): 557–63.

Miles, M. B., Huberman, A. M., & Saldaña, J. (2014). *Qualitative data analysis: A methods sourcebook* (3rd ed.). Los Angeles: Sage.

Moerschell, L., & Novak, S. S. (2020). Managing crisis in a university setting: The challenge of alignment. *Journal of Contingencies and Crisis Management, 28*(1): 30–40.

Morrow, B. H., & Lazo, J. K. (2014). Coastal emergency managers' preferences for storm surge forecast communication. *Journal of Emergency Management, 12*, 153–60.

Morss, R. E., Lazo, J. K., & Demuth, J. L. (2010). Examining the use of weather forecasts in decision scenarios: Results from a US survey with implications for uncertainty communication. *Meteorological Applications, 17*(2): 149–62.

Rainear, A. M., & Lin, C. A. (2021). Communication factors influencing flood-risk-mitigation motivation and intention among college students. *Weather, Climate, and Society, 13*(1): 125–35.

Roth, F., & Prior, T. (2019). Utility of virtual operation support teams: An international survey. *The Australian Journal of Emergency Management, 34*(2): 53–59.

Saldaña, J. (2013). *The coding manual for qualitative researchers*. Los Angeles: Sage.

Simms, J. L., Kusenbach, M., & Tobin, G. A. (2013). Equally unprepared: Assessing the hurricane vulnerability of undergraduate students. *Weather, Climate, and Society, 5*(3): 233–43.

Spinuzzi, C. (2013). How can technical communicators study work contexts? In J. Johnson-Eilola & S. A. Selber (Eds.), *Solving problems in technical communication* (pp. 428–53). Chicago: The University of Chicago Press.

Tracy, S. J. (2013). *Qualitative research methods: Collecting evidence, crafting analysis, communicating impact*. Chichester: John Wiley & Sons.

Ulmer, R. R., Sellnow, T. L., & Seeger, M. W. (2017). *Effective crisis communication: Moving from crisis to opportunity*. Sage Publications.

Walsh, L., & Walker, K. C. (2016). Perspectives on uncertainty for technical communication scholars. *Technical Communication Quarterly, 25*(2): 71–86.

Wernstedt, K., Roberts, P. S., Arvai, J., & Redmond, K. (2019). How emergency managers (mis?) interpret forecasts. *Disasters, 43*(1): 88–109.

Yin, R. K. (2014). *Case study research: Design and methods* (5th ed.). Los Angeles: Sage.

Part II

EXPLORATIONS AND EXAMINATIONS

Chapter Four

Nimble Pedagogies for a Liquid Time

Disruption, Accommodation, Collaboration, Reinvention, and Compromise

Diana Ashe and Colleen A. Reilly

A brief online search for disaster pedagogies may give the impression that catastrophes that challenge educational institutions happen elsewhere in the world. From earthquakes and tsunamis in Japan (Shiwaku & Shaw, 2016) to sea level rise and typhoons in Taiwan (Wang, 2019), disasters are discussed by scholars and educators in terms of the disruptions that they cause throughout the world but much less often in the United States. We in southeastern North Carolina know very well that disasters, including recent Hurricanes Matthew, Florence, Dorian, and Isaias and the COVID-19 pandemic, pose immense challenges to our ability to maintain the continuity of instruction at institutions of higher learning in our region. In fact, the full range of crises challenging educational institutions are increasing everywhere (Schlachte, 2019). This reality contributes to the already unstable environment in which universities find themselves culturally, financially, and socially and reinforces Green and Gary's (2016) conception of our moment as a "liquid time"—a time in which "anomalies . . . are the norm; we are living with permanent uncertainty" (p. 47).

As tenured faculty who run our university's Center for Teaching Excellence and Center for Faculty Leadership, we have been at the center of every disruption to our campus in recent years and have helped our colleagues face the many uncertainties that these disasters have posed. Such permanent uncertainty has been the case for many of our colleagues who came up for reappointment to assistant professor in Spring 2021, for example. The whole of their careers at the University of North Carolina Wilmington (UNCW) has been punctuated with sequential disasters and resulting uncertainty. They arrived at UNCW in August 2018 just prior to Hurricane Florence making landfall on September 14. Some had their new offices, labs, and burgeoning experiments destroyed by water from severe damage to the main science building, and others experienced lengthy evacuations from Wilmington and serious damage to their homes. The other disasters referenced above hit one after another, causing the state of mitigation in which the colleagues participated to be their true normal as new faculty at UNCW. In this persistently unstable environment, they have had to learn to persevere and adapt.

For our staff of the Center for Teaching Excellence, Hurricane Florence left all of our own homes damaged in varying degrees. The drudgery of cleaning up and dealing with repairs and insurance (or the lack of insurance) and assistance programs added a layer of work and a steep learning curve to so many on our campus and in our community. Even as this was occurring, we were all figuring out how to get back to work, how to salvage courses that had been canceled for a record number of days, and how to meet learning objectives when everyone was learning to cope, while dealing with the shocking destruction of our campus, with buildings rendered useless and networks of white air tubes like tentacles looping out of every window and door, blue tarps protecting roofs, and one parking lot newly taken over by portable buildings housing temporary science labs. With streets lined with piles of debris everywhere we looked, nothing seemed stable. Many of our colleagues considered leaving and heading to somewhere less prone to this kind of disaster—but disasters, we all know, happen everywhere. And, as if to prove that point, the pandemic soon followed, everywhere.

In response to this liquid time, Green and Gary (2016) argued that we all need to develop dynamic and flexible pedagogies that assist students to focus on process over product and exploration over conclusions, learn to be comfortable with a constantly emerging knowledge base, and meet this fluid environment with creativity and curiosity. The editors of this volume assert that "disruption, accommodation, reinvention, and compromise" are "defining aspects of pedagogical responses to disaster in the 21st century." We concur but add another crucial aspect to their list: collaboration. Our chapter details how, as faculty developers, we encourage our colleagues to meet current and future uncertain moments through forging nimble pedagogies that draw heavily on each of the five strategies. In addition, we encourage the use of established approaches such as backward design, universal design for learning (UDL), and transparency in learning and teaching (TILT) to bring needed clarity, accessibility, and consistency to these times that are all too murky and unpredictable.

CONTEXT: OUR CENTER FOR TEACHING EXCELLENCE AND CENTER FOR FACULTY LEADERSHIP

The Center for Teaching Excellence has served the UNCW faculty for 30 years; the Center for Faculty Leadership, more than 15. In that time, the institution has grown rapidly, and the unit has innovated to keep up with emerging needs and pedagogies. With 1.9 FTE of faculty developers aided by an administrative associate, we serve nearly 1,000 faculty members in their teaching and leadership development needs. Every area of programming was altered by the pandemic in 2020, bringing the need for additional time allocations for the faculty developers on the staff to plan and execute increased and drastically altered programming in every area of operations.

We spent much of the additional time assisting faculty to shift teaching modalities suddenly in Spring 2020 and then more intentionally during Summer 2020 in preparation for the Fall semester. For example, after UNCW shifted to all remote learning in Spring 2020, we partnered with the Office of Distance Education and eLearning (DEeL) to develop the Keep Teaching and Keep Learning websites and offer a conference-style program during the extended "Spring Break" in March 2020 to support this change. With a bit more lead time in Summer 2020, we developed two online course design institutes enrolling 60+ faculty, created and screened more than 900 applications for course development funds to support faculty in shifting modalities, and spearheaded the summer Adapt 2020 conference alongside DEeL, offering sessions to hundreds of faculty as they made modality shifts. To enhance our skills and ethos, we completed the seven-course program from Quality Matters (QM) to earn the Teaching Online Certificate. Even with all of our preparation and previous experience, supporting so many was quite challenging and, at times, even overwhelming, giving us empathy for the analogous experiences of our colleagues and students during this uncertain and difficult period.

DISRUPTION: THE MOMENT EVERYTHING CHANGES

The very nature of crisis is that it cannot be ignored. At a certain point, we recognize that our carefully crafted syllabi and course schedules are not going to work in the face of unfolding circumstances. For faculty developers who also teach, this means letting go of the semester's planned workshops and programs along with our own syllabi and course schedules—and needing to rethink both on the fly. Disruption is overwhelming in part because it presents a ton of work, and we often don't know where to begin.

It's not just the instant workload that is overwhelming, of course, as classes aren't being canceled because the university won the MegaMillions and has instantly doubled its endowment. Crisis disruptions are often frightening and sad and almost always uncertain. When trees fall on your house while you are out of state, as happened to one of our colleagues during Hurricane Florence in 2018, figuring out what to do about your belongings and your child and your cat loom large and parallel your need to determine what to do about your syllabus and your students (who are also worried about their belongings, their families, and their pets).

Disruption, like every aspect of crisis response, is not a stage that you go through to get to the next stage. There are lots of recommended strategies for the early stages of disruption, many of which are the same recommendations given for stress management at any other time: things like mindfulness practice (Pecore, 2020), yoga and other exercise, connecting with friends and colleagues, and harnessing productive narratives and sensemaking to manage crises and move through them (Block, Bryant Block, & Peters, 2012; Gigliotti, 2016). Disruption characterizes every point of a crisis and may predict some permanent shifts as well. All of these aspects are not only recursive but are happening simultaneously throughout the crisis situation—yet another reason why crises feel so overwhelming.

So, what do you do when disruption hits? How do you handle that moment when you realize that your best-laid plans are best saved for some future semester? We recommend taking a few steps:

1. *Let yourself be upset.* You might feel angry or saddened or afraid or disappointed or flat-out crushed that your hard work is now for naught. You can absolutely own that reaction. Find ways to express that reaction safely, such as by speaking with a friend or colleague or posting to a social media site; understand that you might grieve this experience for some time to come, so consider setting up a friend connection or other way to work through it.
2. *Communicate with your students as soon as you can tell them anything at all—even if you communicate just to say that you are aware of the situation and you will get back to them as soon as you know more.* Your students are having these same reactions and have the additional stressor of a total lack of control over what happens in their classes, so regular reassurance that you are going to handle the situation for your class will be a balm to them and could save you from many frantic emails as time passes. For example, you can use the course email and announcements portion of the learning management system to reach out to students and let them know when you think you may have concrete information to share.

3. *Examine your course materials with crisis goggles on.* Crisis goggles allow you to see your syllabus, schedule, and assignments only through the lens of your course's student learning outcomes. When a crisis forces you to reduce your course's face-to-face time or number of assignments, put on your crisis goggles and seek out anything that does not directly contribute to the student learning outcomes. For instance, you might combine two assignments into one or focus an exam on the essential content that is directly related to the course learning outcomes. Although it may be painful to eliminate anything from your course, if you must take something out to meet new time constraints or minimize demands in the face of a crisis, the material that isn't contributing directly to student learning outcomes can go first.
4. *As you shift from regular operations to crisis operations, determine how you want your class to run during the crisis and then communicate this to your students and, as appropriate, to your department chair.* We advocate communicating this information redundantly because people under stress (and this includes your department chair as much as your students) may not look in the places you expect them to look for information. Post in your learning management system in more than one place (for example, post a new schedule in the Calendar or Syllabus section, point out the changes in the Announcements, and then offer an Overview within the next Module as well) and make sure your department chair has access to necessary information in more than one place as well (via email and your campus's intranet or backchannel information system, for example, or by cc'ing a departmental administrative associate).
5. *This may be the hardest one: If the disruption is a long one and your class will be severely altered, work at finding something positive about the change.* Can you help your students create a Slack channel or Discord server to help each other through the crisis? Can one of your projects in the class be converted to something that helps students understand the crisis or think about it in ways that pertain to course content? Some students will say that they are tired of hearing about the crisis—and they are—but they do need ways to think about it and comprehend its causes and consequences. Does your discipline offer them ways to dig deeper? In Reilly's senior seminar in Fall 2018, for instance, she added a brief reflective video assignment to make up some of the time lost to the hurricane—this video allowed students to articulate their learning and reflect on their experiences during the storm.

Disruption is critical when thinking about disaster pedagogy in part because one of the worst things we can do is pretend there is no disruption, to maintain our expectations and schedules as though there were no crisis at all. Shoehorning a course plan written during relative calm into a semester of crisis is confusing and frustrating for students and will only cause more problems. In the aftermath of Hurricane Florence, for example, many of us received grateful responses from students even when we emailed them just to let them know that we did not yet have concrete information about when classes would resume and how our course schedules and assignments would change. The act of making contact and acknowledging the disaster was reassuring for students although it was not accompanied by firm plans. Accepting that our plans have been disrupted frees us to make necessary changes and to ensure that powerful learning still takes place. It may not be the learning we had planned or hoped to see, but our students will remember our roles in their learning and in helping them through their own crises. Following these steps will enable you to be steady for your students and not add to the strain.

COLLABORATION: THERE'S A UNIVERSE INSIDE THE UNIVERSITY

As faculty members, we have specializations that are shared with few others on our campus. As administrators, we are part of a small office that provides services different from any other office on campus. Specialization is one of the ways that universities as organizations avoid too much redundancy and overlap between units. Our offices, departments, and courses are clearly defined by separate mission statements and university catalog descriptions. There is typically very little "stepping on toes," and boundaries are clear. During regular times, this can be a good financial strategy and help the university run smoothly. During a crisis, though, it means that the university may or may not have the culture of collaboration needed to adjust quickly and engage in transdisciplinary knowledge making (Vanasupa et al., 2014).

We are lucky to belong to a unit with a long history of collaboration at a university that is very relationship-driven; we are even luckier, probably, to have been working here for a very long time—each of us has been at this institution for at least 20 years. During the aftermath of Hurricane Florence, for example, we were able to leverage our connections and call upon a clinical psychology professor to speak to the faculty twice about "The Emotional Aftermath" and collaborate with the Office of Applied Learning and the Office of Undergraduate Studies to offer Applied Learning Recovery Grants that helped faculty rethink their courses in response to almost a month of lost instructional time.

When the COVID-19 pandemic hit in early Spring 2020, this history of collaboration reached new levels inside and outside the university. We worked with our colleagues in DEeL to create a five-day virtual conference on Zoom for faculty retooling their courses for the suddenly remote end of the semester. The most important sessions covered communicating with students, understanding how to use the Canvas learning management system, and altering assignments and learning activities for remote delivery. With permission from colleagues at the University of North Carolina at Chapel Hill, North Carolina State University, and Indiana University to adapt their content, we worked with DEeL again to create a Keep Teaching page for our faculty and then, with permission from the University of Iowa, to create a Keep Learning page for our students. There was no time to create all the content our faculty needed, and we remain grateful to these institutions for sharing their work with us during the crisis. Collaboration—inside and outside the university—was the only way we could have met the vast needs before us.

We kept connecting with other units to offer programs that made sense for the emerging needs. In the summer, we borrowed an idea (again with permission) from the University of North Carolina at Greensboro for a summer virtual conference called ADAPT 2020, held in collaboration with UNCW's DEeL. We put our own spin on the content, of course, and several other campus units contributed to a successful event with 25 sessions, 13 campus offices presenting, and more than 1,200 attendees. Some of the most useful sessions covered how to teach synchronously on Zoom, how to alter your course policies and course syllabus for online contexts, and how to use transparency in learning and teaching (TILT) principles to make all your policies, assignments, and schedules clear to students. Because we, as faculty developers, stay active in our statewide organization, we can borrow great ideas and hope that our colleagues will borrow ideas from us as well. Our colleagues expressed to us that they were grateful for our guidance and advice in this time of crisis. The evidence for this can be seen in the participation we had in these programs and all of our programs during Summer 2020. We usually have 20 faculty attend our summer course design institutes each May. In Summer 2020, we had 60 faculty enroll in two four-week sessions. They were excited to explore how to meet this moment of crisis through improving their pedagogical approaches.

To continue to bring faculty together and help them collaborate into the Fall semester, we held eleven sessions over the course of several weeks called Modality Meet-Ups. Each session was reserved for faculty teaching in a specific modality: synchronous online, asynchronous online, face-to-face, and hybrid in a few varieties. Faculty members who were experienced in teaching in that modality volunteered to facilitate each session's informal conversation, and colleagues from DEeL were often there to help. Bringing faculty together to share ideas and simply connect can make all the difference. In addition, we held four weeks of programs throughout the month of November to welcome new faculty to the institution called Newvember. Each week asked a different subset of the campus to participate in welcoming our newest colleagues in a different way, asking for all hands on deck so that those faculty who joined our institution during this time of crisis would gain a sense of belonging despite the remoteness and strained circumstances.

For faculty, collaboration in a crisis can happen in much the same way that it does for us at the program level and, similarly, goes better in a crisis if the connections are already there. Long-standing tradition dictates in many universities that faculty are typically generous about sharing course materials with one another. Make it a practice to put a citation on borrowed course materials so that your students see you giving credit to a colleague—a practice that demonstrates how credit for intellectual property works and values the labor involved in creating course materials.

There are numerous books written about collaboration (Lemon & Salmons, 2021; Simmons & Singh, 2019; Walsh & Kahn, 2010), but here are some ways for you to launch and nurture collaboration during a crisis:

1. *Use all of the networks you are already a part of, from your academic discipline to your department itself.* Many disciplinary groups held workshops and gathered shared resources tailored to their discipline at the start of the pandemic, for example. Reach out to those same groups for help in dealing with the crisis you face. Chances are good that someone has already faced it and will be able to offer insight and help. Our statewide faculty developers organization shared resources during Spring 2020 related to creating video lectures and forming community through using tools like VoiceThread in online courses. We could draw on those resources for our programs.
2. *Put out a call in your department or your discipline's list for a virtual meeting to share ideas.* You can use a simple sign-up sheet and shareable documents to allow everyone to contribute. We have attended these meetings about everything from improving diversity and inclusion to holding virtual New Faculty Orientation. Every time, we have come out of them glad we attended. Our North Carolina faculty developers group held an online meeting in Summer 2020 to share ideas synchronously and through a Google doc for teaching in hybrid settings in particular. We used and conveyed the ideas they shared, such as strategies for doing group work with students who are both in person and online by creating group sharing spaces in the Canvas learning management system or in Google docs for students to share resources and ideas with all group members.

3. *Check social media for specialized groups forming in the face of the crisis—or form one yourself.* Facebook is home to Pandemic Pedagogy and the Higher Education Learning Collective, among others, either formed during the COVID-19 crisis or ramped up because of it, that host thousands of faculty and staff.
4. *When you do something that works in response to a crisis on your campus, share it!* Tell your colleagues, tell your center for teaching and learning, post it on social media. Be as generous in sharing your ideas as you hope that others will be with you. We directed our colleagues to use Microsoft Teams to share example assignments and resources. Additionally, we helped some of our new colleagues in Fall 2020 to get on Yammer to share ideas and bond during their unusual first semester at UNCW.
5. *Once you are collaborating with a colleague or group, set role expectations up front.* Be sure that all parties know what the goals of the collaboration are and what each member is expected to share. A crisis is already stressful, so double your efforts to communicate well in collaborations to prevent misunderstandings that make things worse. In both Summer and Fall 2020, we worked together with our Office of Distance Education and eLearning (DEeL) to create numerous workshops and the Keep Teaching site, for instance. We had to clarify with our colleagues who would lead each session, who would be responsible for recording and editing the video, and who would advertise the programs. Being clear about the expectations allowed us to seamlessly meet the needs of our colleagues and avoid duplicating efforts. For more guidelines on successful collaborations, see Lemon and Salmons (2021).

Collaboration is always a part of our professional lives. Crises just make it, like everything else, more urgent. We think crises make us more grateful for collaboration, too; the isolation that often comes from a crisis can be ameliorated by connecting in these ways with your colleagues who are facing the same struggles you face.

ACCOMMODATION: STAYING COMPASSIONATELY NIMBLE

While we are struggling in a crisis, our students struggle alongside us. Managing the ways their experiences will affect our classes—and managing our own responses to them—is a daunting and seemingly endless task. In the social media groups mentioned above, faculty often seek advice for handling specific student situations and challenging emails. Schlachte (2019) reminds us that we need to develop ethical and affective pedagogical responses to disasters and their almost inevitable recurrence in order to support our students. Having an ethical and affective framework is especially important because, as we have experienced during recent hurricanes and the pandemic, disasters have disproportionately negative impacts on students of color, lower-income students, and students with disabilities (Schlachte, 2019). We can communicate care and compassion through the language of our syllabi, the flexibility of our policies, and our willingness to address current hardships directly through course projects and materials when relevant to our subject matter. You might include a course policy that allows students to submit one or two select assignments late, for example, to assist students who are recovering from a natural disaster or are sick or caring for a sick loved one during a pandemic. Alternately, you might alter a writing assignment in a science writing course to suggest that students communicate scientific information to nonscience audiences about the natural disaster or the pandemic illness that may prompt them to learn more about the information on their own and improve their own situations.

Consider some of these strategies to help you decide which accommodations make sense for your courses:

1. *Create multiple pathways through course content.* Rather than requiring every student to complete the same assignments in the same way and in the same order, consider offering students options where possible. Could students select whether to complete a research essay or an exam to satisfy a learning objective? Could students complete, say, any six of a list of ten activities for one of your modules, allowing them some choice over their work? Could students determine which assignments weigh most heavily? According to the Eberly Center for Teaching Excellence and Educational Innovation at Carnegie Mellon University, "Creating a grading scheme that provides students with some flexibility in determining how their points get weighed across course assessments can also reduce cheating" (Eberly Center, 2020).
2. *If you want to make bolder changes in your course to respond to the crisis, you could try a new form of grading*: specifications grading, in which work is grouped into bundles and graded on an altered pass/fail scale (Nilsson, 2014); contract grading, which assigns no grades until the end of the semester, relies upon negotiated standards, and allows for revision, enabling students to determine more about their own experience (Inoue, 2015); or even ungrading, which veers even further from traditional classroom relationships and centers student autonomy (Flaherty, 2019). Whatever changes you make, though, clarity and consistency should lead the way; adding to student anxiety by introducing unclear or

inconsistent new ways of organizing course materials and grading will only make things worse for everyone. Communicate openly, clearly, and redundantly.

3. *Know your campus's resources that are likely to connect to the crisis at hand—and link those services' contact information to your course's site in the learning management system (LMS).* Depending upon what crisis you face, it is likely that you and/or your students will need to reach out to the professionals on your campus in counseling services, advising, student health, financial aid, online learning, and other areas. Finding their contact information and adding it to your LMS site makes sense for everyone and can save you time. Create a Campus Resources page and place it prominently in your site, then mention it in and link it to an announcement to the class. When students know where to turn, they get the specific help they need sooner—and they are less likely to turn to you with problems outside of your wheelhouse.

4. *In addition to the changes you make in your course itself, consider shifting your responses to student questions and requests as well.* Thinking in advance about how you will respond to students' individual needs will help you retain your equanimity as the crisis wears on—and can help you make some offers to the whole class that might head off problems before they arise. Will you allow presentations to be submitted via video recording or VoiceThread rather than an in-class performance? Will you allow attendance problems to be made up by viewing recorded lectures or otherwise engaging with course content and completing alternate assignments? For legitimate reasons, students will request specific, additional accommodations during a crisis. Offering options in advance that are available to everyone and have clear deadlines and submission information will make your job easier and your students' journey less stressful.

We encourage participants in our programs to create multiple pathways through course content, develop policies with maximal flexibility to accommodate student experiences, allow students to have choice and agency in assignments and course projects when feasible, and review all course assignments and policies through the lens of diversity and inclusion (see Columbia Center for Teaching and Learning, 2017). One relatively painless way that we often recommend to faculty to incorporate flexibility is to offer students options when completing small assignments. For example, if you ask students to post to a discussion board, require that they do so a specific number of times during the semester but offer a larger number of opportunities. That way, students can skip some posts when they are overwhelmed with other tasks or particularly troubled by crisis-related activities. With compassion and empathy, consider whether your approach allows for engagement and inclusion of every student and every circumstance that the crisis presents.

REINVENTION: THE ONLY WAY OUT IS THROUGH

When a crisis is protracted, we may need to reinvent our courses and our approaches entirely. During Summer 2020, for example, we hosted two online, four–week, course design institutes (CDI), one in June and one in July, during which we provided colleagues with strategies to develop their courses with change at the center of their designs and attitudes. We had hosted a Course Design Institute for several years before, always in person, in a networked classroom for a week. Trying it remotely over four weeks with two cohorts to manage the increased demand was a new challenge entirely: We reinvented it in the same way that we and our colleagues were reinventing our courses.

Specifically, we encouraged our faculty participants to infuse flexibility and become nimble in two main ways: structurally and relationally/compassionately. To be structurally nimble, faculty can emphasize transparency in their materials and course structures, create materials for multiple modalities, develop multiple ways for students to navigate the course based on their circumstances. Likewise, becoming relationally nimble involves incorporating compassion and empathy into course materials, assignments, and structures to account for the toll that uncertainty and actual disasters take on the ability of all students, but especially those at risk, to engage in learning and succeed in our courses.

To reinvent your course so that it is more structurally nimble, we recommend these possibilities:

1. *Convert some or all of your assignments using the Transparency in Learning and Teaching approach (TILT).* In this liquid time filled with change and uncertainty, the clarity emphasized by using TILT strategies offers reassurance to faculty that can be transferred to their students. The great thing about the TILT approach is that it is systematic—faculty can follow the guidelines on the TILT site (https://tilthighered.com/tiltexamplesandresources) to make their assignments transparent in ways that are easily recognizable and clear. As TILT resources indicate, the approach focuses on articulating for students many of the assumptions that underlie faculty's course materials, approaches, and assignments (Winkelmes, Boye, & Tapp, 2019). Thus, applying TILT requires you to analyze why you are teaching what you are teaching, why you selected the materials that you

include in your courses, and why you ask students to complete specific assignments and assessments. Upon completing an analysis of your purposes and motivations, which are often very well grounded but unarticulated, you are ready to make this information available to students.

Using the TILT approach does not require you to change what you are teaching or the assignments you include in your courses; the TILT analysis will help to reaffirm the legitimate purposes and contributions made to student learning by your approaches. In some cases, you may discover that an assignment or activity does not contribute to the overall purpose of the course, relate directly to students achieving what is articulated in student learning outcomes for the course, and/or falls short of helping to move students to the next level of understanding of the course materials. In this case, the TILT approach can help you to complete a more extensive overhaul of your course materials and assignments.

Many of the participants in our 2020 summer course design institute (CDI) sessions used the TILT approach to revise one or more of their assignments and clarify their course policies and structures. For example, one of our faculty participants, an anthropology professor, redesigned her global health infographic assignment for her medical anthropology course using TILT principles. This led her to clearly articulate the purpose of the assignment, connect it to relevant course SLOs, and outline precisely the format and deliverables to be submitted by students. Even more significantly, this professor provided detailed instructions for how students might approach completing the assignment—these incorporated a list of free infographic software that students could use and a heuristic for audience analysis for the final product. Finally, she also included a set of questions that would guide students through a self-reflection after developing their infographic design that asked them to consider the success of that design, reflect on the importance of using graphics to communicate across language barriers, and recognize the skills that they learned through completing the project.

As the professor explained in a reflection that she uploaded with her final revised assignment, through the TILT approach, she gained a better understanding of the role of this assignment in her course and was able to provide her students with a much clearer and more thorough assignment prompt. Not only will such a prompt help students to be more successful in completing the project, it will also decrease their level of uncertainty in this changeable learning environment, provide them with flexibility in completing the project through providing access to a multitude of free applications, and assist them to better understand the material via the use of critical reflection.

2. *Make sure that your course student learning outcomes, module or section objectives, course activities, and assessments are aligned.* Take this opportunity to check that every assignment and activity meets the objectives for its module or section and for your course learning outcomes. Even better, show your students how these activities and assessments align with the learning objectives so that they know why they are completing each component of the course—a key idea behind TILT and an important motivator.

   Not only did TILT help our faculty participants (and us) revise and clarify assignments, this approach, in conjunction with our other grounding philosophies of backward course design and Universal Design for Learning (UDL), also enabled our participants to become more structurally nimble through a process of reflection and in-depth analysis about their courses' designs, content, and policies. Most of our faculty participants submitted revised course materials at the completion of each CDI session, and a constant theme in those materials and corresponding reflections was a realization of the need to articulate the alignment between course SLOs, module/section objectives, learning activities, and assessments. Several participants, including a faculty member in French and one in Music, submitted tables presenting their newly conceived alignments of SLOs and learning activities and assessments. Although mapping these course elements seems like a simple exercise and straightforward process, the improvement to course structures and the clarity of instruction was potentially transformative. For example, through the mapping exercise, a French professor determined that she needed to change her course assessments and replace the brief discrete essay assignments in her capstone course with a multistaged, course-long project that would allow for a sustained drafting and revision process to better allow her to meet the course SLOs related to writing intensive courses.
3. *Use the learning management system (LMS) as the home base for your course.* To be maximally prepared for crises, we encourage structurally nimble pedagogical designs through planning all course interactions, activities, and assessments/assignments to be delivered in multiple modalities: face-to-face (f2f), hybrid (in all its definitions), and asynchronously and synchronously online. All preparation begins with considering course student learning outcomes (SLOs) and creating the most flexible ways to assist students to accomplish those outcomes regardless of context. To this end, we encourage faculty to treat our campus's learning management system (LMS), Canvas, as the center of their courses; preparing all materials in and through this system helps them to shift the methods of course delivery in response to the pandemic or the arrival of another storm. Not surprisingly, in Fall 2020, those shifts had to be made.

Designing courses for the use of multiple modalities while developing a complete course presence in the LMS helps to increase stability and clarity for students. All students can learn to rely on the course information in the LMS when attending synchronous online course meetings and f2f meetings. In this liquid time, constructing a course home in one reliable space provides students with surety and comfort—if they get sick or miss a synchronous meeting, they know where to find all instructions, schedules, and materials.

The LMS facilitates course spaces that are clearly structured, easy to navigate, and open to multiple paths of navigation to accommodate alternate patterns for student explorations. If you don't know how to use your LMS in these ways already, your campus's center for teaching and learning or center for online learning may be able to help. If your campus does not have these resources, your colleagues—or an internet search—will provide you with resources. The LMS used by your university will have user materials of its own to guide you as well. We advocate LMS-based design that helps our faculty participants to move away from structuring courses around assessments, exams, papers, or projects, and advocate creating learning modules instead that address specific SLOs for the course, contain a range of instructional activities, and incorporate multiple means of assessment, some of which are low stakes and formative.

4. *Use the tools in the LMS to monitor your students' engagement with the course—and keep in touch.* The LMS not only provides many tools to help you to better organize your courses and broadcast the structure to students, such as modules, the course calendar, and announcements, it also provides you with tools to monitor students' interactions and participations with the course through the system's metrics. In Canvas, you can view student engagement through New Analytics and find out immediately when and how often students are interacting with the course materials. For each student, you can see at a glance a dashboard of all assignments and their performance on them, page views organized by week, and communications from the student and the instructor in the course. Use this information to determine when students need assistance. In times of crisis, students may need more encouragement and individualized attention than usual. Decide which circumstances, such as not logging into the course for specified periods or missing specific assignments or exercises, will prompt you to reach out to students and offer support. Using the LMS as a course home makes these circumstances visible even though the students may not be physically present.

5. *Develop different pathways through your courses for different students.* During a crisis, students are experiencing our courses so differently and

may have life challenges and situations that require faculty to build in some level of choice and flexibility for how they can engage with our courses. As universal design for learning (UDL) principles emphasize, all students can be assisted by the course materials and structures created for students who are experiencing disruptions. UDL also emphasizes the need for clear policies and structures to help at-risk students, students with disabilities, and all students at once (Higbee & Goff, 2008). The level of choice offered to students does not have to be radical in order to be effective. It can be as simple as offering students a choice of low-stakes assignments or providing 12 exercises for students to complete but only requiring them to complete 10 of them.

Planning courses to incorporate this level of flexibility certainly requires additional effort prior to deployment; however, it can improve learning experiences for your students—encouraging more active learning and applied projects in place of routine lectures and exams—and preserve instructional continuity regardless of disaster type. Additionally, you can repurpose the materials for use in future semesters.

6. *Set dates to reach out to your students.* Even when students are engaging well with the course, it is worth the extra trouble to reach out on specific dates and check in with them during a time of crisis. You can schedule these extra communications, whether they are emails or extra videos or announcements in the LMS, in advance by thinking about the students' experiences in the course. Would a check-in that expresses admiration for students' efforts work best after every exam or major assignment? Would a check-in make more sense a week before each major deadline, outlining the support available as students complete the project? You know your course best, so think about how you can anticipate the biggest stressors and emphasize your presence and availability to your students as they navigate the crisis.

COMPROMISE: DECIDING WHAT GETS LOST—AND HOW TO PROCESS THE LOSS

Crises always bring compromise. No matter what, crises require sacrifices of some kind, whether it's as minor as lost time to reconfigure ruined plans or much, much worse. Perhaps the hardest part about dealing with compromise as faculty and as faculty developers is that we don't get to decide which sacrifices we will make: we don't decide what will be destroyed in a natural disaster or who will fall ill in a pandemic. The one place we retain some control is in our courses. The compromises we make in our courses to adapt to a crisis are within our locus of control and may ameliorate the experience of the crisis for us and for our students.

Here are the points that we recommend for you to keep in mind when determining what stays and what goes:

1. *With your crisis goggles on, cull everything that doesn't directly contribute to student learning outcomes (SLOs).* If an activity or assessment does not improve outcomes in the course, then now is not the time to keep it. Save it for another semester.
2. *Focus your energies where they will do the most good.* Use the analytics in the LMS to see which materials your students actually use. If you are spending enormous amounts of time creating detailed review packets and nearly no one is accessing them, or if you are recording elaborate video lectures that no one is watching, now is the time to reassess. If you aren't ready to drop the materials altogether, consider creating shorter versions and checking to see whether they are used more readily. Don't have good analytics for this? Then send your students a survey to find out which materials are the most helpful to them.
3. *Keep doing what you enjoy as long as you can use it in another semester—and let your current students know that it's optional.* Perhaps you originally planned to ask students to use an advanced application, like Adobe InDesign, to complete an assignment but the crisis causes a time crunch that prompts you to use something that students already know, like Microsoft Word. Even when you know that most of your crisis-period students won't be able to take advantage of the more advanced software, you can still provide them with the information and tutorials about it. Students who have used it previously might individually select the more advanced option. The key is to emphasize to your current students that its use is optional; accomplishing the assignment goals is the most important outcome. Additionally, this is a great opportunity to collect feedback on materials for a later semester from those students who do try it.

The hard part about cutting back on the assignments, videos, and activities that we have created is that we like them. It stings! That's where the processing comes in: We have to figure out the best ways to let go of What Might Have Been while we are scrambling to make the best of What Is. A few of our favorite ideas for processing the losses that come with crises:

1. *Acknowledge the loss.* Find a trusted colleague who is willing to swap tales with you of the things that you are saddest about losing specifically in your classes. Give some space to the legitimate grief you feel

and don't worry about whether it is as significant as the next person's suffering.
2. *Connect with your students' losses.* Focusing on the needs of your students in your classes right now will help you keep the loss in perspective. The crisis took opportunities away from your students—whether it was study abroad, internships, face-to-face classes and labs, or being able to participate in a live graduation ceremony—and supporting their process will help you make your way through your own. For example, when you meet with individual students to check in about their work in your course, you might also ask them about what plans they had to alter in response to the crisis and provide them with any guidance about making up those experiences in the future.
3. *Nurture yourself and your creativity.* We survive crises through disruption, collaboration, accommodation, reinvention, and compromise. We can't do any of those things without resolve and creativity. Know what you need to replenish your energy and to feed your creativity and give yourself permission to do those things. It may be exercise, mindfulness practice, naps, time with family, or any number of other possibilities. Whatever it is, strive to continue it as much as the crisis will allow so that the losses you feel will seem smaller than the strength you have left.

CONCLUSIONS

All five of these aspects of crisis—disruption, collaboration, accommodation, reinvention, and compromise—are challenging. None of us would choose to disrupt our lives suddenly and unpredictably. But when we consider these aspects in their verb form, they seem more positive, more hopeful: to disrupt may result in loss but may also provide unforeseen opportunities; to collaborate is to join strengths to build something better; to accommodate makes room for others; to reinvent is to create new possibilities; to compromise is to allow for other views of the way forward. When UNCW struggled to find a way forward after Hurricane Florence, the *Chronicle of Higher Education* (Crowe, 2018) included a comment from then president of the UNC System Margaret Spellings about all of the help offered to the campus from the state System and from the local, state, and federal government to bring the campus and its community back together: "Everybody is aware that it could be you next time, so it's just heartwarming to see the collaboration and the teamwork and the generosity of spirit that's been at play here in the last week."

At UNCW in 2021, we can see both progress and continued disruption. The buildings damaged by Hurricane Florence have now been fully rebuilt. New student housing has been completed to replace the apartments that were damaged beyond repair and have since been demolished. On the other hand, while the trailers that temporarily housed the science labs and courses have recently been removed and the parking lot will soon be repaved and reopened, few cars regularly park on campus as many of our courses are still being delivered online due to the pandemic. Likewise, the occupation of new student housing is well below prepandemic levels. Tangible effects from our cascade of crises remain as does our need to continue to adapt. As we prepare for the Fall 2021 semester, we wonder about the possibility of returning to in-person learning and some semblance of the campus culture we left. Uncertainty persists for us all.

Our liquid time necessitates revisioning how we approach university teaching at all levels from our assignments to our interactions with and relationships to our students. We cannot rely on our courses being delivered in the spaces and using the strategies upon which we have always relied. The external chaos brought on by present and future disasters must be mitigated through increased planning, flexibility, and a different sort of certainty, namely our confidence in the important learning experiences that we can offer our students and deliver in a myriad of ways. As faculty, we need to create transparent, accessible, and rich course materials and learning opportunities so that the robust education we provide can be one of the constants for students in this liquid time. We are already equipped with the skills and tools to do this; each new crisis just tells us that the time is now.

REFERENCES

Block, S. H., Bryant Block, C., & Peters, A. A. (2012). *Mind-body workbook for stress: Effective tools for lifelong stress reduction.* Oakland, CA: New Harbinger Publications.

Columbia Center for Teaching and Learning. (2017). *Guide for inclusive teaching at Columbia.* https://ctl.columbia.edu/resources-and-technology/resources/inclusive-teaching-guide/

Crowe, C. (2018, October 5). Nearly one month after Hurricane Florence, this campus is still picking up the pieces. *Chronicle of Higher Education.* https://www.chronicle.com/article/nearly-one-month-after-hurricane-florence-this-campus-is-still-picking-up-the-pieces/

Eberly Center for Teaching Excellence and Educational Innovation. (2020). Use criterion-referenced grading. https://www.cmu.edu/teaching/solveproblem/strat-cheating/cheating-06.html

Flaherty, C. (2019, April 2). When grading less is more. *Inside Higher Ed.* https://www.insidehighered.com/news/2019/04/02/professors-reflections-their-experiences-ungrading-spark-renewed-interest-student

Gigliotti, R. A. (2016). Leader as performer; leader as human: A discursive and retrospective construction of crisis leadership. *Atlantic Journal of Communication, 24*(4): 185–200.

Green, L., & Gary, K. (2016). Pedagogy for a liquid time. *Studies in Philosophy and Education, 35*: 47–62.

Higbee, J. L., & Goff, E. (Eds.). (2008). *Pedagogy and student services for institutional transformation: Implementing universal design in higher education.* Minneapolis: University of Minnesota.

Inoue, A. (2015). *Antiracist writing assessment ecologies: Teaching and assessing writing for a socially just future.* Fort Collins, CO: WAC Clearinghouse and Parlor Press. https://wac.colostate.edu/books/inoue/

Lemon, N., & Salmons, J. (2021). *Reframing and rethinking collaboration in higher education and beyond: A practical guide for doctoral students and early career researchers.* New York: Routledge.

Nilsson, L. (2014). *Specifications grading: Restoring rigor, motivating students, and saving faculty time.* Sterling, VA: Stylus.

Pecore, J. L. (2020). Teaching mindfulness for pandemic times. *Curriculum and Teaching Dialogue, 22*(1/2): 163–165.

Schlachte, C. P. (2019). *Before the aftermath: A pedagogy for disaster responsiveness* (Publication No. 13808800) [Doctoral dissertation, University of North Carolina at Greensboro]. ProQuest Dissertations Publishing.

Shiwaku, K., & Shaw, R. (2016). Introduction: Disaster risk reduction and education system. In K. Shiwaku, A. Sakurai, & R. Shaw (Eds.), *Disaster resilience of education systems* (pp. 1–10). Japan: Springer.

Simmons, N., & Singh, A. (Eds.). (2019). *Critical collaborative communities.* Leiden, Netherlands: Brill/Sense.

Vanasupa, L., Schlemer, L., Burton, R., Brogno, C., Hendrix, G., & MacDougall, N. (2014). Laying the foundation for transdisciplinary faculty collaborations: Actions for a sustainable future. *Sustainability, 6*: 2893–2928. doi:10.3390/su6052893

Walsh, L., & Kahn, P. (2010). *Collaborative working in higher education: The social academy.* New York: Routledge.

Wang, J. (2019). Framework of school disaster education and resilience: Context and structure. In I. Pal, J. von Meding, S. Shrestha, I. Ahmed, & T. Gajendran (Eds.), *An interdisciplinary approach for disaster resilience and sustainability* (pp. 313–38). Singapore: Springer.

Winkelmes, M., Boye, A., & Tapp, S. (2019). *Transparent design in higher education teaching and leadership: A guide to implementing the transparency framework institution-wide to improve learning and retention.* Sterling, VA: Stylus.

Chapter Five

Studying Abroad During a Time of Disaster

An Exploration of Pitfalls, Pivots, and Possibilities for the Future

Kara Pike Inman, Nicole Desjardins Gowdy, and Jason Kinnear

For decades, higher educational institutions around the globe have actively sought to enhance their global dimensions and increase the number of students who engage in global educational experiences (Altbach & Knight, 2007; Larsen & Dutschke, 2010; McCabe, 2001; McCallon & Holmes, 2010). As these increases in participation occur, it is integral for both educators and administrators to consider the unique needs of this growing student population, particularly in times of crisis. This chapter provides a brief overview of the types of disasters experienced by education abroad participants, describes the risk management response and decision-making processes undertaken by international educators, explores the challenges students experience when disasters strike abroad, provides recommendations of how faculty and administrators can best assist this unique population during crises, and considers new opportunities uncovered by the current COVID-19 situation for the future of international education.

The field of education abroad has a long history of monitoring and managing complex situations in a variety of forms. Within just the last 20 years, international educators have worked with students abroad experiencing wars, civil and political unrest, terrorist attacks, epidemics/pandemics, nuclear disasters, and natural disasters, while also reacting to fears of being abroad in the wake of domestic incidents like the attacks on the United States on September 11, 2001. In spite of the potential risks associated with international travel and study, universities have recognized the importance for students to gain global perspectives, positioning education abroad experiences as an integral component of institutional practices and academic programs (Altbach

& Knight, 2007; McCabe, 2001). Given this emphasis on global experiences, the number of college and university students who study abroad on an annual basis has increased rapidly, with participant numbers more than tripling over the past two decades. During the 2018–2019 academic year alone, more than 347,099 U.S. college students participated in an education abroad experience for academic credit (Institute of International Education, 2020).

For students, studying abroad may fulfill course requirements for graduation; provide international internship, service-learning, or research opportunities; increase proficiency in another language; facilitate critical engagement with local and global issues through a new lens; assist in developing personal and professional skills valued by employers; and satisfy departmental or institutional global experience requirements (Allen, 2010; Anderson & Lawton, 2015). Although student motivations for participation also include cultural engagement, travel opportunities, and personal growth (Pope, Sánchez, Lehnert, & Schmid, 2014), the ability to earn academic credit is integral to the experience. When disaster situations interrupt student experiences abroad or necessitate that students end their international experiences early, students face a variety of challenges. These challenges can include financial hardship, emotional stress, logistical obstacles, dislocation from support networks, and a lack of academic continuity.

WHERE IS EVERYBODY?

A key component of mounting an effective response in a crisis is knowing where students are and how to reach them. A number of tools are available to assist with tracking and locating students during their travel abroad. At a minimum, program administrators should keep program dates, locations, lists of students, and contact information easily accessible to identify which students may be in a particular location when an incident occurs. Students should be encouraged, if not required, to notify program staff when traveling away from their program's primary location. Travel registration systems with a dashboard accessible to program administrators can help faculty and staff locate students immediately; however, they also rely on student compliance in registering their travel (including any personal side trips). As an example, during the Paris attacks of November 2015, the University of North Carolina Wilmington had a number of students who were spending the semester studying there. Additionally, several students who were studying in Ireland for the semester had traveled to Paris that weekend. Since these students had registered their travel away from Ireland with their home university, all students who were in Paris at the time of the attacks could be accounted for quickly. Similarly, when attacks occurred on airports in Brussels and Istanbul, students who were not studying in either city but whose flights routed through these airports were impacted. As these students had shared their flight itineraries and travel plans via a travel registry system, their home institutions could reach out to them, confirm their well-being, and connect them with assistance (e.g., travel logistics, counseling services, etc.) as needed. These enhancements in systems provide a welcome addition to our field and are a far cry from the work staff had to undertake in previous years. For example, immediately following the terrorist attacks of September 11, 2001, education abroad staff relied primarily on phone calls and emails to partners abroad in an attempt to account for students, a daunting activity that took hours to identify the locations of students.

* * *

VIGNETTE: Dealing With the November 2015 Paris Attacks

At 4:00 p.m. on a Friday afternoon in the Study Abroad Office, one normally starts to wind down—sure, there is the knowledge that students in Europe are out and about, many of them have traveled to other cities and countries, but in the many years of working in education abroad, there haven't been too many phone calls and when they do come, they are usually later, mostly around 8:00 p.m. or later when the bars tend to close in many European cities. The calls are often related to alcohol abuse; however, local partners and sometimes other students are there giving help to the affected student. Once I know the student is being cared for, and the appropriate persons have been notified, I can return to my weekend activities.

Friday, November 13, 2015—shortly before 4:00 p.m., I receive an update from one of my French news agencies with the horrible news that there have been numerous shootings and bombings in Paris, France. Immediately, my risk management training comes to the forefront: I start checking on our students currently studying in Paris. I'm on our database in no time and pull up all their information. Very quickly, I start receiving notices from our partners abroad and check them to see which students have already been contacted, which students have reported in and so are safe. We had less than 10 students in the Paris area. I'm also listening to the live French news (I'm fluent in French) and hear more about the details of where the attacks have taken place; I learn about the attempted bombings at the Stade de France where a France/Germany soccer game is going on. I start making phone calls and, surprisingly, I get through to some of the students, most of them are with their host families or are not in the affected areas of Paris.

There is one student that I can't reach, and I think she may be traveling outside of Paris. Then I think of all the students who may be in Paris—I quickly get on the STEP (Smart Traveler Enrollment Program) website but it is sluggish and I realize few of our students have uploaded their weekend travel information. I am certain that we have students from all over Europe who may have traveled to Paris for the weekend. I am the Director for Continental Europe programs and can access the database for all these students. I watch live what's happening at the Bataclan concert hall as well as other places in Paris. I am now the only person in the office and it is close to 6:00 p.m. I still haven't heard from some students. I write an email to ALL the students in Europe (except those in Paris)—I just want to inform them, let them know we know what has happened, that we are in contact with students in Paris and they are safe (except for that one) but most importantly, I ask them to report in on their location and how they are doing.

I want to reassure them that if they are not in France, they are probably not in danger; I request that they contact their families and reassure them. I ask if any traveled to Paris and, if so, to report back to me via all means available (sms, WhatsApp, email, phone call) about their well-being. During this time, I am also constantly reporting to the director of our office as well as the provost and chancellor. Very soon, I start to receive messages from students—so many are fine and thank me for contacting them and giving them news. They report on other students traveling with them, they even tell me if they know which students went to Paris. Some have news from those students.

I head home around 9:00 p.m. and continue to receive messages from students and partners. I find out that there was a group of eight students at the Stade de France for the soccer match, they are safe and back at their hotels. They had come together from England, Italy, and Germany and were in Paris for the weekend. Others from Italy were also there but all are safe. I still have not heard directly from the one student in Paris; her parents don't believe she was going out as "she doesn't do that much at all" but they can't reach her either. On Saturday morning, she emails me to tell me she was in bed and had her phone off!!! WHEW!

By 3:00 a.m. on Saturday, I have heard back from the majority of the students I emailed. I send out another email reassuring them that students are safe and ask them again to reassure their parents, families and friends, and their program staff. I strongly advise them to enter their weekend travel information in STEP and the UNC travel registry.

I head off to bed around 3:30 a.m. to get some rest thinking about my own friends who live in Paris.

I sometimes share about this night in predeparture orientations as I ask students to enroll in STEP and update it with their weekly travel. Nevertheless, the ability to quickly contact students via our database made it possible to quickly get responses from students.

Only one of the students based in Paris returned to the United States before the end of the semester. Many students expressed their gratitude for the follow-up emails.

* * *

In addition to having a travel registry system, working with third-party providers can greatly enhance the capacity of education abroad offices and faculty program directors to manage and mitigate risk. On-site and U.S.-based staff monitor local conditions in program destinations, keep track of students' whereabouts, and communicate with students and home schools in a crisis. Providers also coordinate on-site emergency response and evacuation, if needed. Most third-party providers will also provide students with local and international medical and emergency evacuation insurance.

When assessing third-party providers for new partnerships, it is important to ask about their overall philosophy and approach to health, safety, and security; communication plans; medical and evacuation insurance coverage; and the provider's general approach to supporting students in a crisis. The Forum on Education Abroad's *Standards of Good Practice for Education Abroad* (2020) offers tools to help assess programs and factors to consider when developing new programs and partnerships. More specifically, the Forum has also developed a set of "Guidelines for Conducting Education Abroad During COVID-19" (2020) that address health, safety, and security considerations among others.

SHOULD THEY STAY OR SHOULD THEY GO?

When a disaster strikes abroad, after accounting for all students and confirming their safety, the next step for education abroad staff is to assess the situation and determine the best course of action for student participants. This typically involves a decision about whether they can remain in the host country or must return home, each of which comes with a variety of challenges. Health, safety, and security should be at the forefront of decision-making about whether to stay or depart; however, the decision for whether to allow students to remain on-site may also hinge on whether their program remains operational, what on-site support is available to students, consistency of access to commercial transportation for departure, changes to travel advisories and other official indicators, and what means are available for ensuring academic continuity.

Remaining in the host country requires constant ongoing vigilance in monitoring and assessing the current conditions and being prepared to shift plans swiftly if needed. Students should be oriented with information and updates on local health, safety, and security conditions as well as local laws and guidelines. These may include restrictions on movement and gatherings; access to medical care and emergency response; availability and limitations of on-site staff support; and potential for local curfews, strikes, lockdowns, and border closures. Responsibilities and expectations should be made clear to students, and the nuances will depend on whether the program remains operational or whether students are choosing to remain on-site independently after a program closes for the rest of the term. In either case, universities must be prepared to advise and discuss with students issues of liability and potential inability to assist with any future travel needs. Students should be well-informed and understand the risk and responsibility they are assuming if they remain on-site. Programs and universities may wish to have students review and sign an updated informed consent or assumption of risk document to include more information about health, safety, and security changes in the new environment.

In some cases, early departure or suspension of on-site program operations will be the best and safest option. During the fall 2019 semester, civil unrest and protests in Hong Kong necessitated weeks of close monitoring and communication with students and home universities to share updates on local conditions. After weeks of watchful advising as the situation escalated, many programs and universities made the decision to return students back home. It is important to consider the impact such a decision will have on students' academics, emotional well-being, and financial capabilities.

Programs should be prepared for the possibility that some students may choose or feel they have no choice but to remain on-site after their program closes and should have a clear plan for how to handle these cases. For example, during the recent evacuations due to COVID-19, students faced ethical and logistical questions related to departure. Some of these dilemmas included fears of contracting the virus during a period of heightened exodus from high-risk locations, potentially exposing other travelers or their families back home to a virus they may have contracted before departing or while in transit, risks of returning to a location that may have a higher prevalence of the virus than the location they would be leaving, concerns about access to health care or local response to the pandemic in the places they would return to, or the challenge of not having a home to which they can return.

In one example during the COVID-19 pandemic, a student whose program closed on-site operations in Europe in mid-March 2020 was not able to return to her parents' home in Asia because they were not a citizen or legal resident of the country in which they lived (as expatriates) and the country had closed its borders to all incoming travelers who were not citizens or residents. The student could not stay in their program housing, nor could they return to their home campus in the United States, which had also closed its residence halls. Furthermore, the student was not a U.S. citizen and as such was not able to enter the United States after the ban on travel from Europe for non-U.S. citizens.

Likewise, the student had no place to go in the country that issued their passport. The student remained alone and in limbo throughout the spring and summer as they waited to learn about their home campus's plans for whether to bring students back for the fall semester as well as for the reopening of borders that would allow her to rejoin her parents. Fortunately, the student was able to secure housing in the host study abroad country through family connections and complete the semester remotely. The home school study abroad office provided financial support for her housing, meals, and onward airfare (as part of their home school comprehensive fee model for study abroad) and checked in on the student a few times throughout the remainder of the semester.

Other students evacuated from programs during the COVID-19 pandemic faced challenges of not wanting to put immunocompromised family members at risk by returning home from locations with high prevalence of the virus. Students experiencing homelessness or abusive home situations did not have a safe home to return to, and when unable to return to their home campus, found themselves needing to suddenly find a solution and funds to live independently for the remainder of the term. One nontraditional student, a single mother whose daughter was abroad with her and attending elementary school, stayed abroad because she did not have a home for them to return to in the United States and also did not want to jeopardize her daughter's academic progress.

Students who have stayed abroad during or immediately after a disaster offer examples of resilience and determination to conclude their academic studies. After events such as September 11, 2001, the bombings in Madrid in 2004 and London in 2005, and the recent COVID-19 pandemic in 2020, students who remained abroad shared stories of their success and gratitude for being able to stay on-site. These stories of continued academic and language learning, coping with shutdowns and curfews, and learning to navigate under increased uncertainty and ambiguity demonstrated students' continual growth and increased ability to cope in unpredictable situations.

* * *

VIGNETTE: Lessons Learned from Cairo

In January 2011, Elon University had six students enrolled at a partner university in Cairo. We had been monitoring reports from the Overseas Security Advisory Council (OSAC) as a matter of routine practice, with particular attention to the growing unrest across the Arab world that had been ignited in Tunisia two months earlier. Heeding advice—from our office and from a local student they had befriended—to avoid the demonstrations in Cairo, five of our six students had accompanied the friend to his family's vacation home near the beach in Sharm El-Sheikh, about 5.5 hours away by car.

Leverage Partnerships and Relationships

In this case the in-country, on-site expertise and knowledge of colleagues at our partner institution and friends of Elon was invaluable. Our students in Sharm El-Sheikh were safe from the protests in Cairo, but their access to television and internet was disrupted. Our office, senior staff, and families were following constant live news from Tahrir Square and other protest sites throughout Cairo. We were also in frequent contact with in-country colleagues.

Our top priority was to safely evacuate the students from Egypt, which would require their return to Cairo. Initially the roads were blocked on the way back to Cairo, so the five students remained at the coast. Once travel was possible, our on-site partners recommended that they go directly to the new university campus, well outside the city, avoiding any attempt to access the students' residences in the city's center. The partner university then transported the students to the airport for evacuation flights coordinated by the embassy.

While safety and evacuation were the immediate priority, quickly identifying and coordinating viable options for the semester was also critical to save their semester. While a return to the Elon campus was one option, the students were committed to spending the semester abroad and the study of Arabic, and the semester abroad was a requirement for several of their majors. At the same time we leveraged existing partnerships with other institutions and programs in the region. We were able to quickly identify two programs, one a university-based program in Israel, and the other a study center-based program administered by a U.S. provider in Jordan. The students—sheltered from the unrest and violence that was occurring in Cairo—were resistant to departing Egypt and felt like they were being forced to leave. Presenting the students with multiple options—return to the United States, study in Israel, or study in Jordan—allowed them to regain some sense of control. Building on an existing relationship with the partner in Israel, we were able to coordinate a phone meeting between the students and the program director. This enabled the students to make an informed decision to opt for the semester in Israel as their best option.

Finally, we took advantage of informal relationships. The sixth Elon student in Cairo was an overseas American citizen, the son of a U.S. executive who led his corporation's Middle East operations at its Cairo headquarters. The student's parents were able to provide insights into status of the American expat community in Cairo, and shared the steps that corporations were taking to protect their employees and their families. They even offered to help our other five students with security and access to cash while the ATM machines were out of service. This situation was not as uncommon as it may seem. Most of us have extensive alumni and parent networks throughout the world. These individuals with a connection to our institutions, and an understanding of our students, can provide important insights that bridge the geographic and cultural divides that can exist even with our strongest partners.

Parental Expectations on Communication

The students were eventually safely evacuated to Istanbul and were then able to continue to Israel a few days later to recommence their semester. Despite this success, some of the parents involved expressed a level of displeasure in a letter to the university president. A review of the facts of the case confirmed, as is indicated above, that we had acted quickly, proactively, and efficiently. However, the parents perceived that the host institution in Egypt and the new host institution had "done all the work." This was perhaps the most important lesson learned. While we understood that we had done quite a significant amount of work in vetting, establishing, and collaborating with quality partnerships, the parents viewed Elon and these institutions very separately. This informed our practice moving forward, both ahead of and during crisis response. Ahead of time, more emphasis was given in promotional and predeparture sessions to underscore the role of our partners. Additionally, during times of future crisis, we were mindful of always communicating frequently directly with parents, even if it seemed to be repetitive information that had been shared by partners and repetitive of our communications with the students.

* * *

If required to return home, having to abruptly depart their host location and cut short their international experience is inherently stressful. Students may face the challenge of changing their return travel arrangements and incurring associated fees. Flight cancellations, airport closures, or border closures further complicate this process as students seeking to return home may not be able to do so or may have to wait for an official evacuation process to occur. Students from multiple U.S. universities who were studying abroad in Peru and Ecuador at the onset of the COVID-19 pandemic were unable to depart prior to border closings.

Some of these students had to locate temporary accommodations as they waited to be contacted by the U.S. Department of State about an available seat on an evacuation flight. Typically, these evacuation flights do not include food or beverage service and evacuate U.S. citizens to a designated U.S. city, which may be hundreds or even thousands of miles away from the students' homes within the United States. One student reported arriving into the United States on an evacuation flight hungry, disoriented, in a city to which he had never been, in the middle of a pandemic, only to then need to hire an expensive one-way rental car to navigate his way to his hometown several states away. In addition, U.S. government evacuation flights are generally available only to U.S. citizens, and programs and universities should have plans in place to support non–U.S.-citizen study abroad participants. In some instances, universities have contracted with private entities to evacuate students at significant expense.

Education abroad staff should engage key stakeholders in decision-making about whether to maintain on-site operations or recall students back home. These stakeholders may include senior leadership, academic deans, student affairs deans, risk management staff, finance office, registrar, legal counsel, and relevant campus committees such as those overseeing the curriculum and academic policy, education abroad, international travel, risk management, and emergency response. The institution's insurance provider and evacuation services provider can also be valuable resources to provide information and assessment. It is crucial that education abroad staff know decisions are aligned with their institution's philosophy and overall approach to crisis management and that they have the support of senior leadership and relevant offices to weigh in on and affirm the decision. Furthermore, ensuring relevant campus faculty and staff are in the loop helps prepare individuals for their role in supporting students and for coordinating a cohesive campus response.

Regardless of whether the university decides to recall all participants or allow students to remain abroad, clearly communicating policy and decision-making procedures to campus stakeholders and parents is critical. No matter what is decided or which path is taken, education abroad staff will likely hear from parents who disagree with the decision. In spring 2020, as campuses were figuring out the best course of action for students at home and abroad during the COVID-19 pandemic, staff were inundated with calls from parents, some who argued that decisions were made too quickly to force students to return, while others thought that the call to come home was not made fast enough. In other cases, when students chose to remain overseas or when students were not required to return, parents called the education abroad office to demand that students be forced to return. Developing consistent communication plans and remaining on message is key to helping staff navigate the intricacies of communicating with parents and families.

* * *

TECHNOLOGICAL LIMITATIONS

Depending on the circumstances within the students' host country, technology and transportation services may be unreliable or unavailable, leaving students stranded with limited communication ability. When earthquakes, tsunamis, hurricanes, and other natural disasters impact students, regular electricity and Internet services can be inaccessible for days or even weeks. When the University of North Carolina Wilmington was hit by Hurricane Florence in September 2018, parts of the city and surrounding area were without power for a week or more, and the campus was shut down for a full month. International students who had evacuated with friends or via an official campus evacuation process may have thought they would only be gone from campus for a few days, then found themselves stranded in unfamiliar locations for several weeks. Students who did not bring their laptops with them or who relied on campus computer labs for technology access were particularly disconnected. Additionally, some campus housing was damaged to the point where students could not return and had to be relocated to off-campus housing or hotels for the remainder of the semester.

In 2010, when the Eyjafjallajökull volcano erupted in Iceland, concerns that the volcanic ash would damage aircraft engines led to the largest air-traffic shutdown since World War II (Rincon, 2011). The eruptions occurred during the middle of many European universities' spring semester at a time when large numbers of universities held their spring or Easter break. Given this timing, education abroad participants who were traveling during this vacation period found their return flights cancelled and had to find creative ways to navigate their way back to their host campuses.

While this navigation certainly provided an excellent opportunity for students to use their problem-solving skills, it also proved to be a stressful and time-consuming experience for many students as they traveled overland or by water instead of via a quick and easy airline return. In both this situation and the hurricane example above, students' ability to access technology and resources at their host campuses were significantly impacted by factors outside of their control. Students impacted in these situations expressed appreciation for course instructors and administrators who exercised empathy and flexibility in these situations.

SUPPORTING STUDENTS

In order to support students holistically during this time of heightened stress, uncertainty, and disruption, faculty and administrative empathy, flexibility, and collaboration with other campus offices, such as financial services, counseling, and student affairs is imperative. As the challenges of the COVID-19 pandemic mounted, Pomona College's Office of Study Abroad, Registrar, Finance Office, Information Technology Services, and Study Abroad Committee worked closely together to pivot and modify academic and financial policies to offer flexibility and support to students whose programs had been disrupted.

These changes included extending the Pass/No Credit grading request deadline until the last day of class, allowing students to reduce course loads, waiving specific course requirements (such as host country language courses), modifying the withdrawal fee policy to better support students whose programs might no longer be offering the opportunity to earn a full semester of credit, providing prorated room and/or board refunds regardless of whether the student's program refunded these expenses, and shipping laptops and WiFi hotspots to students for use at no cost to the student. During this same time, the University of North Carolina Wilmington, like many universities around the United States, partnered with its counseling center to offer designated sessions to students who had returned home early due to the pandemic so they could discuss their experiences as well as the sadness and stress that they felt in having their experience cut short.

As students depart from the academic experiences they have been pursuing abroad, providing these students with as much academic continuity as possible is crucial. During the COVID-19 outbreak in spring 2020, many programs switched to online learning, which allowed students to continue their quest to obtain academic credit for their experience. However, students expressed frustration with many aspects of this situation, such as a greatly diminished interaction with fellow students and instructors, as well as struggling to stay engaged with online learning while based in a different time zone. Some students found themselves waking up in the middle of the night to join online synchronous lectures at 3 a.m., particularly when instructors did not provide recordings of these lectures as an alternative. These students shared the difficulties they felt in trying to focus on course material during a peak time for sleeping as well as a great appreciation for those faculty members who were willing to be more flexible in offering options for them to engage with course material asynchronously.

Students who were taking courses taught in their nonnative language also expressed struggles when their coursework shifted to an online format. While taking face-to-face courses abroad, these students had the benefit of gestures, facial expressions, and other visual cues to assist them in discerning meaning from lectures and class discussions (Gregerson, 2007). However, when these courses went online, many faculty would display a slide show with voice-overs rather than showing themselves on the screen or would teach via prerecorded lessons that inhibited students' ability to ask for clarification. Language-learning or nonnative speaking students in these situations no longer had the ability to ascertain meaning from nonverbal elements of speech or confirm their understanding of course material through live or immediate interactions with their instructors.

Structural changes to an institution's academic calendar could also benefit students whose international experiences are impacted due to crisis situations. For large numbers of students who were planning to spend their spring 2020 semester studying in countries like Germany, South Korea, Japan, or Peru, their semesters abroad had not yet begun at the time when their home universities began calling students to return home due to the COVID-19 pandemic. In these countries, the first semester of the calendar year typically begins in March or April, in contrast to most U.S. institutions whose semesters begin in January. Since these students' international experiences were cancelled before they began, but their home institutions had already been holding classes for two or more months, some found themselves in situations where they were not able to earn academic credit for the spring 2020 semester. However, students in this situation whose home institutions offered block course schedules were more fortunate in that they could enroll in courses for the second part of the spring semester, thus still being able to progress toward graduation. Although this benefit of block course scheduling was illuminated by the COVID-19 pandemic, it could also be advantageous to other students who experience disasters while studying abroad.

Finally, for institutions that offer embedded faculty-led programs in which an education abroad experience is part of a larger academic course, it is essential that the faculty leaders consider ways to achieve the same or similar learning outcomes if the travel component of the course cannot take place. As a result of the COVID-19 pandemic, many faculty members whose courses had embedded travel experiences scheduled to take place during spring break or at the end of the spring semester had to quickly pivot to find virtual tours, online guest lectures, alternate assignments, and other creative ways to make up contact hours and achieve learning outcomes that were intended to be fulfilled abroad. Some institutions now require their faculty to include academic continuity plans as part of their proposals to lead faculty-led education abroad experiences.

MAKING A PLAN

The key to successfully responding to a disaster abroad is to ensure that campus officials develop and implement an emergency action plan to handle a global crisis. Despite many campuses working diligently to address local and domestic situations, a global crisis may bring about new challenges for university officials. Education abroad staff should be able to connect with other risk management staff and groups across campus, working together to muster campus resources to support students who are abroad.

The University of North Carolina at Chapel Hill utilizes a Risk Management Advisory Committee for Education Abroad (RMAC), which draws individuals from Campus Police, Dean of Students, Risk Management, academic units, and a variety of the global offices across campus. As a disaster or pandemic unfolds, groups like this can meet to discuss a situation as it evolves, examining current conditions to provide guidance to university officials regarding the status of travelers abroad and helping to guide policy and practice on campus. Such advisory groups are also crucial for postevent debrief, exploring what went well and areas of practice and policy that need revision in anticipation of future calamitous events.

Maintaining clear expectations, guidelines, and support structures is essential to the success of international education endeavors. Campuses should have well-articulated travel policies for students, faculty, and staff, outlining requirements such as travel registration, insurance, and any rules or restrictions related to high-risk travel. In the case of faculty-led student travel, it is common for institutions to have a review process for such trips, to consider the academic imperative of the travel, health and safety risks and precautions, and the structure for support for the faculty leaders and students. There should be a clear process for communication with the home campus during the time abroad and specific contacts identified for general and emergency support. Universities should develop and deliver training for faculty leaders to equip them with the tools to respond in an emergency and to familiarize them with the policies, procedures, and individuals that will guide and support their leadership while abroad.

New Opportunities and Conclusions

After any disaster or global crisis impacting international education, educators should seek to learn from the experience, continually update and improve services and responses, explore ways to meet the needs of students impacted by global disasters, and find ways to provide global educational opportunities to all interested students. Throughout the most recent pandemic, international educators have focused on discussing other possibilities for future global opportunities. While virtual exchanges, Collaborative Online International Learning (COIL), and remote global internships are not new initiatives, recent border closures, travel restrictions, and social distancing measures have shifted focus from programmatic options that rely solely on physical student mobility and have increased the prevalence of these virtual modes of global learning. The benefits of these virtual global learning options are vast, particularly in terms of increasing student access and inclusion, not only during times of disaster, but also as a supplement and complement to traditional forms of international education.

The COVID-19 pandemic enriched educators, students, and institutions with tools to navigate global learning in a virtual environment. This has also set the stage for responding to future disasters, as programs and institutions are now much more prepared to switch to a remote learning if needed. As we reimagine global learning in the 21st century, many institutions are asking whether virtual exchanges and remote global learning have a more permanent place in our international education portfolios. Virtual global learning programs may provide increased access to groups traditionally underrepresented in (or excluded from) study abroad including first generation college students, students from low-income backgrounds, student athletes, nontraditional students, and undocumented students.

As programs and institutions consider these options, it is imperative to remain aware of other disparities in access that may still exclude certain students. These disparities may include not having technology needed to participate in such opportunities, views on the value of virtual experiences, language skills necessary for participation, and the cost of these programs in addition to regular tuition.

Educators should be mindful of these potential disparities as institutions around the globe embrace opportunities for students to engage in remote global internships, virtual exchanges, online guest lectures from faculty at partner institutions, remote research collaborations, and other online collaborative activities. Additionally, virtual options should complement, not replace, education abroad experiences that involve physical travel. As educators around the globe strive to improve in areas of diversity, equity, inclusion, and justice, it is critical that work continues to remove barriers of participation to all education abroad experiences rather than simply seeing virtual opportunities as a separate but equal option for certain types of students.

Through shifts in the safety and infrastructure of both home and host destinations, ebbs and flows of participation, and situations that required innovation and problem-solving, education abroad professionals have demonstrated tenacity and creativity in maintaining global learning opportunities for students. A key factor in this success is the overall preparedness and professionalism of emergency response in the field of education abroad. This competence is crucial to help students, families, and institutions maintain confidence in the overall safety and transformative power of global education experiences.

REFERENCES

Allen, H. W. (2010). Language-learning motivation during short-term study abroad: An activity theory perspective. *Foreign Language Annals, 43*(1), 27–49.

Altbach, P. G., & Knight, J. (2007). The internationalization of higher education: Motivations and realities. *Journal of Studies in International Education, 11*(3–4), 290–305.

Anderson, P. H., & Lawton, L. (2015). Student motivation to study abroad and their intercultural development. *Frontiers: The Interdisciplinary Journal of Study Abroad, 26:* 39–52.

Forum on Education Abroad. (2020). *Guidelines for conducting education abroad during COVID-19.* https://forumea.org/resources/guidelines/conducting-education-abroad-during-covid-19/

Forum on Education Abroad. (2020). *Standards of good practice for education abroad, 6th edition.* https://forumea.org/resources/standards-6th-edition/.

Gregersen, T. S. (2007). Language learning beyond words: Incorporating body language into classroom activities. *Reflections on English Language Teaching, 6*(1), 51–64.

Institute of International Education. (2020, November 16). Open doors data: U.S. study abroad. Retrieved from https://opendoorsdata.org/data/us-study-abroad/

Larsen, D., & Dutschke, D. (2010). Campus internationalization and study abroad. In W. Hoffa & S. Depaul (Eds.), *A history of U.S. study abroad: 1965–present.* Lancaster: Whitmore Printing.

McCabe, L. T. (2001). Globalization and internationalization: The impact on education abroad programs. *Journal of Studies in International Education, 5*(2), 138–145.

McCallon, M., & Holmes, B. (2010). *Faculty-led 360: Guide to successful study abroad.* Charleston: Agape LLC.

Pope, J. A., Sánchez, C. M., Lehnert, K., & Schmid, A. S. (2014). Why do Gen Y students study abroad? Individual growth and the intent to study abroad. *Journal of Teaching in International Business, 25*(2), 97–118.

Rincon, P. (2011, April). Volcanic ash air shutdown the "right" decision. *BBC News.* https://www.bbc.com/news/science-environment-13161056#:~:text=The%20outpour%20of%20ash%20from,were%20affected%20by%20the%20shutdown.&text=The%20ash%20ejected%20in%20the%20early%20phase%20was%20light%20and%20powdery

Chapter Six

Thinking Through Disasters

Critical Analysis and Research in College Composition Courses

Melissa Sexton

In the fall of 2021, I went back to teaching in-person classes for the first time since the beginning of the COVID-19 pandemic. I also launched a new and timely literature course that semester: an introduction to fictional disasters and dystopias. As the students and I adapted to sharing space and having discussions while wearing masks, we also talked about why this course felt so important to us. "Why do you want to be here and read these stories?" I asked the students on the first day of class. "Why do you *still* want to read these stories now, as we are going through our own disasters?" Many of the students were fans of disaster and dystopia stories, just like I was; as we talked, we did not seem to find these stories hopeless or frightening, but somehow relatable and even comforting. Rather than seeming strange, it seemed particularly necessary to share disaster stories while coming back to a university that was not only navigating the ongoing challenges of the pandemic but had also weathered closures and disruptions from multiple hurricanes in recent academic years. Ground down by our own times of disaster, we were eager to discuss stories that somewhat reflected our own emotional experiences.

Although my 2021 class was new and gave me new evidence that it can be effective to teach about disasters, it was only the latest in a series of courses I have taught in the past few years that have focused on this topic. In writing and composition courses as well as in literature courses, I have asked students to think about the kinds of stories we tell about disaster, in news media as well as in fiction and films. In all these courses, I have discussed why such narratives do more than reflect real-world experiences of disaster; I have argued that our consumption and analysis of these stories can also shape our responses to events we may face in the future.

My academic interest in disaster stories grew out of my work in ecocriticism, which emphasizes the reciprocal relationships connecting texts and the world. Environmental writers reflect and build on their experiences of the natural world, but their texts also affect and shape the world in turn. Historically, cultural values have emphasized diverse settings, from rugged wilderness to pastoral simplicity; these aesthetic ideas about how nature should look and these textual stories about how nature should be have affected the kinds of environments people have valued, built, and preserved. Too often, the stories we tell about the environment have also been disaster stories, exploring the catastrophic impact human actions have had on the natural world and on our own communities. Just as environmental texts both shape and are shaped by the material world, the stories we tell about disaster not only reflect the material conditions of past events but also shape the emotional reactions people may experience in the future.

Indeed, in *A Paradise Built in Hell* (2009), Rebecca Solnit argued that the stories we tell about disasters matter. Far too often, Solnit explained, disaster films and news coverage depict people "as hysterical or vicious in the face of calamity . . . [as either] victims or brutes" (2009, p. 8). The circulation of such stories fuels new fear and violence during later catastrophes: "Often the worst behavior in the wake of a calamity is on the part of those who believe others will behave savagely and that they themselves are taking defensive measures" (2009, p. 2). Looking at the aftermath of Hurricane Katrina, for example, Solnit demonstrated how media narratives about "looting" helped fuel fear and violence directed against Black communities, including vigilante violence within New Orleans neighborhoods and even an armed blockade of a bridge leaving the city by members of the neighboring community of Gretna (2009, pp. 232–304). Stories of disaster that dehumanized survivors fueled dehumanizing behavior in the real world. By studying the stories we tell about disaster, we can become familiar with these patterns and challenge these "cheap, familiar stories" that depict people as selfish, "hysterical or vicious," rather than accepting a cycle of reactionary violence (Solnit, 2009, p. 221, p. 8).

As I have built disaster-themed classes—and rebuilt these classes when real-world disasters struck—I have aimed to help students develop such critical thinking about the complexities of disaster narratives. When we look critically at historical disasters, as well as at films and narratives about disasters, we can find complex stories that reject simple separation of survivors into passive victims or vicious perpetrators. Solnit also argued that, without diminishing the suffering disasters create, we can recognize counternarratives, stories that imagine people in rich, complicated relationships to their environments and each other. Solnit was particularly interested in the compassion, creativity, and resilience communities often display in the midst of the suffering caused by disasters.

"In the wake of an earthquake, a bombing, or a major storm, most people are altruistic, urgently engaged in caring for themselves and those around them," Solnit argued, drawing on examples including Hurricane Katrina, the 1906 San Francisco Earthquake, and 9/11 to document the communities of mutual aid that can spring up under extreme circumstances (2009, p. 2). Becoming aware of the social compassion often on display during disasters can empower those surviving these events to reach out in empathy rather than fear or anger to those suffering alongside them. Thinking about disasters can also help us assess the social patterns we accept in less extreme times. With their "disruptive power," disasters can "topple old orders and open new possibilities," exposing pre-existing injustices within society and providing opportunities to rebuild community structures in more just ways (Solnit, 2009, p. 16). But to translate these positive frameworks onto our own experiences, we must first recognize disasters as complex events; we have to re-examine the assumptions our disaster stories make about who we are—as humans, cultures, and collectives.

I first introduced disaster units into my college-level composition courses precisely because studying these events offered an opportunity to combine critical thinking, research, and interdisciplinarity. In recent years, as I have not only taught *about* natural disasters, but also *through* them, I have developed another, related goal for my disaster units: to help students engage with these complex stories as a way of understanding their own disaster experiences.

After experiencing a string of hurricanes including Hurricanes Matthew, Florence, and Dorian, I wondered whether it would be helpful to students to keep thinking about the topic of disaster. On the one hand, such discussion offered some framework for processing the events. In the aftermath of the storms, as students faced the destabilization of their routines and expectations, I hoped rereading disaster stories critically would help students cultivate their own narratives of hope and resilience while also acknowledging the frustrations, grief, and loss they may be working through. However, teaching through disasters also made me grapple with pedagogical contradictions: Although units on disaster can feel empowering to some students, giving them context and tools for reconsidering their experiences, such units can feel exhausting to students already overwhelmed by the disaster coverage taking over their social media feeds and the effects of disaster destabilizing their daily lives.

In this chapter, I will share some of my own stories about teaching through disaster, discussing some of the specific events that I and my students experienced in order to illustrate how my classes navigated these contradictions. I will talk about the readings and assignments that offered students tools for analyzing disasters and helped students develop their critical thinking skills in the process. I will also talk about some of the strategies I used to create flexibility in the face of student burnout, allowing students to think seriously about disasters while also granting them some distance from the events they were experiencing. By thinking through disasters in my courses, I believe students were challenged to think about complex narratives and were introduced to new approaches to research, all while also having opportunities to analyze and recontextualize the events taking place in their lives. As intensifying hurricane seasons and an ongoing pandemic have made destabilized college semesters a recurring experience, I have wanted to create classes that grappled with and acknowledged the effect this uncertain reality has had on so many students.

TEACHING ABOUT DISASTERS

"Unnatural Disasters" and Hurricane Matthew

In the fall of 2016, I had my first experience teaching through a disaster. I was visiting family in Wilmington, North Carolina, when Hurricane Matthew hit. I had lived through other kinds of natural disasters—I had grown up in the Midwest, with thunderstorms, tornadoes, and blizzards, and I had spent a decade on the West Coast, living through the 2014 Oregon Gulch fire, but Matthew was my first hurricane. I had never experienced the combination of sudden and slow-moving destruction that hurricanes can bring, as rising floodwaters follow behind the initial damaging winds.

When Matthew hit, I was not working in Wilmington—I was actually teaching in Atlanta, but I decided to ride out the storm, wanting to make sure friends and family stayed safe. What I could not have guessed was how the storm would trap me in its aftermath. Outside of town, the Lumber River surged with rainwater, swallowing up highways and homes. Days after the storm had passed, as I tried to drive back to Atlanta, I was startled to find I-40 blanketed in water. On the backroads, my GPS sent me into dead-end after dead-end, water cutting off every route through the southern Carolinas. After hours of looping around flooded backroads, I had to return to Wilmington, where I would end up teaching remotely until the water receded. When I was finally able to drive back to Georgia, days later, I passed boats launching off the highways' shoulders, headed into flooded neighborhoods, and this is the image from Matthew that remains most firmly planted in my memory.

Hurricane Matthew was not only my first hurricane but also my first time teaching a course entirely about disasters while living through one. This course was an introductory writing and communications class, and the readings we were completing for the course were specifically focused on the social factors that complicate disasters. It was called "Un-Natural Disasters," based on a term from Theodore Steinberg's article, "What is a Natural Disaster?" (1996). Like Solnit, Steinberg explored how people make sense of disasters. But Steinberg focused on the idea of "naturalness," asking, "What is a natural disaster in a society that has so thoroughly tampered with nature?" (1996, p. 34). Steinberg assessed the human systems that complicated attempts at "sorting disaster into natural and non-natural categories" (1996, p. 34).

One of his examples that we discussed in the class was an 1889 flood in Johnstown, Pennsylvania. In this event, "heavy spring rains combined with the faulty construction of an earthen dam lead to the tragedy" (1996, p. 33). Steinberg asked if that flood was "natural," an "act of God," or "unnatural," the result of poor human engineering and unjust distribution of environmental risks (1996, p. 33). In class discussions, we extended this question of unnaturalness to rethink the history of Mississippi River floods, including the flooding caused by Hurricane Katrina. Although a hurricane clearly qualifies as a natural disaster, there were many human factors that exacerbated the aftermath of Katrina, from the climate change that may have intensified the storm, to the unequal responses of police departments and government agencies, to the levee failures resulting from long histories of unjust infrastructure development. Thus, we discussed how environmental justice, including the differing levels of risk and damage various communities faced, was a vital component of the complex narratives we could tell about disasters.

During class discussions, we also applied these questions about environmental justice and unnatural disasters to Hurricane Matthew. In the weeks after the hurricane, my students were researching and putting together group presentations about various unnatural disasters. Student groups had to choose a disaster and explain how the idea of its unnaturalness could help us recognize complex economic and justice issues affecting the event's outcome.

As I taught them remotely, cut off by the flooded highways, this kind of unnatural disaster was playing out in real time; many places like Princeville, North Carolina, and Lumberton, North Carolina, were devastated by floods, and Black communities with a long history of flood damage were dealing with further displacement (Bidgood, 2016). Some student groups decided to address these events in their projects, examining how present-day environmental justice issues were part of a long and complicated history of displaced communities and uneven environmental risk. (For a complete list of readings for this course, please see A1; for a list of suggested topics provided to students before this research presentation project, see A2).

Environmental Justice and Disaster Films

This group presentation project for the "Un-Natural Disaster" course encouraged students to think critically about historical examples of environmental injustice. We also studied some of the very types of movies that, according to Solnit, can perpetuate shallow understandings of catastrophe, depicting humans as either helpless or violent. After watching these films, we discussed how their stories depicted human relationships to the natural world. Did such depictions invite agency or despair? And how did these stories challenge or perpetuate instances of environmental injustice?

For example, we watched Christopher Nolan's 2014 film *Interstellar*, which depicted a world suffering from food shortages caused by an undefined blight. The film suggested space exploration as a possible solution to this ecological collapse, depicting global disaster as the catalyst for technological innovation and, ultimately, humanity leaving Earth behind entirely. Along with the film, students read an article by Noah Gittell (2014), which argued that the film's escapist space story provided reductive choices: "Mankind can either leave the planet behind, or it can stay here and die." Read through Gittell's framework, *Interstellar* imagines a world where most humans are helpless and only select scientific heroes will be able to offer salvation—and then, only salvation for a few. In our class discussions of the film, we considered who gets left out by disaster stories—which communities are left behind when we imagine heroism as exceptional and individualistic, rather than as creative and collaborative forms of response?

The final project for our "Un-Natural Disaster" class asked students to become even more aware of the distortions and erasures that disaster stories can perpetuate. For this project, students created a pitch for their own disaster film, a genre we defined broadly to include not only major blockbusters but also other genres we watched for class, including documentaries like Spike Lee's *When the Levees Broke* and dramas like Benh Zeitlin's *Beasts of the Southern Wild*. Students had to imagine a compelling story about disaster, and they had to draw on some research to do this. They could research a specific technology that might potentially cause a disaster, a specific environment that might be vulnerable to disaster, or a particular geographical region with a history of disaster. Student groups planned a trailer for their films, following the Motion Picture Association of America's guidelines for trailer length; these videos also drew on conventions we observed and discussed in class after watching various disaster movie trailers. Student groups were invited to attend an iMovie workshop through the school library, but they were allowed to use the software of their choice to complete the video component of this project.

Along with making a trailer for their proposed film, students also wrote a rationale, explaining how their imagined disaster exaggerated historical events or realistic threats. The project helped students move beyond research that simply collected facts, encouraging them to instead treat research as a foundation for creativity. And by engaging in their own creative processes of research and fictional exaggeration, students got hands-on experience with the manipulative power of disaster rhetoric. Having themselves reflected on the distance between their research and the stories they created, perhaps students could develop some resistance to the simplistic narratives that, when applied to real-world events, turned disasters into scary, apocalypse myths.

TEACHING THROUGH DISASTERS

Hurricane Florence and Disaster Fatigue

After experiencing Hurricane Matthew and working with students to contextualize disaster narratives, and after seeing the trailers and rationales students created for the "Un-Natural Disaster" course, I clearly recognized how disaster-focused units in composition courses could provide students with opportunities to do research that was creative, critical, and relatable. Crucially, however, during this teaching experience, I was not working with students who were being directly impacted by disaster. While Hurricane Matthew posed teaching challenges for me, forcing me to quickly develop a plan to meet with student groups remotely, for my students, there was both critical and literal distance from the events we were studying and discussing. When Matthew hit the Carolina coastline, my students in Atlanta were not directly threatened by the floodwaters or the winds; their housing was secure and their power was on. The events did not affect their daily lives, but simply highlighted the ongoing importance of studying natural disasters in a time of climate destabilization.

In later years, the disasters I taught through hit much closer to home. In October 2018, Hurricane Florence blew into Wilmington. While the hurricane eventually hit our town as a Category 1, it had ramped up to a Category 4 before reaching our coast. The university closed down, the campus emptied, and large numbers of people, including myself, evacuated the city. My experiences during Matthew and Florence were starkly different. By 2018, I was living and teaching in Wilmington, and it was my home getting hit by a storm. While Matthew had hit the city of Wilmington itself relatively lightly, Florence slowed down and soaked the town, dumping rain on the city for days, damaging buildings and flooding roads in Wilmington itself. While I had been trapped in Wilmington by the floodwaters of Matthew, my husband and

I found ourselves trapped *outside* of the city for weeks, as did many students who had also evacuated. Thus, rather than teaching students online in the aftermath of the storm, after Florence, I found myself watching disaster from a distance, waiting to find out when schools would reopen.

Furthermore, during Florence, students and faculty found themselves experiencing the unnaturalness of this disaster in their own lives. Wilmington as a whole dealt not only with the natural elements of wind and rain, but also with social and economic factors—gas shortages during the weeks when Wilmington remained a virtual island; complicated negotiations about when and how to allow residents to return on limited highways without interfering with utility trucks and emergency personnel. And once we could return to town, we returned to wind and water damage, on and off campus. Many students faced temporary housing reassignments or had family members dealing with damaged houses. Returning in these conditions, I asked myself if studying disasters would help students or if students might be better served by other content. If I planned to keep the disaster-themed material, I wondered, how could I design or modify courses in a way that accommodated students' trauma as they lived through these destabilizing events?

The aftermath of Hurricane Florence thus pushed me to confront disaster as a limiting constraint that challenges teachers and students to complete coursework and attend classes while negotiating material limitations. Just as there are tensions in our cultural narratives about disasters, there are also tensions built into teaching about disasters. While *studying* disasters may reveal empowering narratives about social resilience or create awareness and conviction about environmental justice issues, *studying in the midst of* disasters can exhaust students, making it more difficult for them to read, write, and think carefully. In the weeks after Florence, I was having mold removed from my walls; students were dealing with temporary housing, transportation issues, and classroom reassignments. For students and educators alike, disaster destabilized our campus and classrooms. Uncertain and shifting course schedules combined with makeup work from the missed month of school meant that all of us on campus faced disaster fatigue.

Due to all of these complications, rebuilding a course schedule after Florence took a considerable amount of work. However, at the time, the topic of disaster played a relatively small role in our course: During our research unit, we were only reading one article about hurricanes and unnatural disaster as an example of an interdisciplinary research topic. Thus, although the fatigue I witnessed after Florence highlighted the tensions of teaching through disasters, the modifications I had to make to the course content that semester were relatively small: I allowed students to choose between a number of readings and research topics. Students who wanted to continue reading about hurricanes could do so, using research assignments to contextualize their experiences, while students who preferred to avoid the topic could simply choose to write about a different subject.

Repeated Disaster: Hurricane Dorian and COVID-19

While the modifications required by Florence were minor, recognizing the impact of disaster burnout became more important to my teaching and planning during the next few semesters. During 2019 and 2020, as I started teaching classes with a greater emphasis on research, I returned to designing units focused on unnatural disasters. In these writing courses, I again planned to teach students Steinberg's article (1996). I also planned to introduce the concept of the Anthropocene, the recently designated geological epoch marked by the dominant influence of human activity on the earth ("Working Group," 2020). In this unit, students would complete a series of shared readings (see A3) and then select a research topic connected in some way to these concepts (see A4). Having a shared research concentration for the entire class meant that students would not be isolated while working on individual projects; instead, they could better peer edit fellow students' work and enter into collaborative conversations about what they were learning. Moreover, because studying disasters can lead to such rich conversations about cultural narratives, historical context, and complex systems, disasters would work well as the topic for this kind of classwide, interdisciplinary research unit.

However, during these semesters, disasters repeatedly destabilized our campus. In 2019, Hurricane Dorian hit Wilmington. It closed campus for only a week, but the fatigue felt real, given the lingering exhaustion from the impacts of Florence. Then, as the COVID-19 pandemic spread through the spring of 2020, we, like so many others, transitioned to online teaching, and I again asked how I could make my existing disaster units accessible to students while also taking potential student trauma and burnout seriously. In these instances, the study of disasters was a substantial part of my courses. Given the constraints of semesters already upset by schedule shifts, I did not want to throw out pre-existing units and rebuild my courses from scratch. Instead of rewriting my courses, my goals became to offer students some options that felt manageable and to clearly explain to students why discussing disasters could provide us with context and narratives to help us process our experiences. Ultimately, I identified three key reasons why the disaster units were so valuable: They challenged students to develop critical thinking; they helped students approach research from an interdisciplinary perspective; and they challenged students to broaden their conception of what research might entail.

1. Critical Thinking Through Research

One reason I began teaching about disasters was to avoid reductive, clichéd thinking, specifically about climate change. My goal was not to avoid contentious subjects, but rather to encourage students to move away from reductive binary debates—forced to see themselves as either "pro-life" or "pro-choice," for instance, or either "pro-gun" or "anti-gun." Falling into these kinds of rehearsed positions prior to doing any research or reading goes against the principles of inquiry, an openness to reasoning and changing one's mind that has long been influential to my teaching (Gage, 2006). To avoid such polarization and reductive thinking, complex problems and narratives can be productive topics of study. Climate change is a potentially controversial topic, but it is also an insidious problem that defies simplistic solutions. Looking at climate as one of many complicating factors at work in specific unnatural disasters allowed my classes to start thinking about climate destabilization while moving beyond possible pre-existing commitments students may have had to believe or not believe in climate change.

2. Interdisciplinary Approaches to Research

The diverse problems presented by disasters also offered students opportunities to discuss interdisciplinary research and how such research is often necessary to solve real-world issues. The environmental problems we face cannot be solved without an interdisciplinary grasp of how technological, social, and economic issues are affected by the stories and arguments we make about the environment. Discussing disasters can help students recognize the ways in which stories, social systems, and natural systems overlap and affect each other. Studying Katrina, for example, exposes this complexity: On what do we blame the hurricane's aftermath? Infrastructure failures, historic and institutionalized social injustices, carbon-fueled climate exacerbations, political failures, or cultural narratives about looting and urban violence that slowed compassionate responses from city systems and neighboring regions? The answer, of course, involves all of these systems.

Researching disasters can help students sort through these many layers. In particular, for students going through disaster and watching the systems around them being challenged, learning more about these systems can empower them to see how their own fields of study can help tackle a world of intensifying disaster. For instance, I have written elsewhere about how I talked with students about the New Orleans levees as an engineering problem but also a problem involving economics, politics, cultural stories, and environmental justice issues (Sexton, 2020). I told students that I believe it is essential for engineers to know about environmental justice issues so that they can learn to see these many layers involved in such technical problems.

Similarly, in 2019 and 2020, I asked students to think about how their own academic interests or major fields of study related to questions about the Anthropocene, the unnaturalness of disasters, and environmental justice. What, I asked students, do disasters mean for hospitals and nursing homes? How do disasters affect real estate? How do disasters show up in music, literature, art, and film? By researching different aspects of disasters, my students were able to create projects that fit some of their interests while also remaining part of a larger research community in the classroom.

Furthermore, as I explained to my students, developing the ability to do this kind of creative synthesis of ideas was valuable to their overall academic careers; they would not always be given free rein on research in their courses, and the ability to connect a given topic to their own major or career interests could be a proactive strategy for completing academic projects in many of their classes. Such connections could also help them come up with creative topics to research in their own fields of study as they went on to more advanced coursework.

3. Broadening Conceptions of Research

In addition to reading the articles about disasters and the Anthropocene to start the research unit, my research-focused composition classes also discussed disaster films together. For example, we watched *The Day After Tomorrow* and read Michael Svoboda's article, "The Long Melt" (2014). Svoboda discusses a 2004 *Environment* article, which found that "*The Day After Tomorrow* generated more than 10 times the news coverage of the 2001 IPCC report" (Leiserowitz as cited Svoboda, 2014, p. 34). We also read Jen Christensen's "Cli-fi (climate fiction) on the big screen changes minds about real climate change," which asserts that popular films about climate change "help people believe in actual climate change, even when Hollywood's version of the science is a bit off" (2019). While disaster movies can perpetuate stereotypes about helpless victims, as Solnit argued, these studies on *The Day After Tomorrow* suggested that such films can also have more positive effects. Some disaster films appear to motivate people, dramatizing real-world threats in a way that has a more significant emotional impact than research alone.

Therefore, watching *The Day After Tomorrow* and reading these articles introduced students to diverse approaches to research. Research could mean familiarizing yourself with what many different critics say about a text; research could mean finding sociological studies that catalog human responses to films; research could mean watching a series of disaster films and learning about the history of a genre. Thus, thinking about disaster films provided students with some distance from current events while also encouraging them to broaden their understanding of research, all while becoming more aware of the rhetoric and stories pop cultural texts can perpetuate about disasters.

4. Final Research Project

The final project for these courses again asked students to craft their own stories about disasters; in these cases, however, rather than asking students to imagine their own fictional dystopian or apocalyptic stories, I asked students to create projects that made significant claims about disasters and that presented these research-based claims in ways that were accessible to a general, public audience. Rather than writing a formal research paper, students instead created public-focused interventions: newsletters, websites, or videos that offered specific takeaways for the audience. This framing pushed students away from reporting data and asked them to think in terms of reasoning and evidence: Given the goal you are trying to communicate to your audience, what evidence or reasoning from your research could best help support this point?

The urgency of disasters also helped students shift from report to argument, as they considered what they wanted audiences to do, change, or become aware of based on this research. In the final projects, some students made suggestions about disaster preparedness plans for hospitals or nursing homes or insisted on the importance of developing beach nourishment plans. Other students explored why dystopian films remained so popular or talked about the repeated appearance of historical disasters in popular music. Thus, while thinking about important composition topics like audience, argument, and significance, students also had an opportunity to consider questions about what we can learn from experiencing as well as studying disasters.

CONCLUSIONS

As an environmental scholar, I have long been interested in the kinds of stories we tell about disasters. And as a writing instructor, I have long been interested in helping students challenge assumptions and think critically about the world around them. When I began teaching about disasters, my courses drew on my interests to help students achieve these goals. These units worked because disasters are such complicated events, tangling together the effects of human and natural systems. These units also worked because stories about disaster play a powerful role in news media and in popular narratives.

However, after my own experiences with hurricanes, I found myself more eager than ever to analyze the disasters that have changed my life and my teaching. I believe that such analysis can also help composition and literature students, not just to think critically or approach research in new ways, but also to navigate abrupt changes to our classrooms and campuses in the aftermath of hurricanes and pandemics. In a world of climate destabilization, more students may have to deal with campuses changed or challenged by disastrous events. Complex narratives can thus help students to recognize that the meaning of their own disaster experiences can also be complex.

In the fall of 2021, as we returned to campus and continued to teach through the COVID pandemic, I saw again how valuable complex narratives can be. As I addressed student fatigue, brought on by changing safety guidelines and modality shifts, it felt important to acknowledge that disasters can be meaningless, the source of both tedious fears and acute suffering. Disasters can prevent us from sticking to our plans and can challenge us to be flexible, even when dealing with the most basic of daily tasks like coming to class and setting up schedules. But disasters can also be significant; they can offer "disruptive power" (Solnit, 2009, p. 16).

Wearing our masks, shifting between online and in-person classes, my new literature class reminded me that stories about disaster can reveal social anxieties and expose ongoing injustices. Navigating the tensions of disaster requires sophisticated critical thinking; such thinking can help students in their academic work and in their larger civic lives, as they build community while suffering through the losses brought on by their pandemic experiences. Complex narratives name and validate the destructive outcomes of disasters, but they also illustrate that destruction and suffering do not always erase hope or the potential for positive change. Complex narratives recognize that events from the past can shape our present, but also that the stories we craft in the present can alter our abilities to empathize, hope, and create different futures. My hope is that thinking through disasters can help students acknowledge their suffering and fatigue while also cultivating a belief in their own complexity, compassion, and resilience.

Appendix: Course Resources

In this final section, I provide examples of some course reading lists and assignment topic suggestions discussed in this chapter. For complete bibliographical information on course readings, please see the final references list. The course materials are organized as follows:

1. A1: Course Readings for English 1102, "Un-Natural Disasters," Georgia Institute of Technology (2016)
2. A2: Suggested Topic Ideas for English 1102, "Un-Natural Disasters," Georgia Institute of Technology (2016)
3. A3: Course Readings for English 201, College Reading and Writing II, University of North Carolina Wilmington (2020)
4. A4: Suggested Topic Ideas for English 201, College Reading and Writing II, University of North Carolina Wilmington (2020)

A1

Course Readings for English 1102, "Un-Natural Disasters"

- Part 1: Historical Views of Technology
  - Edward Burtynsky, *Water*
  - Ralph Waldo Emerson, "Works and Days."
  - E. M. Forster, "The Machine Stops"
  - Fritz Lang, *Metropolis*
  - Frank Norris, excerpts from *The Octopus*
- Part 2: When the Levees Break: Disastrous Floods
  - Silpa Kovvali, "What 'Beasts of the Southern Wild' Really Says"
  - Spike Lee, *When the Levees Broke: A Requiem in Four Acts*
  - Pare Lorentz, "The River 1937"
  - John McPhee, "Atchfalaya"
  - Ted Steinberg, "What Is a Natural Disaster?"
  - Benh Zeitlin, *Beasts of the Southern Wild*
- Part 3: Films and the Rhetoric of Disaster
  - Roland Emmerich, *The Day After Tomorrow*
  - Noah Gittell, "*Interstellar*: Good Space Film, Bad Climate-Change Parable."
  - Christopher Nolan, *Interstellar*
  - Ted Nordhaus and Michael Shellenberger, "Apocalypse Fatigue: Losing the Public on Climate Change."
  - Michael Svoboda, "The Long Melt: The lingering influence of *The Day After Tomorrow*."

A2

Suggested Research Topics for English 1102, "Un-Natural Disasters"

- Environmental justice and the Mississippi River: Develop our definition of this term and find specific, historical examples in this region.

Texts to consider: "Atchafalaya," *The River, When the Levees Broke, Beasts of the Southern Wild.*
- The Mississippi River and delta land loss (including, possibly, the effect of levees and dams on silt).
   Texts to consider: "Atchafalaya," *Beasts of the Southern Wild*
- Climate change and hurricanes (What links exist between hurricane severity and climate change?),
   Texts to consider: *When the Levees Broke, Beasts of the Southern Wild, Sharknado*
- The history of Mississippi River levees (When were major improvements made to the levees? What did these improvements entail? What drawbacks did such projects face?).
   Texts to consider: "Atchafalaya," *The River, When the Levees Broke, Beasts of the Southern Wild.*
- Historic floods (background on major events that could include [but are not limited to] the 1927 Mississippi river flood and the 1965 Hurricane Betsy).
   Texts to consider: "Atchafalaya," *The River, When the Levees Broke, Beasts of the Southern Wild*
- Dynamiting the levees (What happened in 1927? What evidence exists for and against dynamiting in the 1965 Betsy incident?).
   Texts to consider: *The River, When the Levees Broke, Beasts of the Southern Wild*
- The relationship between agriculture, erosion, and flooding.
   Texts to consider: "Atchafalaya," *The River*

A3

Course Readings for English 201, College Reading and Writing II

- Key Theoretical Texts
   - Theodore Steinberg, "What Is a Natural Disaster?"
   - The Smithsonian, "What Is the Anthropocene?"
- Supporting Articles
   - Jen Christensen, "Cli-fi (climate fiction) on the big screen changes minds about real climate change."
   - Ted Nordhaus and Michael Shellenberger, "Apocalypse Fatigue: Losing the Public on Climate Change."
   - NPR, "When the Levee Breaks: Ripples of the Great Flood"
   - Our Changing Climate, "*The Day After Tomorrow*: Why Cli-Fi Matters"
   - PBS, *A Tale of Two Rivers,* excerpt—Mississippi Flood, 1927

- Films
  - Roland Emmerich, *The Day After Tomorrow*
  - Spike Lee, *When the Levees Broke: A Requiem in Four Acts*

A4

Suggested Topic Ideas for English 201, College Reading and Writing II

- Historically significant disasters (in the United States; in North Carolina; in your home state/town/region; in a particular country)
- Fire management in the American West
- Flood management in the American South
- Levee building—as an engineering issue
- Levee building—as a socioeconomic issue
- Major environmental justice cases (in the United States/globally)
- Climate fiction—What was/is its impact?
- Disaster films—How have they affected public discussion?
- Public health issues related to environmental disasters
- Computer modeling—how accurate are our models (for flood/storm prediction)?
- Musical responses to disaster (1927—legacy of *When the Levees Broke*; How did hip hop communities in New Orleans respond in the aftermath of Hurricane Katrina?)
- News coverage of disasters—How has it changed in the past decades? What role does the Weather Channel play in our perceptions of disaster?
- Climate change coverage—How has the coverage of this issue changed in the media?
- Sea level rise—What can humans do now to prepare for this problem? What kinds of building challenges do we face? What might this do to real estate or investments?

REFERENCES

Bidgood, J. (2016, December 9). A wrenching decision where Black history and floods intertwine. *New York Times*. Retrieved from https://www.nytimes.com/2016/12/09/us/princeville-north-carolina-hurricane-matthew-floods-black-history.html

Burtynsky, E. (2010). Water. *Edward Burtynsky*. Retrieved from https://www.edwardburtynsky.com/projects/photographs/water

Christensen, J. (2019, February 8). Cli-fi (climate fiction) on the big screen changes minds about real climate change. *CNN*. Retrieved from https://www.cnn.com/2019/02/08/world/climate-change-movies-eprise/index.html

Emerson, R. W. (1870). Works and days. *The complete works of Ralph Waldo Emerson: Society and solitude,* (vol. 7). Retrieved from https://quod.lib.umich.edu/e/emerson/4957107.0007.001/1:11?rgn=div1;view=fulltext

Emmerich, R. (Producer), Gordan, M. (Producer), & Emmerich, R. (Director). (2004). *The day after tomorrow.* [Motion picture]. USA: 20th Century Fox.

Forster, E. M. (1909, November). The machine stops. *Oxford and Cambridge Review.*

Gage, J. (2006). *The shape of reason: Argumentative writing in college* (4th ed). New York: Pearson.

Gittell, N. (2014, November 15). *Interstellar*: Good space film, bad climate-change parable. *The Atlantic.* Retrieved from https://www.theatlantic.com/entertainment/archive/2014/11/why-interstellar-ignores-climate-change/382788/

Gottwald, M. (Producer), Janvey, D. (Producer), Penn, J. (Producer), & Zeitlin, B. (Director). (2012). *Beasts of the southern wild.* [Motion picture]. United States: Cinereach/Fox Searchlight.

Kovvali, S. (2012, August 16). What "Beasts of the southern wild" really says. *The Atlantic.* Retrieved from https://www.theatlantic.com/entertainment/archive/2012/08/what-beasts-of-the-southern-wild-really-says/261228/

Kramer, S. (Producer), Morreale, A. (Producer), & Polin, D. B. (Producer). (2002). A Tale of Two Rivers. *Great projects: The building of America.* [Motion picture]. USA: Great Projects Film Company.

Latt, D. M. (Producer), & Ferrante, A. C. (Director). (2013). *Sharknado.* [Motion picture]. USA: The Asylum.

Lee, S. (Producer/Director), & Pollard, S. D. (Producer). (2006). *When the levees broke: A requiem in four acts.* [Motion picture]. USA: 40 Acres and a Mule Filmworks.

Leiserowitz, A. A. (2004, November). Before and after *The day after tomorrow*: A study of climate change risk perception. *Environment, 24*(9).

Lorentz, P. (Director). (1937). *The river 1937.* [Motion picture]. USA: Farm Security Administration.

McPhee, J. (1989). Atchafalaya. *The control of nature.* (pp. 3–92). New York: Farrar Strauss Giroux, 1989.

Nolan, C. (Producer/Director), Obst, L. (Producer), & Thomas, E. (Producer). (2013). *Interstellar.* [Motion picture]. USA: Paramount.

Norris, F. (1901). *The Octopus.* Boston, MA: Houghton Mifflin Co.

Nordhaus, T., & Shellenberger M. (2009, November 16). Apocalypse fatigue: Losing the public on climate change. *Yale Environment 360.* Retrieved from http://e360.yale.edu/features/apocalypse_fatigue_losing_the_public_on_climate_change

Our Changing Climate. (2017, July 21). *The day after tomorrow: Why cli-fi matters.* [Video file]. Retrieved from https://www.youtube.com/watch?v=YqhyGKPbHLU

Pommer, E. (Producer), & Lang F. (Director). (1927). *Metropolis.* [Motion picture]. Germany: Parufamet.

Ray, S. J.. (2010). Eco-collapse: Fear, disaster, and nature in U.S. Culture. *Association for the Study of Literature and the Environment.* Retrieved from https://www.asle.org/syllabi/eco-collapse-fear-disaster-nature-u-s-culture/

Sexton, M. (2020). Teaching the Anthropocene: Technology and environmental justice. *Resilience, 18*(1), 26–31.

Solnit, R. (2009). *A paradise built in hell: The extraordinary communities that arise in disaster*. New York: Penguin.

Steinberg, T. (1996). What is a natural disaster? *Literature and Medicine, 15*(1), 33–46.

Svoboda, M. (2014, November 5). The long melt: The lingering influence of "The day after tomorrow." *Yale Climate Connections*. Retrieved from https://yaleclimateconnections.org/2014/11/the-long-melt-the-lingering-influence-of-the-day-after-tomorrow/

When the levee breaks: *Ripples of the great flood*. (2011, May 18). *NPR*. Retrieved from https://www.npr.org/2011/05/18/136427246/when-the-levee-breaks-ripples-of-the-great-flood#:~:text=Archives%2FGetty%20Images-,A%20levee%20on%20the%20Mississippi%20River%20in,the%20Great%20Flood%20of%201927.&text=Archives%2FGetty%20Images-,Along%20the%20mighty%20Mississippi%20River%2C%20rising%20waters%20carry%20musical%20echoes,river's%20long%20history%20of%20floods.&text=%22This%20song%20is%20a%20documentary,the%20flood%2C%22%20Brown%20says

Working Group on the "Anthropocene." (2020). Retrieved September 28, 2021, from http://quaternary.stratigraphy.org/working-groups/anthropocene/

Chapter Seven

How Do You Learn to Teach When You Can't Go to School?

Teaching Teachers in the Age of Virtual Living

Alice Hays, Jouselin Martin, Alexandra Chapa-Kunz, and Wade Branch

Lately I have been trying to recall what it felt like to work in a physical classroom and interact with students in person. The memories are there, slightly hazy through the fog of a global pandemic and the year-long stint of stay-at-home orders. As I approach each new hurdle in my credential program, figuring out how to be a teacher to my students in a way that is functional in a virtual space while being measured by the standards of a physical classroom, I question my decision to pursue this path. When the mechanisms that judge my students' success and my capabilities continue to spin as though we are not existing in new territory, I question my sanity for hanging on. Despite the fears, stress, and worry about my ability to teach effectively, I know I want to be there for my students. I focus on their experiences right now in the isolating world of virtual school giving them as much support as I can, even as I simultaneously muddle through my own isolation.

—Alex Chapa-Kunz (Kern High Teacher Resident, 2021)

It was 1994. The scuffling sounds of tennis shoes on the tiled hallway served to emphasize the tightening knot in my stomach while my sweaty hands gripped the piece of chalk. I glanced over to my cooperating teacher who nodded comfortingly at me, with a look that said, "You're okay . . . you can do this." I stumbled through my first day of trying to teach these restless 9th graders, while my cooperating teacher deftly stepped in and managed the most unruly of them for me, allowing me to figure out what sorts of things landed with kids and which of them sailed completely over their heads. All of this was done in the classroom, and through the eye rolls of students, side conversations, or enthusiastic responses, it was easy to see when my lesson was a flop or a success.

As I am now teaching student teachers in the year 2021, we are all battling a new sense of normal. Our teacher candidates are faced with screens full of black boxes and unfamiliar names. As of March 2021, California high schools have been remotely teaching for a full year. Some of our least experienced teacher candidates have never set foot in a classroom as an instructor. Instead, they are now teaching virtual classes full of students they have never met, and in many cases, have never even seen. As teacher educators, administrators, and experienced teachers on school sites, we must ask ourselves, what sort of ramifications will this training have on their ability to become excellent, quality face-to-face teachers who stay in the profession for the long haul?

TEACHER TRAINING

Typically, a teacher goes through structured coursework at the university level, which ultimately culminates in a series of field experiences. The intention of the field experiences is to give students opportunities to spread their teaching wings with the support of qualified university supervisors in addition to strong mentors in the classroom. The more time student teachers get in the classroom, the more prepared they are, and the more likely they will be to stay in the profession (Zhang & Zeller, 2016). As such, there has been a growing movement to implement internships within education programs that follow a medical residency model.

These residency programs are fostered by creating partnerships between universities and local school districts with the goal of "building better instructors from inside the classroom" (NCTR, 2021). A critical residency program component is the active involvement of mentors who incorporate research-based practices taught at the university level into their own work, while also guiding student teachers through the tumultuous experience of teaching. Unfortunately, this year's virtual experience has created an emergency situation for all teachers, regardless of their level of skill and experience in a face-to-face classroom. Not only are they tasked with modeling good teaching and coaching student teachers, but they are having to learn how to pivot into a virtual world they may have no experience with. In addition to that, the K–12 students that they are working with are also experiencing a pandemic. Nothing is normal.

Many education programs use an exit survey, and a typical question that is asked of the students is how effective they expect to be in various areas. This "belief in one's capacity to organize and execute the courses of action required to produce given attainments" (Bandura, 1997, p. 3) is known as self-efficacy. A teacher who has a high sense of self-efficacy is linked with student success (Hoy & Spero, 2005; Mulholland & Wallace, 2001), so it is in our best interest to foster this in our teacher candidates. According to Hoy and Spero (2005), a teacher's sense of self-efficacy can improve most significantly during their student teaching year through experiences in which they have some type of mastery. It is difficult to develop this sense of self-efficacy when students do not have an opportunity to practice teaching in person.

Teaching is a constantly evolving profession that demands continuous improvement. It is critical that individuals have a sense of efficacy around the career if they are to grow into teachers who change their students in meaningful and significant ways (Ross, 1994). Unfortunately, not all teacher candidates are seeing behaviors that model efficacy. The following reflection from one of our Kern High Teacher Residents, Wade Branch, showcases these struggles:

> I have noticed that one of my greatest battles this semester is the desire to complain. Our world has experienced quite a year. Who are we in the education field to assume that such a year would be any different for us? We are feeling the ripple of difficulties felt the world over. What is our only option as teachers? To persevere. What is the only option that students have? To persevere. We all have the right to be frustrated, confused, over-worked, under-motivated, and weary; however, dwelling on those things will not help us move forward. We all have been tasked with just grinding through a tough time where we could find excuses in abundance and reasons to complain in no short supply. The teachers that have been successful, in my estimation, have been the ones who spend more time finding solutions than talking about the problems. I have sat through countless meetings this year, expecting to hear conversations about how to teach. Instead, I have heard hours of venting and problem magnification. I believe that we all are tasked with mustering an extraordinary amount of stamina and perserverance right now.

Although the idea of teachers complaining in the lunchroom is nothing new (Gonzalez, 2013), the prevalence of these grumblings may be occurring in more areas and in more significant ways. Our teacher candidates cannot, and possibly should not, always be shielded from negativity in their placements. Supporting our student candidates as they develop the discernment to distinguish between destructive negativity and constructive criticism, and the emotional resilience to cope with both, is an important aspect of teacher training. It is our hope that our students see role models who are doing the work to move through difficult times as a means of learning how to develop their own efficacy. The virtual environment makes those observations and discoveries less available and is something to take into consideration in the future.

CLASSROOM BEHAVIOR MANAGEMENT

One of the biggest concerns for new teachers is often classroom management. As Eisenman et al. (2015) stated, "Most teachers view classroom management strategies as tools to control student behavior" (p. 2). As multiple scholars have argued, classroom management is about so much more than keeping students in line, and is instead a way of supporting student learning (Eisenman et al., 2015; Emmer & Stough, 2001; Wong & Wong, 2018). Although there is typically some focus on management within teacher preparation courses, everyone who has set foot in a classroom recognizes that without the tangible experience of dealing with students, many of the theories are just that. Our student teachers need experiences that help them learn how to create positive teacher-student relationships, how to understand students' psychological needs, how to use instructional methods that facilitate optimal learning, how to maximize on-task behavior, and how to use a range of counseling and behavior methods to deal with serious behavior problems (Emmer & Stough, 2001).

Imagine, if you will, that a student has walked into your classroom and is full of anger about something that has nothing to do with you. You ask them to participate in a tangible way, and it results in a full-scale tantrum, with the student cursing you out. Your fight-or-flight reaction may kick in, leaving you shaking and sweaty. You have seconds to think through how best to defuse this situation and there are 30 other pairs of eyes watching to see how you will respond.

Everything in your management class spoke about all the pre-emptive work you should do to avoid this ever happening. You create rapport with students, you lay out expectations which are co-developed with students and you create an engaging curriculum that prevents students from wanting to check out. Unfortunately, it is very rare that students get an opportunity to role-play an event of outward defiance during their coursework, and even if they do, it is unlikely to be accompanied with the physiological response that happens when it is real.

The teacher has choices they can make that may de-escalate or escalate the situation, but without mentorship or guidance, they may inadvertently escalate the event. And ultimately, without going through the event, one does not know how one will react in the moment, making it difficult to imagine options for when the moment arises.

In our current pandemic pedagogy, which relies solely on online classes, the solution for when a student uses inappropriate language in the classroom is to move that student to a waiting room or mute their microphone. I have heard my student teachers talk about the agony of fumbling to move them out of the room quickly. While this may certainly be a bit panic inducing, the definitive move to make in a situation like this is clear, and relatively simple. The student teacher does not have to talk down an angry student, nor do they have to decide whether or not they should call for security, potentially adding fuel to the fire. They simply click a few buttons on their screen and the immediate problem is resolved. There are still decisions that must be made about how they will address the issue with the student in question along with the other students, but the "mute" button gives them time to think.

Although this is an extreme example, student teachers are equally unprepared to manage the more mundane, yet equally important aspects of classroom management. In fact, it is the ability to manage these smaller, everyday events that may help prevent more extreme situations from happening.

And our student teachers recognize this missing piece. Those who have spent any amount of time working with adolescents realize that there is a critical gap in their experiences. Even those student teachers who have mentors who quickly adapted to the virtual world and developed routines quickly—a hallmark of strong classroom management—feel unprepared to be in the same physical space as their students. As Alex Chapa-Kunz, a Kern High teacher resident, so eloquently explains:

> I have spent the last year adapting in-person theory and practices to a virtual space and there is a proud accomplishment to the growth I have experienced. This is at times eclipsed by the knowledge that I will have to relearn or learn for the first time how to maintain my management skills in a physical space. I have a deep awareness that my first year in person will bring many challenges I will have to overcome on my own that I might have experienced in the program just one year earlier.

All of this is not to say that there are not classroom management issues occurring in the Zoom classrooms. The task of keeping students on task is significantly more difficult for this pandemic-era cohort of teachers. While there are no side conversations happening in the classroom that teachers must refocus, no students getting up to sharpen their pencil in the middle of an important discussion point, and no students not-so-secretly texting in a group chat, our current student teachers are having to contend with an entire world of distractions. Paradoxically, it is unfortunate that the off-track student behaviors are not impacting the student teacher's ability to move through the lecture at the speed they had previously imagined. Their attention is not being pulled away from their intended lesson objective, and the student teacher may wrongly believe they are successful at achieving their goals.

With only a black box representing the student, our student teachers have no idea what student behaviors they may be competing with, and as such are not learning the tools they need in terms of pacing and pulling students together. Most importantly, the immediate reflexivity/flexibility demanded of good teaching is not a muscle that is being developed and flexed.

The teacher candidates I work with worry that all of the practicing they are doing, and all of the work they are putting into developing lesson plans will be irrelevant without face-to-face management skills. And as a teacher educator, I have a certain level of misgiving about putting my teacher candidates into in-person classrooms on their own next year without being able to give them experiences to support their ability to succeed.

ENGAGEMENT

A second aspect that is critical for new teachers to learn about is how to engage students in learning. Engagement is defined by Marks (2000) as including "attention, interest, investment and effort students expend in the work of learning" (p. 155). There are three types of engagement, including affective (showing positive emotions during class), cognitive (mental effort), and behavioral (time on task, attention, participation, and question asking) (Wang et al., 2014, p. 518). Teachers typically measure these forms of engagement by looking at body language, eye contact, verbal signs of affirmation, and active participation in the classroom in addition to successful completion of challenging work. In our local district, however, teacher candidates and their mentors are not allowed to require students to turn on their cameras. The general idea is to protect students from exposing inequitable situations to their peers and teachers. What this means is that teachers are presenting content and information to a wall of 20 to 40 black boxes on their screens. They are unable to identify engagement through typical means, and even if the K–12 students are successful in their assignments, it does not guarantee cognitive engagement.

In one case, a teacher candidate was running through the module created by the district for the students and showing them how to access the content through their Canvas pages. The material was a complex poem that students were unlikely to have seen before. The module pages did not include ideas for teaching the concepts, but only the skill of annotation. The student teacher spent time showing students how to annotate, and without any visual cues from the students, the student teacher was not able to spot the need to check for understanding in the moment.

Later, when the teacher candidate asked if there were any questions about the worksheets to be filled out, there were none. As the ability to ask questions is a sign of more developed cognitive processes (Ciardiello, 1998), the lack of questions does not necessarily mean students were comprehending the material. Of course, the silence may also signal disengagement from the class entirely. Although there was an assessment tied with the module, it was something that would not be submitted until the following day, so there was no immediate feedback the teacher candidate could use to assess engagement in that scripted lesson plan. Of course, the scripted lesson plan and reliance on district-developed curriculum during an emergency situation may contribute to the issue, and an increased focus on curriculum literacy with the teacher candidates may be necessary.

This does not mean that the teacher candidates are not attempting to check for understanding throughout their lessons. I have observed them pose questions to the class only to face deafening silence, but also a wall of black screens that give no indication that students have even heard the question. Every experienced teacher knows the feeling of having a question land flat on the floor, not even getting kicked around a bit, but there are generally a few willing students who might finally speak up to save the teacher or teacher candidate from abject defeat. This sense of pressure does not seem to have the same impact in the virtual classroom, however. One student teacher, Jouselin Martin, elaborated on this paradox:

> One strategy we learn as teachers is that of "wait-time" which is supposed to give students enough time to process the question that was just proposed to the class; in the virtual space "wait-time" can go all period when you have no way of knowing if students are even there. You might get one or two students who will respond in the chat, but often it is privately in fear of not having the right answer or being the only one who answers out of the whole class. Without voices heard and student interactions "wait-time" feels like a failed lesson more than a failed question.

The tactics that their classroom instructors and mentor teachers told them to use seem to be falling short of the needs of the virtual environment. The practice-based part of student teaching has not quite been met in ways that will benefit them in the physical classroom next year. This will require a longer grace period for these new teachers, as they find their bearings in the physical classroom through trial and error.

This is not to say that engaging students virtually is impossible. The amount of technology I have learned from my students in the last year has been incredible. Several of our classes have turned into peer-to-peer technology lessons where my students support one another in adapting face-to-face strategies to technology that is both student friendly and district software friendly. My teacher candidates have discovered new digital pedagogies in order to ensure that students are engaged, which I hope they continue to use as these tools encourage some students to engage who may otherwise not participate in a face-to-face full classroom discussion.

Social and Emotional Needs

Another component of good teaching is the ability to recognize the social and emotional needs of students defined as "promot[ing] students' capacity to integrate thinking, emotion and behavior to deal effectively with everyday personal and social challenges," (Greenberg et al., 2017, p. 14). This pandemic-era cohort of student teachers may actually have a slight advantage in this area due to the increasing prevalence of a need for self-care for themselves and students. In a class discussion about their own stress and coping techniques, the talk turned to their students. One of the student teachers responded that she "had more parents this semester email me that their kids are just depressed and have checked out."

When I went through student teaching, these were not common topics of conversation, yet as the following excerpt from Wade Branch shows, the personal challenges the K–12 students are having are significant.

> One of the toughest things about teaching in a pandemic is the psychological battle that has been faced. One day, my mentor teacher got a message from a student telling him that her friend (another student at the school) was contemplating suicide. My mentor teacher had to alert the dean, who contacted the police, who quickly went to the child's home to make sure the child was safe. I mentioned that story to my fellow student-teachers and two other student teachers had experienced the same thing! That is very telling of the mental state of our students right now—that in a group of 20 of us, three have been alerted of suicide danger. This is the result of being shut in. My students rarely turn on their cameras; however, when they do, I often see students lying in bed in the dark. One time, a student was under the covers with his shirt off. Many of our students are lying in bed in a dark room, not socializing, not exercising, and not living normal lives right now. It is hard to see. I took a survey of my class, and many of them said that they are having a hard time—citing their lack of activity, lack of socializing, lack of contact with teachers, and lack of extracurricular activities like sports and clubs. My students admit to being lazy and not wanting to work, but not being able to muster the motivation to continue in this environment.

Although these issues are certainly just as hard to deal with in the physical space, they are exacerbated by not having contact with the individual students. Those moments when students might hang out after class, or when they put their head down all period, and teachers get a chance to check in on them are missing. Educators in this virtual space have to resort to relying on self-reporting by students. Additionally, student teachers are struggling to know how to support their students' emotional health. Several are using videos and emotional check-ins to reach their students, but those are not always well received.

One student teacher detailed her frustration at being told by her university supervisor that she should not play five-minute videos at the beginning of class to support students' emotional health, because they did not directly connect to her content area. Enriquez further explained in the chat, "However, we are supposed to know our kids' needs and I do not think she realizes they are [more] different now than they have ever been."

It is important to note that while our teacher candidates may be more in tune to recognizing students' social and emotional needs through this online space, because they are so much more prevalent, the teacher candidates themselves are also struggling with their own social and emotional health. As Kern High resident teacher Alex Chapa-Kunz explained, "I think in person interactions will be made so much more challenging after being home for so long, for both students and us. We will all need some grace as we step back in those roles."

CANDIDATE EVALUATION DURING A PANDEMIC

Grace, however, is not forthcoming from the education system. The stress that our teacher-candidates are under is exacerbated on multiple fronts. Teacher candidates are evaluated by their mentors, their university supervisors, and ultimately external forces. Our students are required to pass the Teacher Performance Assessment (TPA) before they can be recommended for a credential. This is a significant financial burden as it requires them to register for a support class at the university and to pay $150.00 for each part of the two-part exam. The exams themselves require them to video record themselves teaching, and they must include students in those clips. Of course, the students have not been required to have their cameras on, so this is an added expectation on the teacher candidates. The K–12 students must speak, and the student teachers also have to include a lengthy narrative showing how they have adapted their instruction to meet the needs of three focus students who all must be in the same class period. While this has always been an arduous and daunting task for student teachers, the added barrier of teaching online makes it feel insurmountable. Student teacher, Jouselin Martin, expressed the following:

> The requirements are inequitable in this virtual environment. In a face-to-face classroom, students are not as vulnerable to feeling exposed while teachers are recording. In an online setting, students are having to expose their living

environment. Many students are now full-time babysitters, cooks, maids, and even part time parents. Especially in the lower socio-economic schools. Many students already did these things but before the pandemic it was only after school; now they are having to do it full time and school is now part time. Dealing with problems with engagement and the expectations of TPA makes it difficult to meet the requirements. It seems inequitable to us as aspiring teachers to base our entire year of work, progress, and connection with the students based on 5-minute video clips of us doing something to conform with the requirements. Although the requirements are tasks we should be doing as teachers year round, it is difficult to capture this with the parameters set in an online environment where students can and are choosing to opt out and school districts are not requiring anything from them except for logging on for attendance purposes.

Imagine being asked to prove your worth in your profession under almost the same expectations that are always in place while simultaneously trying to navigate such unprecedented times! What is particularly disheartening is the realization that these pre-service teachers are feeling discouraged by low scores on the exam. One teacher candidate wrote that the TPA "makes me feel like I'm not capable of being a teacher based on the feedback." When the teacher candidates receive their scores, they only receive a score that shows them where they fit in the rubric. None of the feedback is specific to the particular candidate or their situation, and the rubric is somewhat broad including statements such as, "Planned accommodations attend to IEP/504/GATE goals and identified assets and needs between FS2's current developmental or academic abilities and the demands of the lesson, allowing FS2 to fully access content and meet learning goals" (CTC, 2018).

One of my residents, Alex Chapa-Kunz, reacted to our discussion about the TPA rubric with the following:

> In my writing for the TPA submission I kept the rubric next to me at all times, referencing each of the requirements I knew I would be assessed on. Despite this technique there were two rubrics that I received a level 2 [out of 5] score on. While I can read the rubric and see the reasons an assessor may have selected that score, because I have no specific feedback tied to my low score I can only guess at the error I made. This makes improvement as a new teacher especially difficult.

Additionally, several of the students in my residency have expressed that they specifically felt that they had met the demands for the highest box on the rubric but have learned from their TPA instructor that if they did not address everything in the third box of the rubric, the evaluator will not even consider the fourth or fifth boxes of the rubric. This makes exceeding standards particularly difficult, depending upon the assessor.

In examining the TPA report for our particular cohort of students, those who did not pass the exam are those whose students were only seen as black zoom boxes. Every meeting we have had with the mentor teachers eventually focuses on to how to get students to turn their cameras on. Some of the mentor teachers have success with some of their classes, but all of them admit that it is not what they want it to be. These are mentor teachers who were hand selected by their administration and the university residency faculty to support and coach the teacher candidates because of their strengths–one of the main ones being flexibility and willingness to try new things. If our experienced, superior educators are unable to get students to turn on their videos consistently, how can the evaluators expect teacher candidates or pre-service teachers to be successful?

We value the quality of flexibility and responsiveness in our teachers so much so that we evaluate them for these qualities on multiple rubrics and tools. Yet, when we are tasked with being responsive and flexible as an education community, it seems we are unable to do so. This pandemic should be a lesson to all of us.

WHAT HAVE WE LEARNED?

Learning how to teach in the pandemic begs us to answer the question about what teaching truly is. Is it simply developing a curriculum that is narrowly focused on content, or is it more than that? The pre-service teachers in our classrooms chose the teaching profession to work with students, as opposed to simply teaching content. Without the face-to-face interactions our students need, are we truly teaching them to teach? What ultimately will happen when they step foot in the classroom? What strengths have they gained, and what weaknesses have we missed?

In order to think through what this year's cohort of pre-service teachers will need, we need to consider the ways in which we support new teachers in gaining a sense of self-efficacy, developing classroom management, increasing engagement, and addressing social-emotional learning. Although students in this cohort will presumably have finished their university programs by the end of the school year, I would like to extend the suggestion that the university should continue to support these students into the following year.

Potential ways universities might support their new graduates include affinity groups, workshops and alumni gatherings. Merriam Webster defines affinity groups as "people having a common interest or goal or acting together for a specific purpose." Affinity groups can significantly impact the way a new teacher perceives their identity (Gee, 2001), and affinity groups may develop in accordance with who you are associating with in addition to the physical spaces being occupied (Bullough, 2005; Gee, 2001). Our teacher candidates will have new adjustments to make as they transition into the physical space both in terms of how they connect with their colleagues and students, and how they make sense of their school site. Providing opportunities for both first- and second-year teachers, who have spent much of their time learning how to operate in the virtual world, to begin to discuss how to transition to the physical space will be powerful and important.

One way universities could create peer affinity groups is by hosting evening or weekend meetings for the cohorts as they work to transition into in-person learning. This could take the form of an informal discussion to give the new teachers opportunities to share their frustration and problem solve, or it may be more structured by the facilitators to address the needs that seem to arise over time.

An additional option may be to host more professional development workshops to focus on the new teacher candidate needs. Often, coursework requires students to videotape themselves teaching, and then share that work with their peers. Teaching virtually allowed the critique to focus primarily on teaching strategies and curriculum development; however, K–12 student behavior did not typically come into play during these discussions. Workshops where students present their work in a nonthreatening way, in order to explore student behavior, might be useful to the new teachers. For example, the Boston Teacher Residency (https://www.bpe.org/boston-teacher-residency/) developed an interesting "game" that allows students to respond to difficult student behavior through a fabricated parental contact, and they asked parents to select the best responses. This could provide the new teachers with safe opportunities to practice events they are likely to come up against before they actually occur.

Additionally, putting these teachers in continuing conversation with university faculty who can provide support may emphasize continual learning, as well as extending the foundation of research-based practices. This would provide the teacher candidates with further opportunities to work through classroom management issues, student engagement, and social and emotional instruction. Another opportunity for universities to further support these new teachers is by hosting alumni gatherings. This provides opportunities for the students to strengthen their affinity groups, identify a community of practice, and find the emotional support necessary to do the hard work of teaching in the classroom.

In addition to these university-led efforts, schools that employ new teachers can support their growth with parallel efforts. For example, school sites would be well advised to consider incorporating professional development and mentoring plans explicitly geared toward these early career teachers and their needs. Although most teachers who leave the teaching profession do so in their first three years, solid mentoring practices can increase retention of new teachers (Elliott et al., 2010). Differentiated mentoring allows for principals and building administrators to focus on the needs that individual teachers have in order to be most successful. The Kansas City Teacher Residency (https://kcteach.org) suggest that coaches touch base with their new teachers bi-weekly, and Elliott et al. (2010) suggest that site leaders provide individualized attention. They also suggested that mentors for the new teachers be chosen intentionally, based upon the needs that the new teachers may have as opposed to simply choosing mentors by longevity or willingness to serve.

Areas that are likely to be high need for new teachers coming out of a virtual teaching space will include classroom management and pacing within a lesson plan. The instruction students have had most likely included theoretical discussion about classroom management and lesson planning; however, the reality of students in the classroom will shift the way new teachers cope with it. School sites ought to consider these specific needs in their mentoring guidance as well as in their professional development workshop planning.

All of this is to say our students aren't sure what they know and don't know. They haven't been left on their own with the students to develop their management or engagement skills in the way that they might have experienced in a face-to-face classroom. One of our resident teachers, Wade Branch, explicated the areas of support he feels he might need, which touches upon this idea.

> After some time in the physical classroom, though, I will benefit greatly from a mentorship program in which I can discuss my own victories and failures with a more experienced teacher. If I could meet once every two weeks to discuss questions and dilemmas, I would enjoy that. After being alone with my own class for even a week, I would be glad to have a supervisor step in, observe, and give me feedback on my work. I would be happy to sit in on a seminar about behavioral theory in which I can talk about the behavior patterns of Jane Doe in my class. The bottom line is that even with the wonderful residency (immersion) program like I am in, there is always the presence of the experienced mentor teacher that my students will respect. Only when I am left without support will I see what my management strategies and competencies are made of.

Ultimately, our student teachers are going into the classroom with experiences that, while beneficial, are not closely aligned with the situations they are likely to face. It is important that administrators, teacher educators, and evaluators continue to be responsive to the situation, even as we move back into classrooms. These new teachers will need extensive mentoring and support from their new colleagues. Their evaluations should aim to be more instructive as opposed to critical, and their peers must lift them up instead of tear them down and bemoan their lack of preparation. I have faith that we can, in fact, learn from this pandemic. I hope our educational system is prepared to embrace this pandemic-era cohort for all that they have to teach us and all that we have to teach them.

REFERENCES

Bandura, A. (1997). *Self efficacy: The exercise of Control*. W. H. Freeman and Company.

Bullough, R. V. (2005). Being and becoming a mentor: School-based teacher educators and teacher educator identity. *Teaching and Teacher Education, 21*(2), 143–155. https://doi.org/10.1016/j.tate.2004.12.002

Ciardiello, A. V. (1998). Did you ask a good question today? Alternative cognitive and metacognitive strategies. *Journal of Adolescent & Adult Literacy, 42*(3), 210–219. https://doi.org/10.2307/40014681

CTC. (2018). *CalTPA performance assessment guide single subject cycle 1* (p. 63). https://www.csusm.edu/soe/currentstudents/caltpa_c1_guide_ss.pdf

Eisenman, G., Carey, S. E., & Cushman, A. (2015). Bringing reality to classroom management in teacher education. *Professional Educator, 39*(1).

Elliott, E., Isaacs, M., & Chugani, C. (2010). Promoting self-efficacy in early career teachers: A principal's guide for differentiated mentoring and supervision. *Florida Journal of Educational Administration & Policy, 4*(1), 131–146.

Emmer, E. T., & Stough, L. M. (2001). Classroom management: A critical part of educational psychology, with implications for teacher education. *Educational Psychologist, 36*(2), 103–112. https://doi.org/10.1207/S15326985EP3602_5

Gee, J. P. (2001). Identity as an analytic lens for research in education. *Review of Research in Education, 25*, 99–125. http://www.jstor.org/stable/1167322

Gonzalez, J. (2013). *Find your marigold: The one essential rule for new teachers*. Cult of Pedagogy.

Greenberg, M. T., Domitrovich, C. E., Weissberg, R. P., & Durlak, J. A. (2017). Social and emotional learning as a public health approach to education. *Future of Children, 27*(1), 13–32. https://doi.org/10.1353/foc.2017.0001

Hoy, A. W., & Spero, R. B. (2005). Changes in teacher efficacy during the early years of teaching: A comparison of four measures. *Teaching and Teacher Education, 21*(4), 343–356. https://doi.org/10.1016/j.tate.2005.01.007

Marks, H. M. (2000). Student engagement in instructional activity: Patterns in the elementary, middle, and high school years. *American Educational Research Journal, 37*(1), 153–184. https://doi.org/10.3102/00028312037001153

Merriam-Webster. (n.d.). Affinity group. In *Merriam-Webster.com dictionary*. Retrieved June 2, 2021, from https://www.merriam-webster.com/dictionary/affinity%20group

Mulholland, J., & Wallace, J. (2001). Teacher induction and elementary science teaching: Enhancing self-efficacy. *Teaching and Teacher Education, 17*(2), 243–261. https://doi.org/10.1016/S0742-051X(00)00054-8

NCTR. (2021). *National Center for Teacher Residencies.*

Ross, J. A. (1994). Beliefs that make a difference:The origins and impacts of teacher efficacy. *Canadian Association for Curriculum Studies,* 45.

Wang, Z., Bergin, C., & Bergin, D. A. (2014). Measuring engagement in fourth to twelfth grade classrooms: The classroom engagement inventory. *School Psychology Quarterly, 29*(4), 517–535. https://doi.org/10.1037/spq0000050

Wong, H., & Wong, R. (2018). *The first days of school: How to be an effective teacher* (5th ed.). Harry K. Wong.

Zhang, G., & Zeller, N. (2016). A longitudinal investigation of the relationship between teacher preparation and teacher. *Teacher Education Quarterly, 43*(2), 73–92.

Chapter Eight

Trauma and Its Lasting Effects After School Shootings

Psychological Considerations for Faculty, Staff, and Students

Anka Roberto

What we have learned from the many school shootings that have plagued our nation over the last decade has provided us with insight into how we can best manage our classroom and learning environments during and after tragedies such as the COVID-19 pandemic. Many of the trauma indicators that we have seen in the aftermath of school shootings and community tragedies are being played out in the current state of anxiety, depression, and trauma responses among our students, faculty, and staff during the pandemic period. These mental health risks are higher than previous outbreaks and in line with rates found as a result of disasters such as school shootings, natural disasters such as Hurricane Katrina, and acts of terrorism such as 9/11 (Wright et al., 2021). In this chapter, we will provide an overview of the impacts of trauma on the mind and body, as well as provide an outline of action steps for leaders and faculty in higher education to initiate in order to adopt a trauma-informed approach while engaging students in the higher education environment.

Imagine teaching in a classroom; a loud popping noise echoes from the adjacent hallway of the building of your lecture hall. To you, the sound is similar to a balloon popping, nothing to be concerned about, you dismiss it and continue with your lecture. To the male student in the front row, the sound triggers an emotional/midbrain response communicating to his logical/cognitive/outer brain, sending messages from his memory bank/hippocampus that somebody has fired a semiautomatic weapon. His eyes are fixated on potential exit routes, as his flight response is initiated. His breathing becomes labored, his skin appears more and more flushed, and his behavior increasingly irrational and paranoid. You notice he is fidgeting in his seat and has asked to stand up in the back of the classroom. Or you are teaching a public health course on the topic of gun violence in America. Students are arranged in small groups for discussion; you notice a usually engaged student sitting in her chair staring at the wall appearing not to be interacting at all with her classmates. Or a lockdown drill takes place during your regularly scheduled class time without warning. A few students begin to look for items they can fight a shooter off with, their fight response initiated, despite being reassured it is only a drill. All of these scenarios are typical of the common fight, flight, and/or freeze response that occurs during a trauma response.

To survivors or victims of a shooting, a trauma response becomes immediately activated due to messages in the brain that start the cascade of the trauma response. Environmental triggers such as smells and sounds activate memory networks housed in the midbrain/hippocampus, sending fight, flight, or freeze messages from the amygdala to the cognitive/outer brain in order to respond to an external threat. The opposing part of the autonomic nervous system, the parasympathetic system which focuses on resting and relaxing, cannot work simultaneously while the sympathetic response of the autonomic nervous system of fight, flight, or freeze is engaged. Thus, it is in our best interest as educators to allow for our student learners to be able to disrupt this response, and initiate the rest-and-relax autonomic response, which also may allow for optimal social emotional learning to take place.

TRAUMA-INFORMED PEDAGOGY

Trauma-informed pedagogy differs from teaching about trauma, and a basic knowledge of trauma and its implications are just the start of the formulation of trauma-informed practices. A trauma-informed educator considers a student's trauma narrative and ensures that consistent, clear, and empathetic approaches are taken in the learning environment for all. While promoting resilience and excellence, educators may assist and mentor students to learn ways to stay within their resilient zone to enhance learning and creativity. Similar to universal precautions in a hospital setting, in which healthcare providers wash their hands and wear gloves during patient interaction to avoid contamination, a trauma-informed educator should assume every student has suffered a traumatic life experience at some point in their life, because as the COVID-19 pandemic continues to impact faculty, staff, and students, we will most likely see many more with trauma-related symptoms in institutions of higher education.

Implementing these guidelines will make a significant impact on the trajectory of our students, faculty, and staff. As the world attempts to return to a state of normalcy after the COVID-19 pandemic, much of what we have learned about the effects of Post-Traumatic Stress Disorder (PTSD) and Post-Traumatic Stress (PTS) related to school shootings can serve as a blueprint for higher education during these pressing times.

ORIGINS OF TRAUMA-INFORMED PRACTICES

As we aim to provide guidelines allowing for trauma- and resilience-informed practices in higher education, it is important to notice where these guiding principles of trauma-informed care came from. The Substance Abuse and Mental Health Services Administration (SAMHSA) formulated six principles of trauma-informed care to allow for organizations to utilize a framework in which policies and practices would not retraumatize individuals rather, promoting a sense of resilience: (1) Safety: Throughout the organization, staff and the people they serve feel physically and psychologically safe; (2) Trustworthiness and transparency: Organizational operations and decisions are conducted with transparency with the goal of building and maintaining trust among staff, clients, and family members of those receiving services; (3) Peer support and mutual self-help: These are integral to the organizational and service delivery approach and are understood as a key vehicle for building trust, establishing safety, and empowerment; (4) Collaboration and mutuality: There is recognition that healing happens in relationships and in the meaningful sharing of power and decision-making; (5) Empowerment, voice, and choice: The organization aims to strengthen the staff, client, and family member's experience of choice and recognizes that every person's experience is unique and requires an individualized approach; and (6) Cultural, historical, and gender issues: The organization actively moves past cultural stereotypes and biases, offers culturally responsive services, leverages the healing value of traditional cultural connections, and recognizes and addresses historical trauma (SAMHSA, 2014).

Implementation of SAMHSA's guiding principles of trauma-informed care has the potential to increase resilience in college-aged students. These principles, when consistent, can produce a new generation of young adults who understand the impact of trauma and resilience on the brain and body, while considering protective factors aiding in decreasing symptomatology of PTS and PTSD while fostering resilience. In addition, a model adopted by many universities across the nation utilizes tenets of trauma- and resilience-informed pedagogical practices that include the following elements, similar to those principles from SAMHSA; (1) Trustworthiness and transparency; (2) Support and connection; (3) Empowerment, voice, and choice; (4) Collaboration and mutuality; (5) Social Justice/Cultural Responsiveness; (6) Safety;

and (7) Resilience, Growth and Change. If these are kept at the forefront of every goal and vision, institutes of higher education will be successful in beginning at the right place.

Overall there seems to be a void in higher education with addressing the needs of survivors of such horrific events such as school shootings and violence. Stakeholders in higher education, including students and their parents/guardians, must trust that students are left in capable hands. This is concerning, as counseling centers on college campuses are not equipped to manage symptoms of PTSD because many clinicians are not trauma trained (Xiao et al., 2017). The nation's leading organizations for mental health and traumatic stress recommend college campuses take on a trauma-informed culture to address the post–9/11 student population (SAMHSA, 2014). Experts in the field of trauma recommend college campuses educate, train, and prepare all faculty and staff to better meet the needs of their students by implementing trauma-informed practices and pedagogy in higher education (Hoch et al., 2015). With more than 187,000 children exposed to gun violence in the school setting since the Columbine massacre in 1999 (Every Town for Gun Safety, 2021), one can conclude that many do not feel safe from violence in academic settings.

Surviving a school shooting has been noted to lead to PTSD, major depressive disorder (MDD), generalized anxiety disorder, acute stress disorder (ASD), panic disorder, social phobia, and antisocial personality disorders (Lowe & Galea, 2017). More so, those survivors who were closer in proximity to the shooter seeing or hearing the events and physical injuries or were acquaintances with deceased victims or their families showed a higher prevalence of severe psychological reactions (Hawdon & Ryan, 2012). Researchers have suggested that symptoms of posttraumatic stress led to poor academic outcomes, including college dropout as early as freshman year, cognitive deficiencies, executive functioning impairments, poor working memory, and difficulty with establishing healthy peer/professional relationships (Boyraz, Horne, & Granda, 2017). One can see why this would cause an issue entering an independent living and learning environment such as a university setting. Many students entering college have reported experiencing traumatic life events, such as life-threatening illnesses or accidents, physical or sexual abuse, and natural or manufactured disasters (Boyraz, Granda, et al., 2017). With the current impacts of COVID-19, a trauma- and resilience-informed approach in all institutions of learning may be necessary to address the mental health needs of this generation of student learners. Educating, advising, and mentoring this vulnerable population of young adults highlights the importance of implementing and utilizing trauma-informed practices within higher education institutions. Allowing these practices to be at the forefront of curriculum design for prevention and tactical approaches to meet the student suffering from PTS or PTSD would enable the systems to be ahead of the issue rather than behind.

As faculty and staff implement trauma- and resilience-informed teaching practices, it is imperative to recognize that no two students are alike. Resiliency differs dramatically based on many factors for individuals (Connor & Davidson, 2003). A trauma-informed educator is sensitive to the social emotional learning needs of each individual student. Institutes of higher education must shift focus to understand the landscape in which students, faculty, and staff have come from. Learning from one another, understanding one another, getting to know one another with an expression of empathy, clarity, and responsive to specific life experiences. As we begin a discussion around trauma- and resilience-informed practices, it is essential that we discuss each part of the seven trauma- and resilience-informed practices in higher education. The following trauma- and resilience-informed practices may assist in the development of policies, procedures, and practices that can lead to trauma- and resilience-informed pedagogy competencies.

SAFETY

Physical and psychological safety is integral to the brain's ability to learn (Clausen et al., 2017). Creating an environment in which safety and respect are at the forefront of all members of a learning community is essential to ensure psychological safety. Physical attributes of safety look different than in the K–12 environment. Most college campuses have doors of buildings unlocked; classrooms, residence halls, and common areas are generally open to the public; and gates to college campuses are unmonitored during daylight hours, leaving many college campus environments vulnerable to potential threats, and thus for trauma survivors, transitioning to a college campus can be challenging.

TRUSTWORTHINESS & TRANSPARENCY

In an effort to establish trust in the learning environment, it is also essential to be transparent both for the faculty and students. Trauma symptoms in postsecondary learners may vary, but behaviors may be seen in the following ways among students: difficulty focusing in class or attending class, retaining and recalling information; tendency to miss a lot of classes or coursework; disorganization and missing deadlines; forgetfulness; challenges with emotional regulation; fear of taking risks; anxiety about deadlines, exams, group work, or public speaking; anger, helplessness, or dissociation when stressed; withdrawal and isolation; and involvement in unhealthy relationships (Hoch et al., 2015). As trust and transparency is a goal, it is essential for faculty to foster a sense of accountability among their course workload expectations, their course objectives, and their students. This includes making course expectations very clear, ensuring consistency is practiced, maintaining appropriate boundaries, and minimizing a sense of disappointment. Fostering positive relationships among all individuals is essential in establishing trustworthiness, and this concept resides mostly in communication from faculty and students both verbally and nonverbally. Questions to consider for faculty and administrators while fostering a community of trustworthiness and transparency are as follows:

1. What message does administration, faculty, and staff relay around campus safety protocols, response to national disasters, systemic issues that may impact the college campus, and other relevant current events?
2. Do they involve students and their supporting organizations when responding publicly to current local events, involving students in decision making?
3. Do departments on campus share vision, goals, policy changes, enrollment adjustments, fiscal information, general operation updates to students and faculty, allowing for a level of transparency?
4. When a local, national, or global event occurs like the COVID-19 pandemic, do institutions utilize reliable methods of communication to all personnel and students with the same message?
5. Is there accountability, consideration for other perspectives, inclusivity, transparency?
6. Is information clear, and are policies and procedures straightforward?
7. Is there ambiguity on how incidents are managed?
8. Are specific goals and objectives made clear?
9. Do programs have policies in place to handle situations that arise?
10. Is there clarity around roles, and are personal/professional boundaries in place?
11. Is there equity across all demographics, schools, colleges, departments, and disciplines?

Once trustworthiness and transparency are achieved among the institution as a whole, faculty, and students may feel better able to engage in real and transparent dialogue around course content, current events, and the culture of the learning environment.

SUPPORT AND CONNECTION

Connecting students with appropriate peer and professional resources to support academic, personal, and professional success is essential as we create and foster resilience. Many students are unaware of the availability of resources such as student organizations, offices of disability, and counseling centers. This is an essential time for faculty to educate themselves on the many resources students have access to, because a lack of support and connection can lead to social isolation, anger, and resentment building up, then leading to depression and anxiety. Globally in 2017, 322 million, or one in five individuals, suffer from depression. During the COVID-19 pandemic, a recent meta-analysis conducted by Bueno-Notivol and colleagues indicated a sevenfold increase with a prevalence rate of 25 percent (Bueno-Notivol et al., 2021). This is most likely due to the lack of connection, the increase in isolation, and the inability to trust the media, the nation, and/or the world. Clearly, this is a critical aspect of trauma pedagogy for educators to address.

EMPOWERMENT, VOICE, AND CHOICE

As faculty embrace course content and attempt to enrich the minds of their students, it is essential to also build opportunities to enhance making choices, having control, being heard, having agency, building skills, and developing confidence and competence for all students. Often, trauma survivors report a lack of or loss of control over situations related to their trauma, lacking the ability to choose outcomes that affect them directly. Choice and lack of control cause psychological disruptions that may lead to anxiety-related disorders such as panic disorder, generalized anxiety disorder, and obsessive-compulsive disorders (Moritz et al., 2018). Offering options for students in coursework, in group work, in classrooms, and dialogue can be beneficial. For example, when constructing a course, is there flexibility with accessing resources? Are there more ways than one to accomplish an assignment? Do students, faculty, and staff receive clear responses about their rights and responsibilities? Are policies and student rights visually represented on syllabi and in the learning management system? Do students, faculty, and staff have a voice in decision making?

Faculty should focus on providing opportunities for students to learn and build upon skills to allow for their success as they gain confidence and competence. Providing opportunities to reflect and express feelings and emotions around a subject area is helpful as well. Creating spaces for innovation and creativity to aspire students to think outside the box may engage, empower, and build students' ability to make choices for themselves. Exercises across curricula that allow for collaboration and empowerment as leaders in their fields of interest are key to fostering empowerment, voice, and choice.

COLLABORATION AND MUTUALITY

Connection has been deemed as a protective factor with trauma survivors, and when one feels a sense of connection to others or their community, resilience factors are more prevalent (Bath, 2015). Each student experiences connection differently based on cultural contexts, social and psychological variables, and the impact the environment has on the individual (Denham, 2008). Thus, it is critical to consider that collaboration is essential for the connection of like-minded individuals to work toward a similar purpose, and that acting as allies rather than as adversaries, as well as creating opportunities to share power and make decisions, is essential in collaborating toward mutuality. Institutions that collaborate across campus and include students in discussions meet this guideline. Students, faculty, and staff should collaborate and connect to allow for perspectives from all to be weighed in systematic planning, service planning, and program development. As the general student population returns to a face-to-face campus environment, there is a likelihood of increased depression and anxiety due to the pandemic's traumatic impacts on college-aged students, which is compelling reason to initiate collaboration and mutuality efforts for students.

SOCIAL JUSTICE/CULTURAL RESPONSIVENESS

A trauma- and resilience-learning environment strives to be aware and responsive to forms of privilege and power, as well as respecting diverse experiences and identities. As racial and social injustices have plagued our nation, all students should have a space to share thoughts and perspectives in a safe and respectful environment. Researchers have noted that risks for secondary traumatic exposure leading to stress are higher for those among marginalized communities (Council on Social Work Education, 2020). In aligning a culturally responsible classroom, educators should work to help empower students to challenge social injustices, as well as facilitate a responsive learning environment to hold space for conversations around intersectionality such as age, ability, gender, gender identity, race, ethnicity, language, religious affiliation, and socioeconomic status. As students take on an objective stance and the learning environment fosters safe and constructive conversation around these factors, educators can allow for students to dialogue about the social order, rather than internalizing within their own systems (Sherwood, Tripplett et al., 2018).

Researchers have noted that in order to provide an environment of cultural responsiveness, it is essential to first develop a level of cultural competence within the learning environment (National Association of Social Work, 2021). This may come in the form of providing information to students to help increase knowledge in an effort to impact value systems. Furthermore, a sense of cultural humility, which addresses systemic issues of oppression (Hook et al., 2013), can come in the form of assignments that link specific content in a course to areas that are impacted by social justice or cultural factors. In an economics course, an example may be the impact of socioeconomic status on supply and demand of production of materials. In an English literature course, it may be choosing a written piece to reflect upon in the area of social justice and impact of societal change. These exercises of humility can be instrumental for students across various disciplines. Practical exercises and approaches to creating a culturally responsive classroom include: (1) Assessing level and knowledge of technology access, (2) Communicate promptly with students in need, (3) Use of inclusive language in course content and written and verbal communication, (4) Attempt to use blind grading to control for implicit bias from the faculty, and (5) Respond to student in a nonjudgmental manner using noncritical language both verbally and in writing (Sherwood, VanDeusen et al. 2021). Consideration of the aforementioned material in response to social justice and the cultural humble learning space along with these approaches may allow for increased connection, empathy, and sensitivity among all learners and faculty alike in higher education.

CONCLUSION OF RESILIENCE, GROWTH, AND CHANGE

Recognizing strengths and resilience while providing feedback to help one another grow and change in the learning environment is an essential factor in adopting a trauma- and resilience-informed approach in higher education. Utilizing the aforementioned principles throughout higher education may allow for growth and resilience among individuals and the learning community. As we approach the end of a global pandemic, the impacts of trauma may continue to have a ripple effect on students in higher education, and it is paramount that educators ensure that these practices are part of their interactions with students.

REFERENCES

American College Health Association. American College Health Association-National College Health Assessment II: Reference Group Executive Summary (2018). Silver Spring, MD: American College Health Association. Retrieved from https://www.acha.org/documents/ncha/NCHA-II_Spring_2018_Reference_Group_Executive_Summary.pdf

Bath, H. (2015). The three pillars of traumawise care: Healing in the other 23 hours. *Reclaiming Children and Youth, 23*(4), 5.

Boyraz, G., Horne, S. G., & Granda, R. (2017). Depressive symptomatology and academic achievement among first-year college students: The role of effort regulation. *Journal of College Student Development, 58*, 1218–36.

Bueno-Notivol, J., Gracia-García, P., Olaya, B., Lasheras, I., López-Antón, R., & Santabárbara, J. (2021). Prevalence of depression during the COVID-19 outbreak: A meta-analysis of community-based studies. *International Journal of Clinical and Health Psychology, 21*(1), 100196. https://doi.org/10.1016/j.ijchp.2020.07.007

Clausen, A. N., Francisco, A. J., Thelen, J., Bruce, J., Martin, L. E., McDowd, J., Simmons, W. K., & Aupperle, R. L. (2017). PTSD and cognitive symptoms relate to inhibition-related prefrontal activation and functional connectivity. *Depression and Anxiety, 34*(5), 427–36. https://doi-org.liblink.uncw.edu/10.1002/da.22613

Connor, K., & Davidson, J. (2003). Development of a new resilience scale: The Connor-Davidson Resilience Scale (CD-RISC). *Depression and Anxiety, 18*, 76–82.

Council on Social Work Education. (2020). *Social work student perceptions: Impact of COVID-19 pandemic on educational experience and goals.* https://cswe.org/getattachment/ResearchStatistics/Social-Work-Student-Perceptions.pdf.aspx

Denham, A. R. (2008). Rethinking historical trauma: Narratives of resilience. *Transcultural Psychiatry, 45*(3), 391–414.

Every Town for Gun Safety (2021). *Gunfire of School Grounds in the United States.* Retrieved from https://everytownresearch.org/maps/gunfire-on-school-grounds/#

Hoch, A., Stewart, D., Webb, K., & Wyandt-Hiebert, M. A. (2015, May). Trauma-informed care on a college campus. Presentation at the annual meeting of the American College Health Association, Orlando, FL.

Hawdon, J., & Ryan, J. (2012). Well-being after the Virginia Tech mass murder: The relative effectiveness of face-to-face and virtual interactions in providing support to survivors. *Traumatology, 18*, 3–12.

Hook, J. N., Davis, D. E., Owen, J., Worthington, E. L., Jr., & Utsey, S. O. (2013). Cultural humility: Measuring openness to culturally diverse clients. *Journal of Counseling Psychology*, 60(3), 353–66.

Lowe, S., & Galea, S. (2017). The Mental Health Consequences of Mass Shootings. *Trauma, Violence, & Abuse, 18*, 62–82.

Moritz, S., Fink, J., Miegel, F., Nitsche, K., Kraft, V., Tonn, P., & Jelinek, L. (2018). Obsessive–compulsive disorder is characterized by a lack of adaptive coping rather than an excess of maladaptive coping. *Cognitive Therapy and Research, 42*(5), 650–60.

National Association of Social Workers. (2021). *Code of ethics.* https://www.socialworkers.org/About/Ethics/Code-of-Ethics/Code-of-Ethics-English

Sherwood, D. A., Tripplett, M. L., Hoyle-Katz, S., & Langereis, J. (2018). Use of technology, pedagogical approaches, and intercultural competence in development. *Journal of Sociology and Social Welfare, 1*(45), 55–76. https://scholarworks.wmich.edu/cgi/viewcontent.cgi?article=4167&context=jssw

Sherwood, D., VanDeusen, K., Weller, B., Gladden, J. (2021). Teaching note-teaching trauma content online during COVID-19: A trauma-informed culturally responsive pedagogy. *Journal of Social Work, 57*(1).

Substance Abuse Mental Health Administration. (2014). SAMHSA's Concept of Trauma and Guidance for a Trauma-Informed Approach, retrieved on https://ncsacw.samhsa.gov/userfiles/files/SAMHSA_Trauma.pdf

Wright, H., Griffin, B., Shoji, K., Love, T., Langenecker, S., Benight, C., & Smith, A. (2021). Pandemic-related mental health risk among front line personnel. *Journal of Psychiatric Research, 137*, 673–80. doi: 10.1016/j.jpsychires.2020.10.045

Xiao, H., Carney, D. M., Youn, S. J., Janis, R. A., Castonguay, L. G., Hayes, J. A., & Locke, B. D. (2017). Are we in crisis? National mental health and treatment trends in college counseling centers. *Psychological Services, 14*(4), 407–15. https://doi-org.liblink.uncw.edu/10.1037/ser0000130

Part III

PERSONAL AND PROFESSIONAL REFLECTIONS

Chapter Nine

Chairing in the Pandemicene[1]

Coronavirus, George Floyd, and the Year of Living Dangerously

Tiffany Gilbert

On June 4, 2020, I had had enough. George Floyd had been dead for nine days, and the furor over the manner of his death had crescendoed into a national wail for justice. Housebound and largely helpless, my fellow department chairs at the University of North Carolina (UNCW) and I did what most academics often do in such moments of crisis: We rattled off solemn emails to our respective faculty and students. Instantly, I felt uneasy, as leadership messages of this ilk can come off as treacly or banal, the bureaucratic equivalent of President Bill Clinton's "I feel your pain"—and not in a good way. I knew that, regardless of what I wrote, I could not sidestep my own experiences regarding race and policing. Thus, in an email to my English department colleagues, I dropped the mask of administrative objectivity and recounted an event from 2012:

> I am existentially exhausted. It is difficult for me to wrap my head around the events of the past week. As I reflect and rage, I think about an incident that took place about 8 years ago. I received my first traffic ticket for expired tags. When the police car signaled me to pull over at the intersection of College and Oleander, I was nervous. . . . He approached the car and pointed out my expired tags. There was nothing to argue about—I had been putting off the inspection. I sat anxiously as he returned to his car to run my license and prepare the ticket. When he returned, he explained the next steps and wished me "a good afternoon." The whole incident, in the main, was pretty unremarkable except for one detail: The ticket misidentified me as a white woman. I always assumed the officer made the mistake, but I eventually learned that, when I first obtained my NC driver's license, the Department of Motor Vehicles presumed to know who I was and mislabeled me in their system. It's frightening, in light of Sandra Bland, to wonder what could have happened if I had encountered a different

police officer. Did a DMV clerical error, which has since been corrected, protect me from a potentially dangerous situation?

When the officer ticketed me, I was enroute to teach a literature class focused on Ralph Ellison's novel, *Invisible Man*. Talk about a "teachable moment" containing multitudes: race, misidentification, policing. Hearing my story, students were both perplexed and amused: Some were more surprised by the fact that this was my first ticket than by the officer's cluelessness. We laughed about this fact and soon settled into a very satisfying discussion of the novel. A month later, a New Hanover County traffic court judge dismissed the ticket; relieved, I tucked the memory of the ticket inside my copy of *Invisible Man* along with my notes. Now, isolated in quarantine, I returned to the ticket episode in my message to faculty because it could have been exponentially worse—especially given the nexus of Wilmington's past and the rise of deadly encounters between police and unarmed Black people during "routine" traffic stops. I had to put the prospect of Black death caused by excessive police force into a personal framework for myself and my colleagues.

The murder of George Floyd, the protests it inspired, and the prolonged dread of the coronavirus pandemic have exerted pressure on all aspects of the academic enterprise—instructional, personal, administrative. Although my chair colleagues and I are united in a fellowship of survival in these hard times, I cannot divorce the travails of this moment from my identity as a black woman academic in the South. What are the intellectual and emotional hazards of "chairing while Black" at a predominantly white institution (PWI) in the vortex of two pandemics—racism and COVID-19? This chapter reflects on department leadership in a time of crisis and moral drift in America. Finally, it contemplates the residual influence of Wilmington's racially violent history on the UNCW chancellor's disastrously inept "All Lives Matter" stance in the face of mass mourning and anxiety.

THE FALL OF FLORENCE

Wedged between the Cape Fear River and the Atlantic Ocean, UNCW was originally founded as Wilmington College in 1947, in New Hanover County, and was renamed in 1969 to recognize its transition from a junior college to a university. As the "state's coastal university," UNCW has survived any number of significant weather events, including Hurricanes Hazel (1954), Fran (1996), and Matthew (2016). The arrival of Hurricane Florence in September 2018, however, brought along a set of challenges that UNCW faculty, students, and staff alike could hardly imagine. Florence's cone of uncertainty, according to meteorologists, fanned out across the entire state of North Carolina, into South Carolina and parts of Virginia. Days before her arrival, residents and students scrambled to evacuate the region, as university personnel activated emergency protocols. Students were instructed to take essentials and depart before roads became too congested; some, perhaps operating under the assumption that the university would reopen soon after the storm passed, left behind computers, PlayStation consoles, and other valuables. Faculty likewise scattered. Fearing the worst from a Category 4 hurricane, some colleagues traveled as far south as Florida and as far west as Texas to escape Florence's reach. My own family and three cats headed north to Richmond, Virginia. Once settled, we did what everyone did—we waited.

Initially predicted to be a Category 4 storm, Florence crossed the shore as a Category 1 on September 14. The hurricane stalled out over Wilmington, drenching the city with more rain than ever recorded from a single meteorological event. Catastrophic flooding washed out major stretches of I-40, I-95, and US-70, leaving Wilmington stranded and inaccessible. The campus, like elsewhere in southeast North Carolina, suffered extensive damage. Hundreds of longleaf pines either lost massive limbs or were brought down altogether, creating a dangerous maze of debris. A number of academic buildings and dormitories were compromised; Dobo Hall, where the biology and chemistry departments are housed, was so badly impacted that it was taken offline completely and shuttered for years for repairs. Water, which breached the roof and cascaded floor by floor throughout the building, destroyed years of scholarly research. Upper administration came to the reluctant conclusion that a swift resumption of normal operations would not be possible. My chair counterparts and I communicated latest developments and game plans to our departments in dense email threads that tested the endurance of even our most patient colleagues. I managed email correspondence from students anxious over renegotiated deadlines and the fate of their grades. Meanwhile, I, too, wondered when the highways would be clear enough to return home. Did our house survive? Would we, in fact, complete the fall semester?

A month would pass before we were able to access campus. Still, we never doubted our recovery; the Seahawk would soar again. The university identified alternative housing for students whose dormitories required water and mold mitigation. Contractors maneuvered trailers into place so that students could complete lab requirements. Many colleagues purged waterlogged offices, ruined books, and papers. The Southern Accreditation of Colleges and Schools (SACS) "forgave" hundreds of instructional minutes, as faculty retrofitted their course plans to accommodate the reduced time in class. The Office of eLearning (OeL) and Center for Teaching Excellence (CTE) provided instructional resources to ease faculty stress as we jerry-rigged the rest of the term. Between appointments with claims adjusters, roofers, tree cutters, and other trades, faculty got back to the business of teaching.

The news of UNCW's salvaged semester made headlines in the higher education press. While there was much of which to be proud, we had experienced enough devastation not to be arrogant: Out of extreme caution, the university shut down for week when Hurricane Dorian, a considerably milder storm system, passed over area in September 2019. No significant damage to overcome, no heroic curricular adjustments to make. After a year of upheaval, we anticipated the spring 2020 semester with excitement: new classes, new students, new discoveries. Little did we know that we were in for the shock of our lives.

COVID SPRING AND THE SUMMER OF GEORGE FLOYD

The spring 2020 semester was hardly two months old when the COVID-19 pandemic absorbed everything into its awful vortex. My department and I were in the home stretch of a second job search when the novel coronavirus began to overtake media coverage in late February. Campus visits, as we know, can be weird under optimal circumstances, because they require all parties to negotiate an awkward tango between professional distance and social familiarity. Over the span of two weeks, we welcomed five candidates to Wilmington with little drama; now, with the search process nearing its end, the sixth visit was thrown into flux. If the candidate had traveled to countries that were then experiencing rapid viral spread, how would we know? How would chairs and search committees modify itineraries to maintain integrity in the hiring process? Chairs received HR permission to ask the candidate to disclose pertinent travel information so that we could, if necessary, adapt the visit accordingly. Fortunately, we were not impelled to alter our plans. As it happened, the department meeting to vote on the hire turned out to be the last act of regular business before spring break and before the virus raged across the country. The date was Friday, March 6, 2020.

Spring break, fraught with nervous restlessness, was initially extended by a week to allow faculty to pivot—a word soon to be invoked ad nauseum—to prepare online instruction for two weeks. Instead of finalizing details for English Studies Week, which was planned for the middle of March and intended to spotlight the major, our administrative associates cancelled room reservations and catering orders. They fielded questions from faculty about the fate of professional conference requests and fast-tracked reimbursements, while I contacted candidates about the search outcome. It was all quite concerning; yet, surely, after surviving Hurricane Florence, we could handle another operational disruption and postponed return? This coronavirus was not a storm that could be tracked, avoided, or even tolerated; rather, it was a brazen plague that did not care about midterms or multimodal presentations. Guidance from the dean and upper administration choked inboxes, as did information about Canvas, the online learning management system to which many of my colleagues across the university would turn for the first time in their careers. The two weeks were hardly exhausted when Governor Roy Cooper issued a "Stay at Home Order" on March 29, 2020, a declaration that guaranteed UNCW would not reopen before the end of the academic year. The loss of regular contact with colleagues and students, commencement, the simple pleasure of coffee with a friend in between classes—and not knowing when we would enjoy these activities again in person—was too much to bear.

Within days, thousands of Americans contracted the coronavirus. The Centers for Disease Control, the National Institutes of Health, state and local officials urged the necessity of taking basic precautions like washing hands frequently, maintaining social distance, and wearing masks. As the number of hospitalizations, then deaths, increased, infectious disease experts noted that Black and Brown people appeared more susceptible to the virus's most devastating effects; comorbidities like diabetes, hypertension, obesity, so prevalent in these communities, intensified the worst symptoms of COVID-19. Conversations about healthcare disparities dominated news cycles. The pandemic was not only a public health disaster, but it had evolved into a racial one as well. If masks had been touted as a means of decreasing the risks of infection, Black men, in particular, raised concerns about profiling. In April 2020, *Boston Globe* opinion writer Aaron Thomas (2020) acknowledged his own fears in a very personal column. A mask may protect him from contracting COVID-19, he reasoned; it could not guarantee his safety from trigger-happy, anti-black vigilantes. Indeed, as pernicious as the coronavirus was, racism remained an enduringly insidious foe.

The tragic case of Trayvon Martin had taught us all the consequences for Black men dressed in allegedly suspicious or threatening clothing and accessories. George Zimmerman, self-designated neighborhood security, accosted Martin, who was walking home from a convenience store. Ignoring police guidance, Zimmerman engaged the eleventh grader in a physical struggle. Fearing for his life, Zimmerman later claimed, he shot Martin, who died from his injuries. Trayvon Martin was only seventeen years old. However, in some news coverage, Martin's image was repurposed to fit a grotesque stereotype of menacing Black masculinity: The teenager in an ordinary hooded sweatshirt was transmogrified into a thug in a hoodie; his pack of Skittles and bottle of Snapple were rebranded as the weapons of a wily criminal. Thomas's hesitation and fear of losing his life while protecting it against a virus, then, was more than justified.

Indeed, not even a pandemic could displace the scourge of racism and unhinged police brutality. While we endured weeks of quarantine, Breonna Taylor's unprovoked killing in Louisville, Kentucky, received more national scrutiny. On the evening of March 13, 2020, she had been asleep when a team of plainclothes police officers, operating under the auspices of a no-knock warrant, entered the apartment she shared with her boyfriend, who fired a single warning shot. The officers responded with a barrage of gunfire, shooting Taylor six times. A black woman sleeping. A 26-year-old EMT, who risked COVID-19 exposure to help others, she never knew what hit her. We had hardly caught our collective breath from the sorrow when, two months later, Minneapolis police officer Derek Chauvin pressed his knee upon the neck of George Floyd, a black man accused of passing a counterfeit twenty-dollar bill. For eight minutes and forty-six seconds, we watched Floyd die. From our couches, we heard him plead for mercy and call out for his deceased mother.

George Floyd's slow death at the hands of police officers during a global pandemic underscored America's absurdist attachment to systemic racism and other narratives of racial anxiety. The spectacle of Black death again became headline news, receiving split screen treatment with ratcheting infection rates. Despite the threat of this pernicious contagion, Americans masked up and gathered in town squares and city plazas to protest yet another incident of police brutality. In the streets and on social media, many united to affirm that Black lives matter. Artists rendered Floyd's image in every possible context, including projecting his face on the graffitied pedestal of the Robert E. Lee statue that anchored the famed Monument Avenue in Richmond, Virginia, for 130 years until its removal in September 2021. How, in this surreal environment in which we are all estranged from routine and each other, would academics respond? Without the interpersonal connections established in our classrooms, how would we engage in this crucial debate responsibly at UNCW?

UNCW, BLM, AND A SHOCKING END

On the university's website, and under the heading "Seahawk Points of Pride," UNCW boasts "a powerful academic experience that stimulates creative inquiry and critical thinking and a community rich in diversity, inclusion and global perspectives." The facts on the ground tell a different story, however. According to institutional data, students who identify as Black or African American constituted 5 percent, or 857 out of 17,499 students in

Fall 2019, and 6 percent, or 991 out of 17,915 students in Fall 2020. In the five-year period from Fall 2016 to Fall 2020, enrollment percentages for this demographic never exceeded 6 percent—effectively unchanged from Fall 1976.[2] Given these statistics, is it any wonder that UNCW is often derogatorily referred to as "UNC-White"?

These numbers are not surprising when considered in light of Wilmington's history. Wilmington holds the ignoble distinction as the only American city to witness the successful overthrow of a multiracial, legally elected government and the massacre of its Black residents.[3] In November 1898, prominent White citizens, with the cooperation of gangs and members of the Red Shirts, a paramilitary terrorist group, marched through the streets arrayed along the Cape Fear River, smashing windows, beating Black people, torching homes and businesses. Even youth was not regarded as a deterrent: Children became targets of this extrajudicial violence as well. Some residents, fearing for their safety, hid in the swamps surrounding Pine Forest Cemetery, the burial ground reserved for Black families of New Hanover County, and relied upon clandestine deliveries of food and medical supplies for weeks. More fled the city, leaving behind property and roots to seek safety beyond North Carolina and an unredeemed, racist South. Half a century later—Wilmington College was founded in 1947—the racial dynamic had scarcely changed. Public school desegregation, though ordered with "deliberate speed" in the Supreme Court's 1954 *Brown v. Board* of Education decision, was not achieved in New Hanover County until 1962; the state did not fully integrate until 1971.[4] Given this vexed local history, and the number and variety of institutions in North Carolina, Black students can simply choose to attend college elsewhere—anywhere but UNCW.

By design or by accident of its youth, UNCW is a strangely ahistorical place. There are no markers or murals to educate visitors about the 1898 massacre that occurred in the city. There are no structures to acknowledge the first Black residential students to graduate from the university. Campus buildings are largely named for rich donors, a common practice at many institutions of higher learning, and for dead White men of varying significance in North Carolina history. Some even bear the names of coastal birds like the pelican, sandpiper, and osprey. Only two buildings are named for women scholars—DePaolo Hall, named after former chancellor Rosemary DePaolo, and Morton Hall, named after former English department chair Shannon Morton.

Within this context of institutional whitewash, and in the wake of George Floyd's televised killing, a contingent of Black Student Union (BSU) members, Black staff and faculty, and the president of the Student Government Association (SGA) held a Zoom conference call with Chancellor Jose Sartarelli and other administration leaders on June 11, 2020. The students came together to discuss how the ways in which the university could demonstrate its opposition to police brutality as well as show its support for the Black Lives Matters movement. They suggested that the university could paint Black Lives Matter on Chancellor's Walk, a quarter-mile esplanade that cuts through the heart of campus. Their request was hardly unique or radical and would have the force of making explicit UNCW's commitment to diversity, inclusion, and equity. The Black Student Union shared the chancellor's appallingly tone-deaf response on its Facebook page: "If you are asking me tomorrow to start painting and decorating the university with Black Lives Matter, that's going to be very difficult because all lives matter." As dismissively obvious as it is passively aggressive, "All Lives Matter" is designed to shut down thoughtful dialogue about systemic racism and its beneficiaries.

Many have opined on the disingenuousness and treachery of "All Lives Matter," including Judith Butler (Yancy & Butler, 2015), who exposed the phrase's inexorable whiteness: "Understood as the sometimes tacit and sometimes explicit power to define the boundaries of kinship, community and nation, whiteness inflects all those frameworks within which certain lives are made to matter less than others." Whiteness, Butler continues, "is less a property of skin than a social power reproducing its dominance in both explicit and implicit ways. When whiteness is a practice of superiority over minorities, it monopolizes the power of destroying or demeaning bodies of color." In light of Wilmington's barbaric racial history, "All Lives Matter" amounts to little more than a form of gaslighting or a clever shorthand to deny the experiences and traumas of the oppressed in order to preserve the comfort of the oppressors. "All Lives Matter" pumps itself up as a kind of totalizing humanism when, in actuality, it is as substantive as wet cotton-candy.

At the same time, its function as a kind of rhetorical kryptonite cannot be understated. Its invocation during this call was not only meant to silence the students, but also to reveal the limits of the chancellor's interest in denouncing police brutality against Black and Brown bodies. I cannot imagine how those students, who were placed in the position of appealing for empathy and redress, felt when the chancellor rebuffed them by repeating this empty slogan. SGA president Matt Talone (2020–2021) criticized the use of phrase and offered the support of his office: "It's important and we do stand with them. We do strongly support all the needs they brought up last night. They're students and SGA's mission . . . to represent the voice and mission of the student body—and if this is their vision we'll do our part to see it through."

News of the disastrous Zoom call circulated through UNCW's social media pages and the local press swiftly. The pandemic had denied us the community of our classrooms and campus offices, the spaces where we could vent, commiserate, and otherwise transform disillusionment into purposeful dialogue or action. Instead, we were all stranded in our digital and analogue bubbles. The chancellor's refusal to paint or otherwise make visually explicit his solidarity on campus mobilized chairs to create their own BLM banners.

A cavalcade to a local copy shop commenced. Within days, my fellow chairs and I across the College of Arts and Sciences, the Watson College of Education (WCE), the College of Health and Human Services (CHHS) used personal money to purchase black and white BLM banners to suspend from the façades of our buildings. To reinforce their positions on the sanctity of Black humanity, many chairs uploaded statements of solidarity to their department websites and emailed similar messages to their majors. In the abstract, these reactions were fine, if not the most radical.

However, as the first Black woman to chair a CAS department in the history of UNCW, narrating this episode for colleagues and English majors in the aftermath of Floyd's death took on a new resonance. It magnified my embodiment in ways that, in my view, could not be ignored, in ways that my predecessors had not been compelled to invoke during their tenures as chair. The moment exposed a strategy for surviving academia that many scholars of Color know too well: "masking" and "spill-outs" (Bain et al., 2017). Considering their implementation in mentoring relationships, Bain et al. (2017, p. 603) explained:

> Masking and spill-outs are tools, employed consciously and otherwise, that help us to navigate the emotional terrain of neoliberalized academia. While spill-outs offer an outlet for the expression of a variety of feelings: excitement, joy, anxiety, self-doubt, or fatigue, for example, masking is often an act of self-preservation. Emotions that may be consequential to one's position or relationships in the academy, if expressed openly, are masked or hidden away, manifesting and usually spilling over elsewhere. Attending to the sites where spill-outs occur exposes the connectivity between our public (professional) and private (personal) selves. Our public selves carry over into private spaces, and otherwise masked or private emotions can also spill out into public settings.

These days, it was becoming increasingly difficult to maintain the mask. As much as I agreed with the protestors' righteous anger and with other chairs on the need for some expression of unity, I wrestled with how much of myself I wanted to invest in this pursuit. Furthermore, I remained skeptical about the efficacy of performative gestures like plastering banners all over campus and departmental posts against white supremacy. Everything felt so hollow, so academic. I was tired of explaining the obvious to those I thought knew better.

With only twenty-three Black tenured or tenure-track faculty on campus, more than anything, I was tired of being the "only one" in most of the rooms I entered. Mary Frances Winters (2020) consolidated these inchoate feelings—the anger, frustration, and exhaustion—I felt in the phrase "black fatigue." For Winters, black fatigue is generational, a kind of psychocultural inheritance that "is a deeply embedded fatigue that takes inordinate amounts of energy to overcome—herculean efforts to sustain an optimistic outlook and enormous amounts of faith to continue to believe 'we shall overcome someday.'" In other words, as Public Enemy declared, "I got a right to be hostile, man, my people are being persecuted!" Why now? Because the chancellor had said the unspoken part out loud? Because we were stuck at home? George Floyd's murder was not an isolated incident; it was as disturbing as any atrocity of its kind. We had witnessed the right-wing hate rally in Charlottesville in 2017, but two hurricanes diverted our collective attention away from the roots of America's existential dependence upon systemic racism and on restoring university functionality. Now, we were surviving a pandemic and, again, trying to make the fall semester happen. What would banners accomplish? What kind of response would they elicit on a deserted campus during the summer break?

Indeed, the banners catalyzed virtual conversations on UNCW's credibility on race and diversity matters. Many critics, including current students and alumni, could not square the university's sudden "wokeness" with its continued employment of criminology professor, Michael S. Adams, who frequently used his social media presence to target UNCW faculty and students as well as to lambast BLM. In July 2016, he tweeted, "Black Lives Matters supporters are either racist, emotionally unstable, or suffering from severe intellectual hernia. Or all of the above."

On May 29, 2020, four days after George Floyd's killing, Adams mocked slavery and the spiritual "Go Down Moses" to complain about Governor Roy Cooper's intensified COVID-19 protocols: "This evening I ate pizza and drank beer with six guys at a six seat table top. I almost felt like a free man who was not living in the slave state of North Carolina. Massa Cooper, let my people go!" In another tweet posted that day, he described BLM protesters as "thugs looking for an opportunity to break the law with impunity." As demonstrations against police brutality multiplied across the country, calls for Adams's ouster grew louder. Whether the university would act could not be guaranteed: UNCW had been burned before, losing against Adams in a 2014 promotion denial suit and ordered to cover court costs, back pay, and raise his salary. The July 2, 2020, announcement that UNCW and Adams agreed to lofty severance, did not prepare us, however, for the coda to this chapter in the BLM banner saga: Mike Adams's suicide on July 23, 2020, one week before his anticipated resignation.

BANNER-GATE AND THE FAILURE OF LEADERSHIP

While Adams's suicide cast a pall on the moment, the urgency of BLM and the coronavirus never abated. On the eve of the fall 2020 semester, we watched the convergence of three disasters: a pandemic, George Floyd's death, and UNCW's public relations nightmare, itself a culmination of the university's failure to comprehend its complicity in a racist regime and the deleterious impact on Black student belonging. Signs enforcing mask use and BLM banners, reminders of the health and racial crises, greeted students who returned to campus. College deans created standing committees on diversity and inclusion to assess and redress racial inequities. A leadership change in UNCW's Office of Institutional Diversity and Inclusion (OIDI) offered the prospect of substantive engagement of these issues that I found wanting post-Charlottesville. Then, a bureaucratic "surprise." On September 18, 2020, the chancellor unveiled, via email, a banner policy that did not exist prior to the proliferation of BLM banners on campus. He explained:

> As it honors and facilitates free expression, the university has policies in place that outline the time, place and manner of such activity. This includes the location of banners and other expressive activity for student events and public events sponsored by external community organizations or individuals. Until recently, we did *not* have a specific policy designated to manage the time, date and place for expressive activities, such as banner placement, by faculty and staff.

The chancellor closed his email with the idea of an outdoor exhibit or artistic installation featuring the banners. I found it difficult to believe that were it not for the Black Lives Matter slogan emblazoned on them, such a policy would not have been codified; an exhibit consisting of identical banners was less consolatory than infuriating.

Admittedly, I had been doubtful about the banners' presence on campus. The longer they were allowed to wave and flutter in the coastal breeze, I realized, the more students felt affirmed. *I* felt affirmed. However, in leadership meetings, we spent an excess of energy fulminating over the chancellor's policy rather than the imperatives animating the BLM message itself. How long were we going to gnash our teeth over the banners' removal or spin our wheels over alternative locations to rehang them?

If anyone harbored any hopes that concerns over the banner policy would dissipate in the COVID haze of the opening weeks of the semester, they were sorely mistaken. Gamely, the Faculty Senate president hosted an open Zoom forum in which faculty, regardless of rank, could learn more about the policy's motivations and tease out the implications of its implementation. The Zoom was a disaster from the start. Many reiterated how the banners only became necessary after the chancellor's refusal to acknowledge BLM or condemn police brutality in a robust manner. The policy, faculty on the call feared, would silence speech. The conversation took a noticeable turn for the worse when it became evident that the chancellor appeared not to comprehend the larger question of human dignity at stake and remained focused on banner placement. "This is NOT ABOUT BANNERS!" I vented in absolute frustration at the tiny boxes on my computer screen.

What the chancellor seemed loathe to engage or acknowledge was the endemic nature of the problem itself: systemic racism in higher education. At one point, he implied that search committees had not done enough to resolve UNCW's problems with diversity. To bolster his credibility, he ticked off a list of future action items: recruiting more faculty of color, expanding the Africana Studies minor into a major, and kick-starting diversity-focused scholarships. In the abstract, these plans sounded good, but did not ring authentic to me in the moment. Would there have been movement on these issues if the banner question had not been handled with such carelessness? Where was the emphasis on cultural change or community building at UNCW? Focusing on metrics or crossing strategic thresholds may gain purchase with trustees and other stakeholders; but, in this meeting, such language further inflamed tensions. Redress required more than bureaucratic rationalizations and endless paperwork that would inevitably land on the desks of those most disadvantaged and wearied from constantly navigating the racial minefields in higher education.

At the end of the forum, I was left more heartbroken than enraged. Perhaps James Baldwin (1985) was right when he wrote in *The Price of the Ticket*: "The price one pays for pursuing any profession, or calling is an intimate knowledge of its ugly side" (p. 302). The ugliness here was palimpsestic in nature: layers of history, power, privilege, and denied access overlay upon one another without clear demarcations. I was also incredibly tired of these types of encounters that never seemed to exact the same emotional toll on some of my university colleagues no matter how much they professed their allyship or allegiance to the BLM cause.

Within days, the chancellor asked to meet and discuss the forum's fallout. I accepted his invitation with a little trepidation; after all, we were not in the habit of talking regularly or extensively. To be singled out, however benign the spirit of the chancellor's request, activated an uncomfortably familiar dynamic: playing the "representative." Given my role as chair and status as a Black woman, I felt this tension acutely. Corbin, Smith, and Garcia (2018) clarify this dilemma: "When one is consistently positioned as the sole purveyor of experiential knowledge for a racially marginalized group, particularly in a setting that requires and/or encourages engagement, the pressure to speak up to, dispute ignorant or malicious statements, or simply 'represent well,' becomes heightened and burdensome" (2018, p. 9). And draining. Even with the interim CAS dean, Office of Institutional Diversity and Inclusiveness (OIDI) interim director, and the provost in attendance, I was concerned that the Zoom medium would distill my personal experience into a monolithic narrative that represented all faculty of color. Nevertheless, what I was seeking from the chancellor, who spent much of his working life in the pharmaceutical industry, was the recognition that an alternative metric of success—one that did not rely solely upon market forces or student credit hour production—was plausible, one grounded in what Lawson (2007) called an "ethics of care." This approach, while feminist in origin, "begins with a social ontology of connection: foregrounding social relationships of mutuality and trust (rather than dependence) . . . [and] understands all social relations as contextual, partial, attentive, responsive, and responsible" (p. 3). Along with the broader institutional goals he enumerated, I maintained that we could expand our priorities to include community building and belonging. After nearly an hour of listening and dialogue, our Zoom ended.

Notwithstanding the cordial tone of our call, the damage had been done; the disastrous faculty forum had wrought more harm and mistrust than I thought possible. Two faculty members submitted a motion of no confidence in the chancellor's leadership to the Faculty Senate. Invoking the violent insurrection of 1898 and the 1971 wrongful conviction and incarceration of the "Wilmington Ten"—nine Black men and one White woman—for allegedly firebombing a grocery store amid integration protests, the motion's authors averred that the chancellor "failed to demonstrate a clear commitment to the principles of equality, justice, and diversity." Senators discussed the motion on November 10—ironically, the same day as the 1898 massacre—but it soon became evident that there were numerous concerns about this action; the motion was postponed indefinitely, rendering it moot. Other colleagues, meanwhile, had prepared language for a motion to censure to express the faculty's displeasure in the chancellor's handling of the BLM question and to reprimand him publicly. As an inglorious coda to the worst year ever, the Board of Trustees denounced the successful vote to censure to the chancellor, which passed on December 8, 2020.

NEW YEAR, NEW HOPE?

The three years from 2018 to 2021 at UNCW have been a surreal blur. Hurricane Florence, though not as strong as had been predicted, devastated the campus and the region. She slouched northward and dissipated, leaving a shattered landscape where we were able to rebuild and reclaim our lives. Then, all hell broke loose. A contagion slouched across the planet and brought unimaginable infection, suffering, and death. Lessons gained from the hurricane became more relevant as the pandemic compelled us to identify "workarounds" to perform our jobs away from campus, postpone or eliminate certain administrative tasks to ease the stress from the ensuing uncertainty, and provide appropriate support for faculty, staff, and students. As we conducted our lives online—doing homework, sustaining relationships, ordering groceries, buying take-out—we waited for science to catch up with the virus and produce a vaccine to liberate us from the grip of this nightmare.

Yet, we remain flummoxed when it comes to matters of race at UNCW. The spectacle of George Floyd's death showed us that not much has changed since the cataclysm of 1898; America's grip on the levers sustaining white hegemonic power has not loosened. The academic industrial complex, like many other institutions, relies on certain structural realities to exist. "'Education' is not innocent or neutral, it is designed to teach peoples to be subject to colonial and capitalist structures (Smith, 2007, p. 141). In this vein, the illogic of "All Lives Matter" denies systemic racism to perpetuate a fantasy of equality. To hear "All Lives Matter," particularly at this school, in this city, glances off the ears like a boxer's stinging blow. Banners may provide, in the short run, a rallying point; they can galvanize sentiment—they cannot substitute for institutional commitment or for policies that engender diversity, equity, and inclusion.

So, what's next? In academia, we often speak the language of outcomes. We design courses with the destination in mind. We strive to equip students with skills suited for the "real world," as well as introduce them to content that challenges them to think about what it means to be human. Contemplating what we want students to carry away with them when the class ends, many scholars have begun the work of decolonizing their syllabi to include other voices. Similarly, we must erect a decolonizing framework in leadership. As chairs, we can rethink departmental philosophies around hiring to ensure that students learn from scholars of color and underrepresented identities. Moreover, given the close proximity in which we work, we must insist upon inclusive spaces on campus. UNCW can survive hurricanes and even a pandemic; but to thrive, she must abandon the supremacist history and systems that perpetuate her longevity.

NOTES

1. I have borrowed the term "pandemicene" from Jenny Reardon, who created "The Pandemicene Project" for The University of California Santa Cruz's Science and Justice Research Center. She uses "pandemicene" to recognize the multivalent impact of the virus on our habits, processes, and systems—everything. "We are going to be asking fundamental questions about how we order ourselves. This pandemic is forcing us to reckon with those questions, and that's all to the good. We shouldn't think any of this is temporary." Retrieved from https://news.ucsc.edu/2020/04/reardon-pandemic.html.
2. This institutional data confirms UNCW's long-standing issues with attracting black students and with recruiting black faculty.
3. David Zucchino's recent account of the events leading the 1898 Wilmington massacre, *Wilmington's Lie*, is one of several important texts on the subject. For more on the topic, see H. L. Prather, Sr., (1984), *We Have Taken a City: The Wilmington Racial Massacre and Coup of 1898*. (Wilmington: Dram Tree Books) and C. W. Chesnutt, and W. Sollors (2012), *The marrow of tradition*. (New York: W. W. Norton Books). Chesnutt's *The Marrow of Tradition*, though fictional, employs the massacre and coup as the inciting event of the novel's drama.
4. North Carolina itself did not reach the Brown's desegregation threshold until 1971, and only after the Supreme Court again decided in *Swann v. Charlotte-Mecklenburg Board of Education* that busing was needed to ameliorate the racial balance. By comparison, Virginia also resisted Brown's mandates and did not fully integrate schools until the 1970s. Retrieved from https://www.oyez.org/cases/1970/281.

REFERENCES

Bain, A. L., Baker, R, Laliberté, N., Milan, A., Payne, W. J., Ravensbergen, L., & Saad, D. 2017. Emotional masking and spill-outs in the neoliberalized university: A feminist geographic perspective on mentorship. *Journal of Geography in Higher Education, 41*(4), 590–607.

Baldwin, J. (1985). *The price of the ticket: Collected non-fiction, 1948–1985*. New York: St. Martin's, 302.

Corbin, N., Smith, W. A, & Garcia, J. R. (2018). Trapped between justified anger and being the strong black woman: Black college women coping with racial battle fatigue at historically and predominantly white institutions. *International Journal of Qualitative Studies in Education, 31*(7), 626–643.

Feldman, K. (2020, June 8). North Carolina university 'aware' of professor's tweets comparing coronavirus shutdown to slavery, calling rioters 'thugs.' *NY Daily News*. Retrieved from https://www.nydailynews.com/news/national/ny-north-carolina-professor-wilmington-adams-20200608-igt3utna6ffajlske2angnjzye-story.html

Governor Cooper announces statewide stay at home order until April 29. (2020, March 27). North Carolina Department of Health and Human Services. Retrieved from https://www.ncdhhs.gov/news/press-releases/governor-cooper-announces-statewide-stay-home-order-until-april-29

Lawson, V. (2007). Geographies of care and responsibility. *Annals of the Association of American Geographers, 97*, 1–11.

Lennon, P. (2020, September 19). UNCW restricts freedom of expression on campus, singles out BLM signs. *Port City Daily*. Retrieved from https://portcitydaily.com/local-news/2020/09/19/uncw-restricts-freedom-of-expression-on-campus-singles-out-blm-signs/

Staff. (2020, July 2). UNCW reaches $500,000 settlement with Mike Adams to avoid costly litigation the school "might not win." *Port City Daily*. Retrieved from https://portcitydaily.com/local-news/2020/07/02/uncw-reaches-500000-settlement-with-mike-adams-to-avoid-costly-litigation-the-school-might-not-win/

Smith, A. (2007). Social-justice activism in the academic industrial complex. *Journal of Feminist Studies in Religion, 23*(2), 140–145.

Thomas, A. (2020, April 5). Why I don't feel safe wearing a face mask. *Boston Globe*. Retrieved from https://www.bostonglobe.com/2020/04/05/opinion/why-i-dont-feel-safe-wearing-face-mask/

University of North Carolina Wilmington. (2020). Banners, posters, and temporary outdoor signs (non-university sponsored individuals or groups). https://uncw.edu/policies/documents/banners,-posters,-and-temporary-outdoor-signs.pdf

WECT News. (2020, June 12). UNCW Black student union leaders "disappointed" by chancellor's "all lives matter" comment during meeting. Retrieved from https://www.wect.com/2020/06/12/uncw-black-student-union-leaders-disappointed-by-chancellors-all-lives-matter-comment-during-meeting/

WECT News. (2020, June 13). Student reacts to UNCW chancellor's "all lives matter" comment. Retrieved from https://www.wect.com/2020/06/13/student-reacts-uncw-chancellors-all-lives-matter-comment/

Winters, M. (2020). *Black fatigue: How racism erodes the mind, body, and spirit*. Oakland, CA: Berrett-Koehler.

Yancy, G., & Butler, J. (2015). What's wrong with "all lives matter"? *New York Times*. Retrieved from https://opinionator.blogs.nytimes.com/2015/01/12/whats-wrong-with-all-lives-matter/

Zucchino, D. (2020). *Wilmington's lie: The murderous coup of 1898 and the rise of white supremacy*. New York: Atlantic Monthly Press.

Chapter Ten

New Literacies, Empathy, and Advocacy

Reconstructing a Pedagogy in Pandemic Times

Suriati Abas

> Water is the first medicine. It affects and connects us all. When a black snake enters into the Earth and poisons the people's water, one young water protector takes a stand to defend Earth's most sacred resource.
>
> —*We Are Water Protectors*, Carole Lindstrom (writer) & Michael Goade (illustrator)

As Katie went on with the narration, faces of resistance emerged. The background music grew louder and louder. And within split seconds, we were scanning through the tribal community. Then, there was a moment of silence. With just a one-sentence closure, the book trailer left viewers hungry for more. This multimodal composition is the first book trailer recently published on Global Story Hour (https://www.facebook.com/GlobalStoryHour/).

GLOBAL STORY HOUR

Initially created as a private Facebook page in Spring 2019, Global Story Hour (GSH) was used to document students' service-learning sessions as part of fulfilling the requirements of a Children's Literature course. The class of 18 college students in a liberal arts college at Upstate New York met twice a week for 1.5 hours per session, and every week, these students read aloud for 10 hours to school-age children either at a local daycare center, a childcare center owned by the university, or a Montessori school. At the end of each session, they uploaded videos of themselves reading aloud to children in the community onto GSH. Another 10 hours were dedicated to participation in two community-based events during school holidays. Although the technological facility for reaching out to a wider audience via GSH was available at that time, some students often cite slow internet connection and inability to upload video files as barriers to avoid filming themselves. However, the pandemic of coronavirus (COVID-19) changed not only the ways in which this course was taught, but also students' mind-set toward technology. In the section below, I describe what it was like in the first six weeks of remote teaching, which was also the last few sessions before the Spring 2019 academic semester ended.

THE PIVOT TO ONLINE INSTRUCTION

The aftermath of the World Health Organization's designation of novel coronavirus as a pandemic on March 11 brought about a hasty transition to remote learning across the United States, altering the mode and delivery of my course immediately following spring break. Although I was well-positioned to dive into a digitized pedagogy, having spearheaded a technology-integrated curriculum for six years, turning my coursework online on a dime was laborious. Given a week for preparation, I decided to conduct synchronous and asynchronous sessions. The rationale for adopting both types of lessons was, to ensure that I could check in with my students to provide opportunities for them to engage in "live" discussions and keep them motivated. While I reconstructed my pedagogy to continue offering a modicum of the learning experiences as promised by the university, I scaled down on the content. One thing that came across very clearly was that COVID-19 is not a purely epidemiological phenomenon. To add on, it is a societal issue that demands immediate response to social emotional well-being. Hence, for my course, the pivot to online instruction constituted three key components: seamless integration of new literacies, empathy (an aspect of social emotional learning, commonly known as SEL), and advocacy to help my students cope with the sudden change.

NEW LITERACIES, EMPATHY, AND ADVOCACY

In planning for the transition to remote learning, I suspended the myth that students born in the digital age are predisposed to be adept at navigating new technologies (Abas, 2021). Although Pew Research Center reported that many youths are now leading "tech-saturated lives" with 95 percent using the Internet, 78 percent having cell phones, 80 percent having a desktop or laptop, and 81 percent using social networking sites, my experiences of integrating technology in my teaching informs me that college students are not necessarily proficient with technology. While technology continues to evolve, educational curricula remain stagnated prior to COVID-19. As Leu (Leu, Forzani, Timbrell, & Maykel, 2015) points out, having acquired the "traditional" literacy of reading and writing does not indicate high competencies in the use of technology. Bearing this in mind, I introduced my students to basic features of Zoom. I instructed them to do simple activities such as using the "mute/unmute" button and clicking on the "raise hand" sign to respond or ask questions. Although this experience felt like teaching a kindergartener or first grader how to behave in class, I did it because I recognized that my students are learning in an "alternate universe" (Ahmad, 2020), a learning environment that is no longer similar as before.

Given the nature of the course, it is mandatory to read many children's books. Although I have introduced my students to free e-books and audiobooks through Libby (https://www.overdrive.com/apps/libby/) and Hoopla (https://www.hoopladigital.com/) at the beginning of the semester, it was only after we went on lockdown that they began to invest more time searching and reading children's books online. The pivot to online instruction additionally provided an opportunity for me to set up a free class account for my students to access Epic, the leading digital library for children (https://www.getepic.com/). Through Epic, I was able to assign books for my students to read and monitor their online reading.

With the coronavirus radically changing our lives, fear of the catastrophe is real for many students as the experience itself. Media feeds, inundated with news of grievances, deaths, lockdowns across the globe, not only create awareness of the fragilities at the present moment but also leave students feeling anxious and worried about their future. To address this conundrum, I built in "empathy" or opportunities for my students to acknowledge their feelings and those of their peers into the revised syllabus. At the beginning of every session on Zoom, I did a social emotional check-in. A day before class, I posted three questions for students to think about before the class meets. For all the sessions, the first question is always, "How are you and how are you feeling today?" (see Table 10.1).

Apart from building empathy into the revised syllabus, I committed to advocating positivity and self-care. Hence, the second and third questions set the stage for developing optimism, helping them to move forward, in unprecedented times. At the end of every week, on Fridays, I send out "A Note to All" messages via the school's learning management system, Canvas, with words of encouragement taken from publicly available internet resources. The purpose is to motivate them to keep learning, exercise self-care, and cope with the on-going crisis which seems to be indefinite. As Chansky (2019), notes, "If we must teach under these circumstances (and we must), we are obligated to serve our students to the best of our abilities with conscientious and humane pedagogies that take into consideration our students' and our own anxieties over and experiences with crisis" (p. 3).

Table 10.1. Elements of a humane, disaster pedagogy

Week	New Literacies	Empathy	Advocacy
1	"mute/unmute" "raise hand" feature	• How are you and how are you feeling?	Inspirational words
2	Breakout groups Join and leave breakout groups	• How are you and how are you feeling? • An object that sparks joy in my house	Self-care tips
3	"Thumbs up" sign and icons to express their feelings virtually Using chat to respond	• How are you and how are you feeling? • A word/two words that is/are important to me at this moment	Inspirational words
4	Sharing screens to present an idea	• How are you and how are you feeling? • How do I invite positivity in my life?	Self-care tips
5	Online Presentation	• How are you and how are you feeling? • Share a motivational saying with us	Inspirational words
6	Online Presentation	• How are you and how are you feeling? • What are you grateful for?	A message for my peers

PANDEMIC POSSIBILITIES: EMBRACING OPPORTUNITIES

Typical of service-learning courses, opportunities were created for students to serve the community as part of their learning process. For this course, my students worked in trios to do read-alouds at a community site that matched their personal schedule. Adhering to the state's stay-at-home order which took into effect on March 22, 2020 (see New York State Department of Health Press Release, March 20, 2020), our weekly class routines had to be adjusted. The assignments prepared for the weeks after the pivot to online instruction were altered to fit into the context and current goings-on. Although COVID-19 saddles education with deficits—loss of face-to-face interaction, cancelled school events, disrupted access to physical resources, and other unanticipated issues—it raises new opportunities for developing literacies leveraging the strengths of digital tools.

To ensure that students continue to gain rich experience through community participation, I instructed them to submit a video-recorded read-aloud and book extension activities that parents and/or caretakers could potentially do with their child independently. These activities replaced the in-person read-alouds that have been taking place at the various community sites. On one of our Zoom meeting sessions, I showed them examples of video-recorded read-alouds; some readers choose to be in the video at the beginning of their read-aloud to introduce themselves and the book. Some chose to make themselves visible throughout the read-aloud while others prefer to give attention to the texts and illustrations as they read aloud. All video-recorded read-alouds and lesson outlines were uploaded on GSH and to a shared space on Google drive.

As originally planned, for the final assignment, students had to create a bibliotherapy comprising 10 books that can be used as resources for teaching children about an identified problem and/or issue in the community. Considering the global crisis that we are currently facing, I decided to use COVID-19 as one example. Using a freely available ebook, "My Hero Is You," I facilitated book discussions for my students to think about questions the pandemic raises and how they could use the story to educate young readers. The book, developed by the Inter-Agency Standing Committee Reference Group on Mental Health and Psychosocial Support in Emergency Settings, and supported by global, regional, and country-based experts, came in multiple languages (for details, please refer to Inter-Agency Standing Committee website at https://interagencystandingcommittee.org/iasc-reference-group-mental-health-and-psychosocial-support-emergency-settings/my-hero-you). We looked at several ebooks available from Libby and discussed potential topics with follow-up activities that could be used as bibliotherapy. Overall, the transition to online instruction went smoothly, partly because my students have been introduced to videorecording, online discussion tools via Canvas, and ebooks at the beginning of the course.

CONCLUDING THOUGHTS

As a professor who has experienced teaching in an elementary school during the severe acute respiratory syndrome (SARS) outbreak in 2003 ("Singapore government Press Release, 2003), the pandemic of COVID-19 feels like deja vu. Although I am dedicated to teaching my college students, self-care is still a priority; therefore, I draw boundaries between work and home so that I am not on the screen responding to students' queries 24/7. Having to weather a public health crisis also tells me that the pedagogy I have been holding on to needs to be reconstructed to incorporate three elements: new literacies, empathy, and advocacy. As aforementioned, these are the components that constituted my "disaster pedagogy." Most importantly, as educators, we need to:

1. Exercise care and concern

    Showing care and concern is not new on the teaching agenda. However, the rate at which we are receiving news of deaths due to COVID amplified the need for a disaster pedagogy on the thrust of humanity. Being isolated at home can have an impact on social, emotional, and mental well-being of students. Hence it is important to check in with them regularly and find out if they are coping well with online instruction. As Ahmad (2020) says, during stressful times, staying healthy is more important than the content that needs to be covered. The dual crisis that we concurrently faced, COVID-19 and systemic racism, additionally, taught us valuable lessons about education in America—learning cannot take place if the well-being of students, especially Black, Indigenous, Latinx, and other marginalized communities, is not taken into consideration.

2. Practice the art of simplicity

    Although guided by a syllabus planned for the semester, in a highly stressful situation like this, we should avoid overcomplicating matters. Although it seems ideal to replicate in-person instruction into an online learning environment, this strategy may not benefit students. At a time when everyone is trying to accomodate to the "new normal," students need space to process their feelings and thoughts. Hence, using digital tools that they are familiar with, may take the cognitive load off their heads and thus sustain learning. In my class, I continued to use Canvas, Google docs, and other tools that have been adopted prior to the transition. For a 1.5 hour synchronous session, I presented the content in bite-sizes, allowing students to engage with one another in breakout rooms on Zoom. All the synchronous and asynchronous activities were scaffolded to ensure that students could grasp the content well.

3. Ensure digital equity

    The success of online instruction is partly dependent on whether students have access to reliable sources online. Doing a short survey on students' basic technology needs helps in planning on specific digital tools for teaching and learning. Through my experience of teaching remotely, I realize that some of my students who live in the city do not have internet access at home, and a considerable number of households who do not have internet connection are those who come from less privileged backgrounds or rural communities. This circumstance can make it difficult to continue learning via online education. Despite having digital connectivity, not all inequalities could be addressed. While all of my students embraced synchronous class meetings, there is a flip side to it; synchrony can enact a pedagogy of privilege reaffirming the systemic inequities promoted by a pedagogy of liberation (Freire, 1990/1970). Mandating that students attend face-to-face sessions conveys insensitivity to the impact of pandemic on some households. The students that we are teaching could be returning to disrupted homes, having to accommodate altered schedules, and/or shouldering family obligations.

Putting the experience of reconstructing a pedagogy into perspective, my parting words at the end of any meetings have since been "Stay well, safe, and healthy!"

REFERENCES

Abas, S. (2019). Reading the world—Teaching visual analysis in higher education. *Journal of Visual Literacy, 38*(1–2), 100–109. doi: 10.1080/1051144X.2019.1574120

Abas, S. (2021). Teaching and learning in COVID times: A reflective critique of a pedagogical seminar course. *Journal of Teaching and Learning With Technology, 10*(1). Retrieved from https://scholarworks.iu.edu/journals/index.php/jotlt/article/view/31392

Ahmad, A. (April 9, 2020). Adapting to disaster, episode 2: Teaching in transition. The professor is in. Retrieved from http://theprofessorisin.com/2020/04/09/adapting-to-disaster-episode-2-teaching-in-transition-guest-post-by-dr-aisha-ahmad/

Ahmad, A. (April 10, 2020). Productivity and happiness under sustained disaster conditions. *The Chronicle of Higher Education.* Retrieved from https://www.chronicle.com/article/ProductivityHappiness/248481/

Bedford, A. W., & Brenner, D. (2010). Making contact in times of crisis. Literacy practices in a post-Katrina world. In M. Laurie (Ed.), *Literacy in times of crisis—Practices and perspectives.* New York: Routledge.

Chansky, R. A. (2019). Teaching Hurricane María: Disaster pedagogy and the ugly auto/biography. *Pedagogy, 19*(1), 1–23. Retrieved from https://muse-jhu-edu.proxyiub.uits.iu.edu/article/712779/pdf

Diaz, J. (2020, March 14). Internet providers won't cut off users over unpaid bills for 60 days. *New York Times.* Retrieve from https://www.nytimes.com/2020/03/14/business/internet-providers-coronavirus.html

Freire, P. (1990/1970). *Pedagogy of the oppressed* (M. B. Ramos, Trans.). Continuum.

Kang, C. (2020, May 20). Parking lots have become a digital lifeline. *New York Times.* Retrieve from https://www.nytimes.com/2020/05/05/technology/parking-lots-wifi-coronavirus.html?searchResultPosition=1

Leu, D. J., Forzani, E., Timbrell, N., & Maykel, C. (2015). Seeing the forest, not the trees: Essential technologies for literacy in the primary and upper elementary grade classroom. *The Reading Teacher, 69*(2), 139–145.

New York State Department of Health Press Release. (2020, March 20). Governor Cuomo signs the "New York State on PAUSE" executive order. Retrieved from https://www.governor.ny.gov/news/governor-cuomo-signs-new-york-state-pause executive-order

Singapore Government Press Release. (2003, March 26). Retrieved from https://www.nas.gov.sg/archivesonline/data/pdfdoc/2003032606.htm

Chapter Eleven

In a Crisis, Stories Need to Be Heard

Changing the Digital Landscape to Include Narratives

Kevin D. Cordi

All teachers remember where we were on September 11, 2001. My high school students feared we would be bombed because we lived close to the Lemoore Naval Base in California. They were scared and confused wondering if they would be next, and at the time, we received no answers or guidance.

That day I wondered whether I should continue teaching English or focus more on addressing their fears. I didn't have the answers to their questions, but I decided to listen. These students needed a place to ask questions, talk about their concerns, tell their stories. I realized listening was the curriculum. I listened as a football player broke down to tell me he worried about his family in New York City. One young first-year with tears in her eyes asked, "My dad is in the Navy, will he be okay?" I remember a young student, who hardly talked in class, sharing for an hour how she was scared to go home because she didn't know what was next. Together we listened to the sound of uncertainty and worked to understand it. On that day, students asked for hugs. I freely gave them. I will never forget how I outstretched my arms, not knowing what to say, but trying to say everything will be alright, wondering if the answer was true.

THE INVASION KNOWN AS THE PANDEMIC

Instead of the towers falling this time, my classes were in danger of crashing because of a pandemic. It was not only my classes, but my students. They were asking the same question "Will I be next?" "Am I safe?" and "Will we be alright?" Yes, Uncertainty returned to my teaching, but this time it was on a digital screen.

WRESTLING WITH DIGITAL TOOLS

The pandemic quickly made the household the new classroom. Screens were turned on by all my students. As an assistant professor, I was expected to know how to digitally teach almost overnight. It didn't happen that quickly, it took time. New language entered my teaching world, Microsoft Teams, break out rooms, Zoom controls, but at the time my main concern was not this language, but addressing fear and questions such as "Will we be alright?"

As much as I instinctively knew that I needed to listen on 9/11, I realized that my college students needed to talk and be heard on screens. They had been silenced from going to work, to see family, to religious gatherings, even to the store, and for many, my class was their only daily conversations. They had new stories of not overcoming difficulty and of struggle pent up inside and needed a space to share them. Digital landscapes did not provide a space for stories, unless we recognized it was needed. We could plan assignments, but they needed more than the 'article of the week.' Instead, if we *do* make it part of our curriculum, it will only serve as a holding place to do quizzes, take exams, read articles, and continue to distance our students from real-world conversations.

How could I ignore that they needed a place to share about these experiences? By telling stories, they could address this critical unpredictable time.

Losing Students

I served as the Middle Childhood Coordinator and I didn't want to lose the rich connections that I had made with my students. Upon checking in, I discovered stress levels were soaring. Since many of my students were from rural communities, I had trouble connecting with them. When I talked with them, you could tell they were giving up, and despite my best efforts, I didn't reach them all. There were a few who simply dropped out.

The Story of Email

As a result of losing face-to-face contact, I started to realize the gravity of the words I used in emails and in my responses on Blackboard. My main goal was to show as teachers and professors we cared about our students. I realized using stories moves digital teaching from "distance learning" to connected learning.

Before the pandemic, I would email the students if they were absent and say they were missed and provide the assignments; however, during the pandemic, instead of opening up with an "I missed you in class," I would share about my struggle or simply offer a space to listen. If I expect to know more about my students, I needed to share more of *my* story. The message included personal notes of my mother-in-law's and father-in-law's declining health and the adjustments we made. They realized I too was struggling. Once I created this space, their responses grew to include narratives of struggle, family problems, and calls to help with stress or balance. Because I shared my struggles, they shared their challenges. This helped me negotiate with my students in the crisis.

Need for Stories While Using Digital Landscapes

As students face a screen, they don't have 25 or more classmates in their room and similarly, a teacher can't immediately see a reaction indicating that a student is confused. Unless we work to invite these stories and make spaces for them to be heard, distance learning can be just that, distanced. Stories bring us closer. I realize a few minutes to ask about them and share stories of the day can go a long way in building community. A student, "Jackie," felt the need to email me about the class. She said,

> "throughout our class I've grasped how important it to have a relationship with your students and care for them. The relationship is what leads them to be able to learn in the best way possible. In our class I am greeted by name and we often are asked what is going on in our lives. The connection has made the biggest difference in my education. It has made me want to connect with my work instead of seeing it just as "work." (personal email, March 30, 2021)

Digital Connections

Another way I created a space that I welcomed my students in the community was sending a personal letter in an email. In the letter, I said that I would listen and that they should practice self-care. However, this is not a 'one and done' exercise, we as educators need to deeply listen to what our students are and are not saying. Sometimes it takes work to build a connection. For example, it took me five weeks to discover "Charles" could not get online because he had a poor internet connection. When I called him to see why he didn't contribute to class, there was silence on the phone. Tears fell as he shared how his father was a preacher and was traveling to see members of his church. The problem was his son was observing his high-risk father enter houses that were not safe and thus withdrew because he was helpless to prevent his father's risk-taking. This weighed heavy and affected his energy. School work was not his first concern. I affirmed his story and adapted assignments to be more equitable.

This pandemic served to remind me that school curriculum is not always the first priority, whether a pandemic is or not is occurring, our students' narrative lives and struggles are significant. I listened as students shared they worked three jobs and were now taking care of their parents. I too must value the work they are trying to do with these changes and thus I eased up on deadlines and allowed work to be turned in later—the world did not collapse as a result. Students generally did not take advantage of my leniency and instead often thanked me for understanding. The stories of my students can help me to motivate, negotiate, or plan learning and are the first curriculum that I address especially in times of crisis.

Teaching Students to Respond and Tell Stories

Although story is a way we make meaning, students are not always ready to apply storytelling strategies to how they comprehend information or share in class. Too often we ask for restatement or repeating ideas or a list of facts, instead of spending time telling the story of what they learned. They first need to give themselves permission to use story to create meaning. Ritual and tradition are part of story. I have created a "Permission to Play and Tell Stories" where students give themselves to "take risks," "make mistakes," play, and tell stories. We spend time sharing and reciting this pledge which serves to remind them they are invited to story. Many of my students have asked for a copy of the pledge. Permission to Story Pledge: As educators, one doesn't often share how students are invited to respond. If we are using story as tools for learning, students need to know they are free to use it.

The Importance of *Tell Me*

Aidan Chambers's (2006) *Tell Me* stresses the importance of these words when working with reading and states that instead of asking "why" or "what" questions, we should say "Tell me more about that." He argues that asking why often puts students on the defense but asking a student to tell me more about something implies that "I have made a space to listen to you." In order for my students to learn that they can respond in story, we engage in "Tell Me" Exercises that I created where each student responds with "Tell me." Students respond to each other out of sincere curiosity to know more about what the other student is sharing.

Search for Stories

As noted, students are not used to answering in story. Even though story is pervasive in our lives, students don't stop to value the stories around them. I share with my students how they can develop a "narrative mind-set," which is "the deliberate practice of refocusing so you respond with a narrative intention to address an issue, idea, topic, or belief" (Cordi, 2020), and we engage in "searching for story" exercises to help develop this mind-set. In each exercise, I speak to responding to what I call "in story." This means instead of given an evaluation statement like "I like this," respond in a more narrative way by using words that speak to what is said inside the world of the story that is being shared. Responding in story might seem awkward at first, but after a few tries, students begin to share how it changes their thinking. The exercises might include any of the following:

1. Listen to a professor and share with someone in story his or her teachings.
2. Safely follow a stranger and look for the stories that you might find.
3. Create a story journal that captures the significant actions of your day in story.
4. Instead of answering with yes or no, practice responding in story. Try to make a longer but interesting response with each day.
5. Use story signals to help your friends respond in story.

The Power of Stories: Listening to Story Signals

I have learned by saying what I call "story signals," such as "Tell me more about that," "Do you mind staying on so I can really listen to this," and "Can you help me understand more by sharing more with me after the meeting?" They were signals to students that I have space to listen to them. Digital space can be story space.

This week, after giving an assignment to create using Green Screen technology, a nontraditional student reached out to say he can't do it: "Fail me if you have to." I realized the way that I responded determines his response and said, "Don't worry, I understand, and I assure you will not fail." This led into conversations about balancing being a student, wrestling coach, and a father and the stress of juggling all the roles. From the story signal, I began to understand it wasn't about not being able to do the work, it was pleasing everyone in these roles.

Signal You Can Stay

When students are on digital screens, we need to be available so that students will have the space to share why their work is not going well. Instead of rushing to leave, I tell my students, "I will be the last one off the Zoom call so you can ask questions or simply talk." Many students have taken advantage of this time. This week a student shared she was feeling overwhelmed and just needed a break. She talked about complications at work, family, school, and guilt for not completing assignments. She said she felt like a loser. I not only gave her more time to find balance but offered space to share her concerns. With the extra time, I saw improved work and more attention in class.

Another student showed up in a Zoom call in uniform while working at a pizza restaurant. She is the manager, and no one would cover her shift. On screen, her book was open right next to a pepperoni pie. In the past, I might have said something, but instead, I asked if I could have a discount on breadsticks. I needed to recognize she was there despite the fact that she needed to be somewhere else. I was surprised at how much attention she paid to the class while making pizza.

Reaching Out and Failing

My students' stress levels rose every day. Their daily story was a stressful one. I wanted to address this, so I created a SharePoint resource page rooted in wellness to invite active dialogue and to help cope with the stress. I wanted to have a place for them to reach out and express themselves. I envisioned a place where students could share websites, images, and advice, but I created this with MS Teams and few students responded to it. My students didn't have time to reach out with this new system, it would have been better use of the time to call them and check in more. Simply put, my students needed more than another computer-oriented response to address their stress. They needed someone to listen to them.

I am still learning about my student concerns. Using story for discovery helps me know them but this is more difficult when the voices are found on digital spaces, but if as educators we consider creating story spaces in the digital and nondigital space, we can create a sense of value for our students. We can create a space of reflection, a shared community, a place for possible stories.

Losing and Gaining from Narratives

Whether I am watching two towers fall or my students crumble, there is destruction. During this time, even when the virus has gone away because science has caught up with it, when we are back in the classes, the need for stories will remain. During the pandemic, I gained insight. I will continue to stay in class until the last student has left so that their story has a space to be told. I have learned to ease up on demands that forced deadlines and allow spoken and unspoken results to allow extra time or a respite to restart. I also, whether I am working on digital or nondigital frames, listen more to what is said and not said. After all, merely because the virus has eased does not mean my students are free from stress. When they want to talk, I will listen because their stories matter.

REFERENCES

Chambers, A. (2006). *Tell me: Children, reading and talk.* Jackson, MS: Thimble Press.

Cordi, K. (2020). Rethinking narrative's place in the school and the classroom. *The Currere Exchange Journal, 4*(1), 38–50.

Chapter Twelve

Community Is Always the Answer

Columbus State Community College, Compassion, and Care

Barbara Allen

SAYING YES

On Thursday, March 12, 2020, my vice president called. I quickly moved outside to speak to him from the empty picnic table in front of my office where I work as an assistant director of employee engagement at a community college in Columbus, Ohio. Fragments of the hurried COVID conversations and makeshift recovery plans to redirect work swirled through my thoughts as I sat at the table warmed by the Spring midday sun. I had often worked on special projects for him before, but in the hours and days before the Corona virus felt real, serious, and life changing, I had no idea how transformative this particular call would become for me, my institution, and the outcomes for our students and employee community. I listened carefully to his words.

The entire experience felt suspended in time. He asked me with an unprecedented focus and seriousness to take on what we call Compassion and Care—a program that allows my team to partner with HR to be alerted daily about those employees with timely outreach needs—as some of the most important work we would ever do for Columbus State Community College. As an improviser at heart, when asked, my answer is most always YES in the spirit of new beginnings and discovery. I knew I was all in.

MISSION DRIVEN

That Friday was the first day of our new world connecting through online meetings and informational texts. We wondered, How would we create connection for our college community across distance, technology, fear, and the unknown? I had no idea this new normal would become our powerful new community, but the urgency of the moment drove us forward. For the first two weeks, we spent hours daily on TEAMs considering ideas—what did compassion and care mean and how could we operationalize them? Whom did we serve? How could we live our values in a way to spread joy, connection, and authenticity for our 2,500 employees (administrators, faculty, and staff)?

We brainstormed every day to create a guiding framework and deliverables. We wanted to stay rooted in our college values and create something that felt real, unique, available, and joyful. The Compassion and Care Committee became a vision realized of many individual committee members' hopes and dreams for the health and prosperity of our community in these unprecedented times.

Inspired by our college leadership, we knew a big, bold, and encompassing mission would guide us best into the unknown creating an anchor as we lead this work forward. After a week of fine-tuning, we solidified our mission, which included sharing "messages of inclusion, support and gratitude as we actively reach out and respond to others in timely, authentic and creative ways to promote kindness, prosperity, and belonging."

STRATEGIES

A first step, we expanded our relationships with our internal printing services to create a welcoming and consistent "you belong" messaging. For example, we provided packets of "you belong" cards for senior leaders and the HR team to reach out and respond to individual employees and teams to build personal connections. We created conditions for Compassion and Care alignment across the college building alliances with departments, faculty, staff, teams, and working groups to expand the principles of compassion and care and help them actualize these concepts in their areas.

We have adjusted outcomes, created solutions quickly, and worked to keep students and employees in the center of the solution. Examples include delivering Sunshine bags to "teams of the month" to support the president, turning around correspondence requests within 24 hours, taking resources to our students, utilizing free resources to build curriculum, and saying yes to employee ideas such as graduation signs and stories in the Daily Dose. In the light of the death of George Floyd and the Black Lives Matter movement, we have been able to learn and improve, connect to existing resources, highlight contributors, and scale up quickly to share our outcomes and next steps offerings. We have been able to offer words from our community, share books, opportunities, and messages from our Daily Dose hosts. Specifically, we invested in three main compassion and care opportunities for deep institutional connection.

Focus One: Compassion Outreach Communication

This allows us to partner with HR to be alerted daily about those employees with timely outreach needs of care. We respond with specialized communication including a "You Belong" graphic to be inviting, inclusive, and consistent. For example, our student and employee team have penned hundreds of handwritten cards and made phone calls to personally extend connection. There is power in the personal and authentic.

Focus Two: A Compassion and Care Grassroots Offering, "The Daily Dose"

With connection at its core, this newsletter is emailed weekly (75 issues to date, 2021) as an official college communication extending resources and building community. The content and structure involve a variety of employee and student contributors from across the college representing our community. Weekly, we feature a member of our college community as "The Daily Dose" host who offers their perspectives and individual perspective.

"The Daily Dose" (TDD) started with a solid mission, understanding, and structure allowing us to reach out to our community to invite their contributions and passions early. Employees stepped forward to share their talents. They included a partnership to open caption TDD as well as a public health and nutrition initiative to create weekly videos that are relatable and accessible featuring recipes and strategies during pandemic. We likewise offered a wellness focus in partnership with College Health and Wellness.

A cross collaboration and commitment to diverse voices helped us create a strong editorial team to deliver TDD in a timely manner with creative conversations driven by employee input and broad college representation. Likewise, through our "you belong" email, we welcomed employee ideas and valuable feedback to help us respond and adapt to their needs.

Focus Three: Compassion and Care Goodwill Outreach and Development of Employee and Student Goodwill Ambassadors (GWAs)

An integral "ask" from our senior vice president, in partnership with the Compassion and Care initiative, was to create meaningful leadership opportunities for FWS students. We developed tThe Student Good Will Ambassador (GWA) program, a three-tier approach rooted in empathetic leadership development, stewardship, and community action to serve these students immediately beginning March 2020.

With career services, we scaled up quickly to best serve student employees and supervisors delivering work assignments, troubleshooting, and tracking working hours to keep students in meaningful employment for their academic success crucial for COVID 19. We created professional development/career content as well as spaces of challenge and support for our student employees with weekly meetings, work assignments, and TEAMS meetings called "Connections and Reflections" for students to meet and share. We continue to build an intentional, holistic experience for our GWA student employees focused on a growth mind-set. Students prepare weekly portfolios to have a co-curricular experience from a shared curriculum and we are learning from their reflection and feedback. They are learning about themselves and feel like what they are doing matters.

Our Good Will Ambassadors interact with a curated curriculum, a collection of articles, YouTube videos, poems, and assessments, to build their capacity and growth as leaders rooted in empathy. They are asked to respond weekly in reflection journals as well as in our weekly required meeting, Reflections and Connections. They also create weekly success and gratitude videos shared in our TDD publications to extend compassion to our entire community. As the curriculum has progressed, it is now student generated and this was an unexpected win for us as higher education professionals.

We had not expected sharing personalized, handwritten note cards sent to all 2,500 employees from our students would have such meaning for both our students and employees. The Student Good Will Ambassadors shared on countless occasions how the cards started out as a work assignment but as they continued the curriculum considering our employees as the recipients, they began to personalize the connections to create unique messages. They felt deeply invested in the experience.

One Student Good Will Ambassador, Traci, really captured the Compassion and Care experience well when she remarked that "everyone I have met is so friendly and helpful—I couldn't even believe it!" I could see the impact of her own words seem to wash over her, envelop her, giving her confidence and comfort to let go, release, believe, and trust to be herself. Another Student Good Will Ambassador, Adriana, emphasized the power of kindness and compassion when she noted that "the smallest of actions can make a profound difference."

With this commitment to our students, the Good Will Ambassadors continue as an integrated program that has developed both organically and intentionally. Within the year, over 20 students have participated, four have graduated, and three have been promoted to Senior Student Good Will Ambassador leaders. In fact, students developed their own mission as an extension of the Compassion and Care work to align their actions and gifts and commitment to story/storytelling.

STORY EXCHANGES, HARVESTS, AND PROJECT 2020

In addition to these initiatives, we further developed community spaces for healing and storytelling for the student/employee/community, aligned innovative experiences, and reimagined spaces of connection by offering storytelling harvests (Project 2020). We use peer-to-peer interviews, reflection journals, and videos as well as creative expression through virtual story exchanges to tell the story of 2020. It becomes a telling time capsule of our collective journey and a way forward.

A YEAR LATER, PROMISES MADE, KEPT, AND EXPANDED

As we reflect a year later, we have and continue to build capacity for the Compassion and Care Initiative. Our team has led strategic college-wide community work with a nimble, curious, and scalable mind-set to build partnerships, create deep connections, and invite innovation, resiliency, and belonging. We have worked creatively with a "just in time" mind-set to extend the college's mission, vision, and values and direction inviting belonging, engagement, and innovative participation.

Compassion and care have fostered radical outreach and strong partnership development. Hundreds have been recognized, celebrated, and served with a flexibility in design and delivery. We created consistent welcoming messages for all internal and external constituents and across social media, internal communications both digital and print. We lifted student and employee voices—the Daily Dose Brand—and its offerings to create consistency and belonging. We offered and cocreated content to build trust, invited participation across all constituents, and made spaces for expression and agency. We also created consistent and reliable procedures to support student workers, delivered in-person care packages and employee postcards, supported sensitive employee correspondence, and trained Good Will Ambassadors. We remained responsive to our community through our "you belong" email mailbox to send cards, clarify needs, and build Daily Dose content. We have also archived our Daily Dose efforts, shared resources (constantly updated and vetted), and student GWAs videos and reflections.

As we imagine our new normal, we are rooted in compassion and care. We look forward to where this work leads us. We are humbled as we reflect on the growth we have seen in our students; the generosity of our college community; and the creativity, positivity, and kindness of our coworkers, who offered talent and passion in a difficult time.

Chapter Thirteen

Holdfast

An Education in Disaster

Andy Tolhurst

Living along the southeastern coast of North Carolina, the storms of the eastern seaboard marked and shaped my personal and professional lives in ways both subtle and overt. They brought me to the coast from Pennsylvania. They shaped my decision to teach. They changed and altered the semesters that followed. When I was young, I learned to ride the swells that march ahead of such storms and follow in their wake. Those lessons changed the way I teach, indeed, the way I approach a great many things. Twenty years after having made a home in their path, hurricanes remain a link between a life on the water and in the classroom. Looking back over the list of names and dates kept in little notebooks and class journals, I am reminded of their influence. I see it directly, and I see how they leave lessons long after the cleanup and repairs are completed, and the swell has subsided. They teach lessons of risk, preparation, and adaptability, and they teach resolve.

1986

Go Away, Charlie! The demand is written on the billboard of my favorite surf shop. We are driving along Old Highway 12 back to our little rental house in Nags Head. "What's that mean?" I ask from the way-back seat of the family station wagon. From the front, my dad begins an engineer's explanation for named storms. It's crisp and direct, but I am gone after the mention of high surf and waves. Scenes of ships on stormy seas are mixing with the raised house pilings and hanging electric wires of Old Hwy 12 as it cuts through Nags Head. We pull into the driveway as he finishes, ". . . so it's a risk, but with the prep, we should be fine." That evening we place our mattresses against the ocean facing windows and cover and tape the rest. I have two memories of the storm. First is the smile and resolve on my dad's face as we walked out in the sunshine in the eye of the storm. Second is the sound of wind and surf just beyond the mattress-covered windows bowing from unseen force.

1995

I attend the University of North Carolina at Wilmington, chosen from both *Surfer Magazine* rankings and prominent marine biology programs. Mostly in that order. Hurricane Felix arrives on campus just after I do. Six hundred miles from home and facing campus evacuation, myself and a few friends huddle together in a small SPEC house just off the ICW, watching pine trees bend in half through the bathroom porthole window. The storm passes, and the next day I skip out on work, ignore my coursework, and go surfing. The '84 Buick takes me through a couple flooded roads, the water never rising past the floorboards. I learn the high spots in the road for just such an occasion. The surf is good; my devotion to bio lab is not. While classes are cancelled for the moment, there is a lab practical waiting on return. Standing on the beach, assessing my resolve, I spend thirty minutes or so sizing up a wave I think I can make without the now growing crowd on shore bearing witness to my drowning. I have not been in surf this heavy before, but I have enough of the skills I need, and I have to try. I huck myself over the edge on a larger wave in the set and I can hear hooting from shore as I pull under the lip. All goes black. It was a beautiful wave. I never had a chance of making it. I couldn't tell when I made the decision to go; at that moment it was a risk but a reasonable one. Later, a photographer from shore runs a picture of the bottom turn on the local surf chat board. It gets a little love. I know how it ended. I take a B on the bio lab practical two days later when campus reopens. The competition in the field of biology and my waning effort makes it clear that I need another way to join the sea and a future position that might clear the mounting debt. Turns out that in the surf and in the lab, I was learning a little about assessment, a little about preparation, and a little about resolve.

During the next four years of college there is at least one storm per year, eleven named storms in all. I surf a lot, finding countless barrels along the east coast, driving through flooded roads to get the swells and wind and beach bathymetry to align. I also awake to the loss of life and property. I leave a swimming scholarship to join the ocean rescue squad. It's probably not the most financially sound decision, but the position is rewarding in other ways.

AUGUST 23, 1998

I move into east Asheville St. on Wrightsville Beach with two other English majors. Two days later we move everything of value into my little attic room on the third floor while Hurricane Bonnie curves north-northwestward directly toward our little island. We move to a friend's house in midtown for shelter. One of my roommates is concerned about the time lost on the semester due to canceled classes. He has plans postgraduation. I put our mattresses against the windows and head to the grocery store for ice, beer, and water. After the storm passes, I take the practiced highline drive back to the house on the beach. From the third-story, cramped bedroom, perched atop our valuables and a dresser, I can see the waves firing along a sandbar between Asheville St. and Johnny Mercer's Pier. In Pennsylvania, my mom gets a phone call to turn on the news where she sees her oldest son paddling out behind the weatherman informing people to stay out of the water. Some of the best waves I rode to that point in my life. My only regret was not having a little fresh surf wax. Three days later we move everything back to my third-floor room as Hurricane Charley causes a second disruption in the semester. The concerned roommate has moved his status to stressed. I remember to put surf wax in the bag with my books and we put the mattresses back up against the window.

1999

I graduate and consider job opportunities by time off to surf. There are plenty. Most of them remind me of bio lab. I take a job at a Sylvan Learning Center in Charlotte, North Carolina, figuring it close enough to surf and "a job" I knew as a practiced student. The prescribed curriculum begins to drone. Little Danny's detailed recounting of *Walker: Texas Ranger* episodes keeps me coming back Monday through Friday. His "r" pronunciations are getting better and his smile more frequent. I eventually move to a manager role at the center, which means I get to go in early on Saturday to oversee administration of the SAT instead of travelling to surf. After coding answer sheets and delivering testing supplies to the test administrators, there is little to do for the following four hours. I spend most of the time looking through the newspaper, cruising the internet, or taking the English portion of old SATs. One Saturday there is an ad in the paper for a job fair for Charlotte Mecklenburg Schools. In the interview they ask a bunch of questions about the classroom, the environment at Sylvan, my thoughts on pedagogy, graduation rates, and stakeholder outcomes. My answers are earnest but I'm not sure I know what I am saying. It's all over quickly and someone is shaking my hand and walking me to the door, "Thank you for your time. If you'll follow me, I'm going to have you speak with one last person about a new position here that we think you might fit." For the next school year, I am the AVID Coordinator at the local high school. The AVID pedagogy is sound, but the role reminds me of Sylvan.

The bright spot of the year is the English class I teach for AVID students, and it is a disaster. The lessons have little continuity. We joke and laugh and struggle and argue. Some days, when the lesson goes well, there is a feeling of fulfilment and purpose that I once knew only in the water. Other days are as frustrating as missed waves, bumbling my way through *To Kill a Mockingbird* and dragging them kicking and screaming through *Romeo and Juliet*. I apply what I learned at Sylvan to the school's AVID review and we get the national certification, but I know how the year ended—with the realization I needed more skills. Hurricane Gordon crosses over the coast and closes school the following September. The small second-story, studio apartment on EWT Harris on the north side of Charlotte's sprawl is too far to hear the surf or spy any sandbars.

2001

I enroll in the Watson School of Education at the University of North Carolina Wilmington. My fiancée, Amy, works remote with First Union Bank and my student loans cover the rest. The income is tight and each month we dip a little further in debt. It's not a great career plan, but we are surviving. On September 1, First Union merges with Wachovia, and Amy loses her remote job. My application for internship credit is denied, adding another semester of loans before gainful employment. We slide into a debt that shadows us today. I find a coffee shop within biking distance of the house, where one morning before opening I arrive and beg for a job. The owner, Scooter, is a slightly hefty guy with an apron marked by espresso, coffee, and breakfast sandwiches. He pays me out of the register. Last hurricane season slowed down the development and interest in the area of the shop and his budget is tight. Oddly, he isn't concerned. I admire his resolve and willingness to adapt the plan in order to stay afloat. Hurricane Gabrielle and Hurricane Humberto roll by the coast later that September without landfall, only waves.

One morning, after surfing a little too long past dawn, I am late to open the shop. Scooter stands at the door, "Don't sweat it. I'm a surfer too. Listen, why don't you come over to my house this evening. I've got a little shaping shed behind my house. We can make a board and talk shop." I'm sure this is a congenial way to fire me, but he smiles and heads to the kitchen once I agree. After work I meet him at his place. One of his sons is pulling on one arm, a slightly older sister is hanging from Scooter's waist; behind them, two older boys are flipping off the couch onto the cushions they laid on the floor. "Hey, glad you made it," he says. I offer to come back some other time, but he gently sheds the two children climbing on him and sends them off to play with their brothers. "Shed is out back," he says, "come on."

We stand in the fluorescent light of the shed overlooking a new, white surfboard blank. On the wall is a picture from *Surfer Magazine* of a Scooter before the breakfast sandwich apron. He's on a wave more than twice his height. Scooter is a surfer. For a period in the 1980s and early 1990s, he was a professional surfer. I pepper him with questions about the professional circuit, famous waves, and stories of his travels. He talks about the risk and reward of surfing Pipeline and living to talk about it. His stories of travels to Escondido are laden with misadventure as is apt to occur when travelling in Mexico. He asks me questions about the licensure classes and teaching. I tell him about how one risks financial stability for the reward of when a lesson really lands with a class. How sometimes it's only one student, but it still feels as amazing. About the odds of finding a job and how to afford a move. About the navigation of the newest methodology designed to fix education, and about not letting stuff outside the classroom interfere with the stuff inside the classroom. Scooter says it sounds like surfing storm swells; a lot of preparation, a little assessment, a little risk, and the resolve to see it through. The surfboard lasts for three years before breaking on a reef in Costa Rica. Those pillars of surfing and storm preparation become holdfasts of my pedagogy and life to this day.

2002

I prepare a semester's calendar and syllabus with real consequences for real students for the first time since the job in Charlotte. Gaging state requirements and the demands of the AP curriculum, I take a risk and abandon Shakespeare and Lee to start with Silko and Harjo and Alexie. I'm reminded of standing on shore, judging lineups and timing swells for the chance to make a few powerful waves. I keep my plans in little spiral notebooks with meeting notes and journal entries that catalogue the year. They are easy to pack in bags with wax and towels and books when storms halt a semester. Subtropical Storm Gustav builds to Hurricane Gustav and passes just along the coast. The notebook reads: "The back stairwell nearest my classroom is open from the parking lot." Hurricane Kyle crosses over at the end of the month cancelling another day of classes, necessitating another syllabus update. The year ends with a 20 percent growth in enrollment in the AP program, and 70 percent of the students score well-enough to earn college credit. I know this because we fill out large data sheets cross-referencing every number of every subgroup. It's an odd, time-consuming task, but I'm told it helps and I assume this is the next level. I know Tim and Emily both said *Ceremony* was the best thing they read and discussed in high school. Risk and reward.

2008

Amy and I become homeowners, which changes my preparation for storms. I use the surf forecast to gage severity and arrival of storm conditions, as well as best times to surf. That semester there's a small parental backlash over the pairing of Gilman-Perkins's "Yellow Wallpaper" with Kesey's *One Flew Over the Cuckoo's Nest* in the student syllabus. Administration is deciding what I will be able to do. On September 7, Tropical Storm Ophelia begins meandering off the southeast coast and swell begins to fill in. For the first time in my career, I call a substitute for the next two days. My brother and two friends throw our gear in the truck and make a series of poor decisions, driving through flooded roads to arrive in the Outer Banks in the middle of the night. The swell is all-time. Later that semester, every student turns in a paper for the Perkins and Kesey pairing with something honest to say. Administration determines that the assignment should be graded as pass/fail and then given a point value of a lesser weighted assignment. I wonder if there are enough boxes on the data spreadsheet to account for the change, and I remember how easy it was to get a substitute. From 2002 to the end of my secondary teaching career in 2012, there are twenty named storms. The one that looms largest is personal.

2012

While walking down the hall to my classroom, I pass Walter's English III class. He's sitting at his desk, feet up, and *The Crucible* is playing on a screen at the front. Students wander in and out of the room, up and down the aisles. I think that doesn't look so bad, and that's when I know it's time to reassess my plan. For the next four years I find work as a landscape foreman for a small family-owned business. My lesson plan notebooks change over to property notes and managerial to-dos. The work is hard, hot, and long, but I'm making more money and surfing just as much. It reminds me of Sylvan, and bio lab.

2016

I return to grad school with the goal to teach at the university level. There are four named storms in the intervening two years while my notebooks return to lesson plans and journal entries. In my resolve to find a full-time position, I'm reminded of the long circuitous route back to the ocean after Hurricane Bonnie. To help the bleeding in our check account, I work on a landscaping truck when semester course loads are light and in the summer when it's hot. It's a chaotic life, but it's a space I have grown comfortable in with experience and time. It's like a life on the coast, born of storms that wipe barrier islands clean and result in loss of life, and a love for the power and beauty which are also to be had. Both have changed me forever.

2018

Between September 25, 2018, and October 8, 2018, there is one entry in my notebook. It reads: "Hurricane Florence." Our home along the Cape Fear River is tucked out of the wind. The longleaf pines sway heavily, cutting the wind in their tops till it spills back into the open air over the river. Water is our problem. The river is 4,431 feet from my front door. Florence is projected somewhere between the intensity of a 4 and a 5. The floodplain for a category 4 hurricane is 5 feet from my front door. Mattresses on windows won't cut it. During the next 72 hours of the storm, my neighbor and I use several industrial pumps to move 158 gallons per minute from under our houses and out to the river, chain-sawing fallen trees from damning up the process. It's similar to the graduate work, voluminous and steady. Food and water and gas become scarce. Standing in line in the Silver Lake Market, a run-down little convenience store and one of few able to open, the lady at the register keeps her handgun visible on her belt. No one talks much, and the tension reminds me of the anxious moments before making it out of a barreling storm wave. On the fourth day, power returns and roads slowly open. In class, due dates need to be adjusted on the fly, some assignments are abbreviated, and others are withdrawn due to time with a weather eye for permanent work. In between are stolen moments in the sun, smiling and surfing.

There have been more than fifty named storms in my twenty-five years living on the coast, links between a life lived in the classroom and a life lived in their path. The preparation for a storm beforehand mitigates some of the risk, but not entirely. The effort to control what I can and the risk and resolve to ride out the rest is a subtle dance amidst chaos of storm and classroom. It's one I seem to never turn down. I am forever marked by both.

Chapter Fourteen

A Resident Assistant's Reflections on the Pandemic

Kayli Childs

In the spring of 2020, I was working as a resident assistant (RA) at the University of North Carolina Wilmington and completing my senior year of college. Between writing nominations for senior awards, my honors thesis, daily classwork, and my job, I had little to no time for anything else, but it was not hard to follow the biggest news story that was on every channel and in every article: the impeachment trial.

At the beginning of February, news of a pandemic in China was a distant whisper. I remember only one conversation with a colleague about it. Based on what she was reading online, she was afraid that it would wipe out everyone on Earth. I had no means of comforting her because I had so little information about it. She told me that when she expressed her fears to her parents, a few days later she received a book in her campus mailbox from her dad about managing anxiety. In retrospect, it is laughable how wrong we all were about how devastating the pandemic would be.

Soon, spring break released thousands of students all over the United States. All the freshman residence halls closed, and the students went home or travelled to other places in hopes of a fun vacation. The Office of University Relations sent out an email four days before the traditional Spring Break ended explaining that, due to COVID-19, the break had been extended by a week. Despite this, all RAs were mandated to return to campus at the end of the original Spring Break for a staff meeting. If we did not appear for the meeting, we were led to believe we would be fired. Though the email that we received didn't explicitly state this, the subtext was that all staff were replaceable.

So we gathered in a ballroom where the staff members placed folding chairs six feet apart from one another. We all took a seat and the Director of Housing stood at the front of the ballroom and spoke to us. We went over what programming would look like for this specific "flu" and what policy enforcement would look like. Apparently, students were going to be given the option to move out if they wanted to. But if *we* left, we would not be allowed to work for Housing and Residence Life again; whether this was a threat or the truth was unclear. The floor was opened to questions, and for the next three hours we sat and asked questions that nobody had answers to.

On March 17, we received another email from the Office of University Relations. It told us that no students were going to be permitted to stay on campus. They would have three options: they could move out immediately, they could come back and retrieve essential items and return in May to move out, or they could opt to move out entirely in May. We learned that we would be responsible for a massive checklist of residents, figuring out who had what plan for moving out, and manning the front desks of the buildings. Housing and Residence Life also took full advantage of the phrase "other duties as assigned" mentioned in our work contract and had us working an onslaught of random jobs without any form of extra compensation. Students had from March 18 to March 22 to move out, but not all students were able to. Alongside my boss, I helped set up extended housing for these students who had nowhere to go. At this point, none of us were wearing masks. When one student had a mask on in the dining hall that afternoon, it seemed strange.

Throughout this difficult and stressful period, when we were mourning the loss of our school year and, for seniors, our commencement ceremony, Housing's response was significantly below average. Many other schools in the UNC system took action earlier, and UNCW was among the slowest to respond to their students. The communication across departments was also incredibly poor, and there was a lot of confusion. While I know that it was a difficult time, this lack of communication made everything harder.

Index

anti-mask, 10
anti-scientism, 9, 20
Applied Learning, 78
Arab Spring, 4

Bhaba, Homi, 26
Black Lives Matter (BLM), 14, 15, 17, 162, 164, 167, 190
Branch, Wade, 127, 129, 134, 139

Center for Disease Control (CDC), 10
classroom management, 130–2, 138–9
collaboration, 31, 73, 74, 78–80
Columbine Shooting, 146
compassionate care, 81–82
Cone of Uncertainty, 52–55, 158–9

The Day After Tomorrow, 119, 121, 123
digital turn, 26, 39
dimensions of wellness, 186, 191
discourse patterns, 18
Discord, 31–40
Distance Education, 75, 81
disruption, 43, 48, 61, 64, 73–77, 90, 103, 109, 149, 161, 197
dystopia, 109, 120

emergency management, 45–47, 52, 56, 61, 63, 64, 66–67

engagement, 84, 87, 94, 132–3, 136–39, 168,
environmental justice, 113, 114, 116, 118–9, 122, 124

Facebook, 27–28, 34, 66, 81, 164, 173
fanfiction, 39
Fauci, Anthony, 12, 16, 19
Floyd, George, 157, 158, 160

Garner, Eric, 15
Gates, Bill, 12, 16, 19
Gittell, Noah, 114, 122

Hurrevac, 52–53, 54, 62, 66
Hurricane Florence, 1, 73, 74, 76, 78, 90, 103, 115, 116, 158, 160, 169, 201
Hurricane Katrina, 69, 110, 111, 113, 124, 143
Hurricane Matthew, 112, 113, 115
hurricanes, 4, 5, 6, 43–45, 47, 48–52, 56, 67,68, 7382, 103, 116, 109, 111, 112, 116–7, 121, 158, 166, 170, 195

interdisciplinarity, 111, 116
Interstellar, 114, 122
Invisible Man, 158

Kress, Gunter, 26

Lee, Spike, 114
learning management system (LMS), 77, 79, 80, 83, 86, 149, 161, 175

Madrid Bombings of 2004, 99
Martin, Trayvon, 161
masking, 9, 18, 19
McLuhan, Marshall, 27
meteorology, 43, 62

National Hurricane Center, 51, 52

ontological interpretive framework, 25, 28–31, 37–40

pandemicene, 157
Paris Attacks of 2015, 94–95
plandemic, 15–16
post-traumatic stress disorder (PTSD), 145

QAnon, 15–17

Russ, Joanna, 9, 19

school shooting, 143, 145–6
social justice, 145, 150–1, 209
Soja, Edward, 26

Solnit, Rebecca, 110–1, 113, 114, 119, 121
spheres modeling, 61, 64, 68
"spill-outs," 165
Street, Brian, 26
story exchange, 193
story signals, 193
Substance Abuse and Mental Health Service Administration (SAMHSA), 145–6
Surfer Magazine, 196, 199

Taylor, Breonna, 162
Teacher Performance Assessment, 135
transparency in learning and teaching (TILT), 74, 79, 84–86
trauma-informed pedagogy, 143–5, 147
trauma responses, 143–4

universal design for learning (UDL), 86
uncertainty, 43–49
university institutional response, 61, 67–68
un-natural disasters, 113, 114, 115, 122

Zeitlin, Benh, 114, 122
Zimmerman, George, 161

About the Editors and Contributors

EDITORS

Victor Malo-Juvera is professor of English education at the University of North Carolina Wilmington where he teaches courses in writing for secondary teachers, young adult literature, and mythology. He has coedited several books such as *Shakespeare and Young Adult Literature: Pairing and Teaching, Canonical and Young Adult Literature: Pairing and Teaching, Vols I & II, Breaking the Taboo with Young Adult Literature, Critical Explorations of Young Adult Literature: Identifying and Critiquing the Canon*, and *Critical Approaches to Teaching the High School Novel: Reinterpreting Canonical Literature*. His scholarship has been published in journals such as *Research in the Teaching of English, Teachers College Record, English Journal, Teaching and Teacher Education, The ALAN Review, Journal of Language and Literacy Education*, and *Study and Scrutiny: Research on Young Adult Literature*. Victor is on the board of the directors of the Assembly on Literature for Adolescents of NCTE as well as being on the editorial boards of *English Journal* and *Study and Scrutiny: Research on Young Adult Literature*.

Nicholas Laudadio is an associate professor of English at the University of North Carolina Wilmington where he teaches classes in science fiction, horror, popular culture, and literary and critical theory. His research explores the cultural history of music and musical instruments with a particular focus on electronic music and science fiction in the 20th century.

CONTRIBUTORS

Suriati Abas is an assistant professor in the Department of Elementary Education and Reading at State University of New York (SUNY) College at Oneonta. Her research centers on the critical, digital, and spatial dimensions of literacy. Dr. Abas is also the founder of Global Story Hour and honoree of the 2022 Divergent Award for Excellence in Implementation of Literacy in a Digital Age. She has taught literacy theory, methods, diversity, and children's literature courses to preservice teachers.

Barbara Allen has served Columbus State Community College for over 20 years in many different capacities and is currently the Assistant Director of Employee Engagement and Belonging. Barbara has been an improvising artist and educator for over 11 years as a founding member of both Columbus Unscripted and Sassy Do Improv. She was humbled and honored to share improv as an invited speaker at TEDx Columbus Women 2013 and was a featured teller Spring 2015 at the Speak Easy's Annual celebration of story, The Big Easy. Barbara was named Columbus State's Legacy in Leadership Award for 2018.

Diana Ashe is professor of English and director of the Center for Teaching Excellence and the Center for Faculty Leadership at the University of North Carolina Wilmington. She teaches undergraduate and graduate courses in professional and technical writing, rhetorical theory, and, now and then, Appalachian literature.

Wade Branch is a high school math teacher at Golden Valley High School in Bakersfield, California. With undergraduate studies in business administration and career experience in construction, he works to develop practical math skills in his classroom.

Kayli Childs graduated with a degree in English from UNCW (2020) and is currently working in medical and science writing and document design.

Alexandra Chapa-Kunz is an English teacher at Highland High School in Bakersfield, California. She hopes to continue contributing to research that inspires growth and understanding of literacy and equity in education.

Kevin D. Cordi, PhD, serves as an assistant professor and Middle Childhood Coordinator at Ohio University Lancaster. He holds a doctorate in storytelling and education from The Ohio State University. In 2021, he was selected to be a Global Teaching Education Fellow with the Longview Foundation. In addition to being a university professor, he is a nationally known award-winning storyteller and author of *You Don't Know Jack: A Storyteller Goes to School* (University of Mississippi Press, 2019) and *Playing with Stories: Story Crafting for Writers, Teachers, and Other Imaginative Thinkers* (Parkhurst Brothers, 2014).

Hannah R. Gerber is professor of literacy at Sam Houston State University and honorary professor at the University of South Africa. She is past president of the International Council for Educational Media. Dr. Gerber's research has won multiple awards including two-time recipient for the Faculty Excellence in Research in the College of Education at Sam Houston State University and recipient of the Divergent Award for Excellence in 21st Century Literacies Research awarded by the Initiative for 21st Century Literacies.

Nicole Desjardins Gowdy is the Senior Director of International and Domestic Programs at Pomona College. Previously, she directed programs in Africa, Asia, and the Caribbean for college, gap year, and high school students, and served as a Peace Corps Volunteer in Cameroon. Nicole's national efforts in the field focus on support for diversity and inclusion, health and safety, and student development in study abroad through presentations, advocacy, and membership in task forces and working groups. Nicole has an MA in international education from SIT Graduate Institute and a BA in English and communication arts from the University of Wisconsin–Madison.

Tiffany Gilbert is department chair and associate professor of English at the University of North Carolina Wilmington, where she teaches primarily in the areas of post-1945 American literature, film, and popular culture. She has published essays on the films *Carmen Jones*, *Imitation of Life*, *Plenty*, *My Left Foot*, *The Rose Tattoo*, and *The Fugitive Kind*. Her manuscript in progress, *Anna Magnani: Performing in Place*, is contracted with Edinburgh University Press. In addition, she is focused on prioritizing access, equity, and diversity at UNCW by spearheading initiatives related to the 1898 Wilmington Massacre and writing on the role of Black women in academic leadership.

Alice Hays is an assistant professor of education in the Teacher Education Department at California State University, Bakersfield. She teaches credential and graduate courses in literacy across the content area, methods and strategies of teaching, and teaching for diversity and social justice. She taught secondary English language arts for 19 years in Arizona public schools, and her research interests focus on teacher preparation, youth participatory action research, culturally sustaining pedagogy, and young adult literature.

Kara Pike Inman, EdD, is the Director of Education Abroad at the University of North Carolina Wilmington. Additionally, she teaches courses in intercultural communication and international education, and leads two annual short-term education abroad programs. She received her bachelor's degree in international studies, Spanish, and mass communication, her master's degree in international affairs, and her doctorate in educational leadership. She has presented at numerous regional, national, and international conferences; has several publications related to international education; and is the author of a children's book series about travel.

Jason Kinnear currently serves as Interim Associate Dean of Study Abroad & Exchanges at the University of North Carolina at Chapel Hill. Working in international education for over 20 years in ISSS, education abroad, and service-learning positions at several large, public institutions. These roles touched on all aspects of education abroad, including program development, administration, curriculum design and integration risk management, and leading programs. Jason studied abroad in London as an undergrad, earned his MA Educational Leadership from the University of Northern Colorado, and is beginning the CHEI PhD program at Universita Cattolica del Sacro Cuore in Milan, Italy.

Jouselin Martin is a teacher at North High School in Bakersfield, California. She teaches biology and intro to physical science. Her interest in research includes culturally sustaining pedagogy, and social and racial motivators in student success.

Colleen A. Reilly is professor of English and faculty associate for the Center for Teaching Excellence and Center for Faculty Leadership at the University of North Carolina Wilmington. She teaches undergraduate courses in professional and technical writing and graduate courses in science writing, research methods, and genders, sexualities, and technologies. Currently, she coedits the *Journal of Effective Teaching in Higher Education* (jethe.org).

Anka Roberto is an assistant professor at the University of North Carolina Wilmington. Her clinical trajectory is treating clients holistically across the lifespan as she works with children, adults, and families in the aftermath of trauma. Her area of research is posttraumatic growth, spirituality, and resiliency in the aftermath of trauma. She is EMDR (Eye Movement Desensitization and Reprocessing) trained, is level 1 trauma treatment certified, and has authored multiple book chapters and articles in the area of trauma and resilience throughout her years in academia.

Addie Sayers is an assistant professor of Linguistics in the Department of English at the University of North Carolina Wilmington. She primarily explores gender, racial, and sexuality ideologies in her research, as well as the role of language in antiracism and social justice. As a multimodal discourse analyst, she examines how language and other semiotic resources impact meaning-making potentials in both digital and in analog spaces.

Melissa Sexton is a lecturer in the Department of English at the University of North Carolina Wilmington. She received her PhD in American environmental literature from the University of Oregon. Her research interests include new materialist approaches to the environment and theories of the Anthropocene. Most recently, her work has appeared in *Resilience: A Journal of the Environmental Humanities* (Winter 2020) and in the collection *Rediscovering the Maine Woods: Thoreau's Legacy in an Unsettled Land* (University of Massachusetts Press, 2019).

Andy Tolhurst is originally from Pittsburgh, Pennsylvania, and has lived in Wilmington, North Carolina, for the last 25 years where he and wife, Amy Jones Tolhurst, share their lives with two beautiful daughters, Abby and Sadie, and their family dog, Sam. After teaching high school English for ten years, Andy is currently an adjunct professor at the University of North Carolina Wilmington. When not teaching or writing or parenting, he is surfing or skating or fishing as often as possible.

Ian R. Weaver is an assistant professor of English in the professional writing program at the University of North Carolina Wilmington. He coordinates the Post-Baccalaureate Certificate in Science and Medical Writing, and his current research investigates the rhetoric employed in disasters, crises, and emergency management, considering how participatory methods can improve environmental and atmospheric risk communication.

www.ingramcontent.com/pod-product-compliance
Lightning Source LLC
Chambersburg PA
CBHW020331240426
43665CB00043B/439